*the good*
*girls'*
*guide* TO

GREAT SEX

# *the good girls' guide* TO

## GREAT SEX

*by* Thom W. King
*and*
Debora Peterson

*Three Rivers Press*
*New York*

Published by Three Rivers Press, a division of Crown Publishers, Inc., 201 East 50th Street, New York, New York 10022. Member of the Crown Publishing Group.

Originally published in hardcover by Harmony Books, 1997.

First paperback edition printed in 1998.

Random House, Inc. New York, Toronto, London, Sydney, Auckland
www.randomhouse.com

Three Rivers Press is a trademark of Crown Publishers, Inc.

Originally published, in different form, by Dowling Press, Inc., in 1996.

Design by Linda Kocur

Printed in the United States of America

Library of Congress Cataloging-in-Publication Data

King, Thom W.
    The good girls' guide to great sex/by Thom W. King and Debora Peterson.—1st ed.
    1. Women—United States—Sexual behavior. 2. Sex customs—United States. I.
    Peterson, Debora.   II. Title.
HQ29.K545   1997
306.7'082—dc21                                                    96-48956

ISBN 0-609-80176-7

10 9 8 7 6 5 4 3 2 1

First Paperback Edition

# Acknowledgments

If each of us is the sum of all the experiences and people we have encountered in our lives, I think this book is a tangible record of my existence. I dedicate *The Good Girls' Guide to Great Sex* to all the women I've met during my first forty years. Each of the six thousand women who participated in the making of this book has become a contributor to my life. On a more intimate level, I dedicate this book to the preacher's daughter in the closet with me when I was ten, to my next-door neighbor's divorced mom who wore the tight white shorts, to the blond, blue-eyed Canadian high school senior, to the dark-haired accountant with the raft and thirteen cats, to Montana Frenchie and the groove strap girl, and to the ravishing DNA expert who stole my heart with her dark brown eyes and snappy comebacks. This book is my humble effort to acknowledge their influences. The ultimate dedication goes to my mom, Kathleen Peach King, who died on September 23, 1994, as the survey and research were in advanced stages. She was well aware of this project and even contributed one of my favorite stories within. She was the strongest woman I've ever known and continues to be the yardstick by which all other females in my life are measured.

*Thom King*

In raising my three teenagers I have learned to be spontaneous, candid, open-minded, and ready for almost anything at a second's notice. Thanks, guys, for the love, the patience you all exhibit, the individual lessons I learn from you daily, and your relentless humor. In my life, there has never been anything more unconditional and fulfilling than your love. You take me as I am and for that, I thank you. I really appreciate my mother for teaching me the quality values of life, with a forthright aim on the disposal of meaningless muck. You gave me focus. Patrick, thank you for consistently encouraging me to seek the truth and follow my instincts. Sara Wall, thanks for your help and friendship. Now, to Meredith Bernstein, the best literary agent in the world (and she rightfully knows it), your ability to move on a project you believe in is equal to none. We can't thank you enough, but we'll try. Deepest thanks to Elizabeth Cavanaugh and the very efficient staff at The Meredith Bernstein Literary Agency, Inc. To Shaye Areheart and Dina Siciliano I would like to say, "You're the best!" If there were a way to measure the pleasure of working with the two of you, it would register off the page! Of course, it doesn't hurt that you are the greatest at what you do, either. Thank you for your hard work, great judgment, and faith in us. I would like to thank you, Thom, for your eclectic talents and wonderful sense of humor. Working on this project together has certainly been a memorable experience I will not soon forget. Maryglenn McCombs: I would like to thank you for trusting in our book and us. Mary Mazer, of Art That Works, thanks for the perfect cover design to beat all. To Andrea C. Barach, our literary lawyer, thanks for your guidance. And thanks to Linda Kocur, for interior design, Mary Schuck, art director, Camille Smith, production editor, and Elke Villa, our publicist at Harmony Books. The faces of romance, love, and sexual pleasure are numerous. The women who participated in this book came from places near and far, and they opened their hearts and minds to share with us. Therefore, I dedicate this book to the women between the covers. You know who you are. *Bon appetit!*

*Debora Peterson*

# Authors' Note

The authors of this book wish to emphasize our desire that readers practice safe sex. Though this book is filled with sexual adventures, memories, and assorted high jinks, we are emphatically not promoting promiscuous or unprotected sex.

The fact is: sex can kill you. We recommend knowing your partners, taking blood tests, using condoms and barriers, and being safe instead of sorry. Do not participate in high-risk activities.

When in doubt, don't. Period.

These stories are from decades of memories when times were different. Actions and deeds that were merely naughty or scandalous in the past are now potentially deadly.

Years ago a shot of penicillin would fix almost any medical problem. Free love was dangerous but not murderous. But now everything has changed.

When a prevention or cure for AIDS is found there will be a sexual revolution that will make all other social events pale in comparison. We anxiously wait and pray for that day to come soon.

Until then be loving, protected, and safe.

# Contents

# Preface

If knowledge is power, then sexual knowledge may be the ultimate power. *The Good Girls' Guide to Great Sex* is designed to help women explore their sexuality.

By the time you have candidly answered all of the following questions, you will know more about your sexual appetite than you ever imagined. This survey is designed to be fun and enlightening. Thousands of women of all ages, professions, and backgrounds have already revealed their utmost secrets. As you read their comments and desires, you may discover some common bonds or, better yet, get in touch with some new desires. Their experiences can be empowering.

Now it is your turn. We encourage you to take an active part in the survey. Write down your thoughts. Express yourself. And then show the survey to your lover, friends, or co-workers. Better yet, leave it around the house and let whomever you want discover it. Take it to work. Give a copy to your best friends. Instead of inviting the girls over for a night of cards, throw a survey party. Be a part of history. Fill out the survey. We want your experiences. This book is the first volume of a series. Subsequent volumes could include your experiences.

Be candid. Have fun. Tell all! If you feel like writing a twenty-page saga on your interpretation of love and sex, have at it. Reveal your fantasies. Get into what you love, hate, enjoy, expect, can't live without, and couldn't care less about. Increase your knowledge. Get closer to your sensual self!

# Introduction

*The Good Girls' Guide to Great Sex* has been a labor of love for the past three years. What began as a series of casual questions between friends and lovers expanded into a full-fledged cultural phenomenon. Thousands of women of all backgrounds, ages, and experiences have shared their innermost thoughts, fantasies, likes, and dislikes with us. These women came from every part of the nation and over a dozen foreign countries. They were nurses, administrators, waitresses, students, housewives, and executives—a wide spectrum of women.

*The Good Girls' Guide to Great Sex* is simply women talking about sex. Storytelling is the stuff of legends, the passing of histories down through the ages. The Great American Sex Quiz was the vehicle through which we acquired that knowledge. By the time a woman had answered all our questions, she had explored a vast range of human sexuality. Some women gave us short answers, concise and to the point. Others turned in essay-length answers with multiple digressions. Our quiz was used as entertainment by sewing circles, garden clubs, and bridge partners. It was the item of discussion around the cafeteria, the health spa, and the water fountain. Women compared notes, shared opinions, and validated their beliefs. It was a wonderful ongoing source of social intercourse.

*The Good Girls' Guide to Great Sex* started three years ago in a photography studio. In my job as a make-over fashion photographer, I met women of all ages, backgrounds, and nationalities.

Women would come to our studio for complete fashion make-overs. They would choose new hairstyles, play with different looks, and live out make-up fantasies. After hours of preparations, I would escort them to the actual photo studio and take their portraits. They would be nervous and scared. I'd try to put them at ease.

What would begin as idle conversation soon developed into specific questions and topics. My job was to make women look sexy and glamorous. While I was taking their portraits, they told me their life stories. They told me sex stories. I listened. What became apparent through these conversations was that women love sex, romance, being in love, and men. They are fascinated with the intricacies, the subtleties, the nuances, the textures of love. They are also interested in the physical aspect of lovemaking. Every woman had a different story to tell. Most had several. They confided their fears, their desires, their needs, and their secrets. They compared lovers. They gossiped. They showed their other selves. They opened the curtain, just a little bit, and allowed an intimate glimpse into the secrets inside.

Out of the thousands, trends developed. Certain fantasies were repeated. Common needs and desires were expressed candidly. A collective sampling of female thought, wisdom, and passion began to emerge. Those passions became the inspiration for this book.

Call girls, exotic dancers, entertainers, kept women, and mistresses also came through the door. And, just like the nurses, secretaries, teachers, and accountants, they had their own stories, desires, needs, and techniques. In reviewing the stories, I found it increasingly hard to tell who told the stories. Some of the hottest and most sensual stories came from the meekest, most demure-looking women.

Debora Peterson, my partner and collaborator, took my initial thousands of observations and insights and fashioned them into cohesive bits. She took my admittedly male perspective and gave it a female once-over. However, her contributions to the book were far more substantial than that: her in-depth interviews and coffee talk brought out the best from the contributors to this project.

In the final analysis, it seems, *The Good Girls' Guide to Great Sex* is good for the soul. If knowledge is power, then perhaps sexual knowledge is the key to pleasure. Thanks to the women who talked and talked. This book is our effort to reveal their knowledge of pleasure and share the power of understanding with those who desire.

*the good girls' guide* TO

GREAT SEX

# chapter one

# *Preferences*

1. *Describe great sex.*
2. *Describe bad sex.*
3. *When is your favorite time to make love?*
4. *How long should intercourse last?*
5. *Do you make love with the lights on? Off?*
6. *What songs, if any, do you like to hear when you make love?*
7. *Do you like to wear perfume? What is your favorite?*
8. *Do you like your partner to wear cologne? What is your favorite?*
9. *What drives you wild?*
10. *What drives you away?*

## 1. DESCRIBE GREAT SEX.

A lot of touching each other during sex is important to me. I like to feel that my body belongs to my husband and his body belongs to me.

*Susan, 45, seamstress*

I'm still pretty young. I hear that women don't reach their prime until their thirties or something like that, but to me, great sex is when both people enjoy it. If both people are happy, then what more could either of us want?

*Michelle, 23, receptionist*

Great sex began to happen to me at a time in my life when I decided to stop being so self-conscious. In my younger years I was so painfully shy about sex that it made it miserable for me. I felt like someone was watching me. I also felt like my mother would disapprove if I enjoyed it. Women were not supposed to enjoy it, for God's sake! Sex in her generation was for reproduction or for men to enjoy.

*Mary, 52, teacher*

Great sex is when I scream my lungs out, twitch like a maniac, and soak the sheets with my vagina juice. It is mind-blowing and totally exhausting. It is death and ecstasy all rolled into one messy little bundle of nerves.

*Sarah, 22, waitress*

Harder, deeper, faster, longer. More is always better than less when it comes to sex. Good, better, best.

*Jenny, 19, lifeguard*

The one ultimate ingredient that makes sex so magic for me is chemistry. Some have it, some don't. It may be unfortunate but that's the way it goes. Let me get in the same room with a nice guy who can make me zing and look out!

*Ellen, 26, police dispatcher*

Oral, oral, oral. Did I say oral?

*Tresah, 40, nurse*

If a man is really into what makes sex great for both of us, then it will be great for both of us. All selfish lovers should be dropped in the middle of the desert. That would be interesting, don't you think? They could do each other and learn to get along or do without.

*Dianna, 35, telemarketing director*

## 2. DESCRIBE BAD SEX.

Bad sex is an impossibility. Now, there is great sex, good sex, and better sex. But there is no such thing as bad sex. Any sex is better than no sex.

*Louise, 48, dental assistant*

Selfish sex. Hurried sex, when there's no need to hurry.

*Denise, 26, store clerk*

When I don't come either in my lover's mouth or around his penis, that is bad sex. When he ejaculates all over my shirt before I've even taken my blouse off, that is bad sex. When I go to sleep in the middle of intercourse, that is bad sex.

*Charlene, 18, video rental salesperson*

When my lover forgets my name.

*Keneesha, 23, historian*

Sometimes my boyfriend and I have had such mind-blowing sex I've worried about him suddenly pushing me away, clutching his heart, and falling dead with a heart attack. I think that would qualify, don't you?

*Lisa, 32, florist*

## 3. WHEN IS YOUR FAVORITE TIME TO MAKE LOVE?

I like to wake up early in the morning, just as the sun starts peeking through. I throw back the covers, kiss my way down my lover's chest, and lightly bite his flaccid penis. It's my personal wake-up call.

*Sharon, 31, office manager*

I like to fuck in the afternoon on Saturdays and Sundays. The kids are outside playing. The yard work has already been done, and the night lies ahead of us. My husband and I close the door, take a hot bubble bath together, and then make love for a few hours, with candles and incense wiping away the tension. Then we get dressed, throw open the door, and take the kids out for pizza at a place where they have big mechanical bears singing old Beatles songs.

*Liz, 32, administrative assistant*

Call me old-fashioned, but I still like to make love in the evening after a full day of life. I like to fuck my lover's brains out and then fall asleep in his arms, our juices flowing and our hair matted together. The best times are when we wake up eight hours later, still in the same basic position and then start all over again.

*Jill, 28, art instructor*

Whenever I can find time is usually a good time.

*Jessie, 37, manicurist*

Whenever it is the most inappropriate time to have sex, that is when I want it the most. I can be standing up in church on Sunday mornings, holding my boyfriend's hand. While the rest of the congregation is saying holy prayers, I have the strongest urge to suck my lover's penis until it explodes on my pretty little white lace collar. Can I get an amen, Sister?

*Alicia, 23, checkout clerk*

The best time I ever had was when my boyfriend came in early from work, grabbed me in the middle of the kitchen, and pulled me to the floor. He ripped my clothes from my pulsating body, buried his warm lips in my pussy, and licked me until I was screaming with joy. Then he fucked me hard and steady. His face was intense, and my body was completely satisfied. Three o'clock in the afternoon, broad daylight, and I was seeing stars. This happened three years ago and I can remember it like it was yesterday. I've got more if you want to hear them.

*Jena, 29, data processor*

## 4. HOW LONG SHOULD INTERCOURSE LAST?

I like for sex to last at least thirty minutes or so. An hour or two some-times. Wine, cheese, soft lights, music—you know the picture.

*Julia, 30, stockbroker*

As long as both people are satisfied.

*Martha, 36, gas station manager*

As long as it can!

*Wilma, 53, hairdresser*

Good, satisfying sex should last long enough to include foreplay, love-making, and plenty of time to relax afterward.

*Sherrie, 21, dance instructor*

Sex should last for hours, days, weeks. It should be all-consuming. It should be mind-altering. It should make everything else seem totally insignificant. It should change the way I hear, smell, and think. It should. But it never does. So I guess I'm still waiting for just the right combination of person, place, and time.

*Melinda, 40, teacher*

Sex with Mr. Right could be mind-blowing and only last a few min-utes, whereas hours of sex with Mr. Wrong could just be an exercise in sweat.

*Cecilia, 31, flight attendant*

If I had my way, sex would begin and never end. No, seriously, I do love making love, missionary sex, and just plain fucking. Give me all I can have and I'm happy. P.S.: A variety of lengths of time is good. Keeps me interested.

*Jimmi, 36, computer analyst*

## 5. DO YOU MAKE LOVE WITH THE LIGHTS ON? OFF?

I love to see everything. I like to use all my senses, and I even keep my eyes open when we kiss. I have always been highly visual, and you can be sure that I want to see the pounding hips, the glistening drops of sweat, and the look of exhaustion on my baby's face.

*Samantha, 23, disc jockey*

Turn those damn lights off and let my mind's eye fill in the details.

*Jean, 38, dance instructor*

We almost always turn the lights off. My eyes are usually closed anyway, so what's the point?

*Rita, 40, interior designer*

I'm really shy about letting my boyfriend see me naked, so I always turn off the lights. We never have sex during the day, anyway.

*Kimberly, 28, customer service rep*

Fluorescent lights make my boyfriend look like a cadaver, and I'm just not into that kinky stuff. He looks all green and sick, so we turn the lights off. I don't like zombie movies or zombie boyfriends.

*Georgia, 20, hairdresser*

Candlelight is the original mood light, in my book. I love the flickering flames echoing the sensual flicking of my lover's tongue on my clitoris. A scented candle and a vial of essential oils can take the place of a halogen spotlight anytime.

*Nicki, 33, taxi driver*

Part of the excitement is the seeing. Seeing his face tense up, his eyes roll around in his head, the sweat bead up, and the yearning look in his eyes. If I can see him while I'm loving him, it really excites me. Of course he's not bad to look at, either.

*Patty, 49, mother*

## 6. WHAT SONGS, IF ANY, DO YOU LIKE TO HEAR WHEN YOU MAKE LOVE?

Blues, R&B, songs with a slow groove.

*Carol, 33, factory worker*

I like classic rock, loud and pounding. It takes me back to my youth and makes me happy.

*Misty, 38, bookkeeper*

Jungle music. Exotic music from the Third World. Tribal sounds. Weird Celtic pipe music. Medieval chants. I don't want to listen to music I know; I want to be taken to another place. I can always turn on the radio when I'm running errands in my car. When I'm making love I want everything to be special.

*Lily, 34, lawyer*

I don't like listening to music during sex. It reminds me of being back in high school in the backseat of a car. Anyway, it's distracting. Have you ever had sex with someone while he was trying to sing along? It doesn't really add anything to it.

*Clarissa, 31, accountant*

Classical music really turns me on. I like the dynamic passages, the tempo changes, the lush orchestrations. I like the texture, the subtle nuances, the crashing cymbals. Classical music was good enough for centuries of royal command performances. So why should I settle for anything less? When I hear a stirring overture, I want a sexual symphony with as many movements as my lover can conduct.

*Darlene, 42, secretary*

With four kids under the age of ten running around my house, I hear a constant ringing in my ears all day, all night. The best music for me would be total and complete silence. I don't even want to hear the sound of my husband's body slapping against mine.

*Ginger, 27, housewife*

Rap music, rock and roll, and classical. I know that's an eclectic combination, but, hey, I'm a very diversified gal. I've got this remote right beside the bed and whenever I want to change it I can do it practically without missing a beat.

*Tonya, 22, radio station sales*

## 7. DO YOU LIKE TO WEAR PERFUME? WHAT IS YOUR FAVORITE?

My favorite perfume is one that isn't named after a person or a movie star. I don't want to smell like a celebrity.

*Jennifer, 25, sales assistant*

I like rare flowers, essences of spice and exotic lands. I want to take my lover to another place when he is with me, and having a unique and personal perfume is part of my total sensory appeal.

*Jacqueline, 37, massage therapist*

I want to smell like love and warmth for my husband.

*Veronica, 34, legal secretary*

I love to wear expensive, sexy perfume and lots of it. It's a trademark. .

*Roseann, 40, hairdresser*

My girlfriend likes for me to smell like bubble gum, talcum powder, and cotton candy. She wants to be able to eat me up. I'm her baby, and she wants me clean and sweet for her loving mouth.

*Nicole, 23, accountant*

You can't beat cotton and the clean, fresh smell of a good soap. It really makes me feel comfortable to know I'm clean and wherever my baby's lips travel will be a squeaky-clean place.

*Jane, 39, printer*

## 8. DO YOU LIKE YOUR PARTNER TO WEAR COLOGNE? WHAT IS YOUR FAVORITE?

I like the smell of funk, sex, and sweat.

*Ginger, 30, manicurist*

I like to smell pipe tobacco and vanilla. It reminds me of my grandfather and his dark library with all the wonderful books and smells of adventure.

*Linda, 28, artist*

Cinnamon and sandalwood are my favorite smells.

*Maureen, 34, cosmetologist*

I like Old Spice, English Leather, Brut, and cheap shaving lotion. I like the familiar smells of my childhood.

*Jenny, 36, dietitian*

When a man is willing to spend money on a good cologne, I know he will be willing and able to provide me with the better things in life, and that turns me on. A man of culture will take care of himself and me. So when I smell designer scents, I am automatically interested in the man wearing them.

*Leigh, 27, dental assistant*

The smell of urine and leather turns me on. Maybe it is because I grew up on a horse ranch, but the sweet, acrid smell of piss and tanned hides makes me so aroused I can't stand it. And it must be the combination of the two to turn me on. I work in a nursery, and believe me, I smell more than my share of wet diapers all day. And the plain smell of leather in a shoe store doesn't do anything for my sex drive. But put the two smells together and I'm ready to go anytime, anywhere. Put that smell in a bottle and you can have my signed blank check any day.

*Sherry, 32, nurse*

It has been my experience if the chemistry is there between a man and myself, no cologne is better. I really like to smell *him*! I like to smell his testicles, his dick, his chest, arms, shoulders . . . shall I go on? Well, anyway, I like to smell everything about a man I love. No cologne.

*Elizabeth, 42, corporate manager*

## 9. WHAT DRIVES YOU WILD?

Eye contact. Talking without saying a word. Talking with our eyes. Soft, contented breathing. Smooth hands. Manicures. Cleanliness. Flowers. Small, loving gifts. When he treats me as if time is standing still. Undivided attention. Communication. Connecting after sex.

*Bette, 41, poet*

Oral sex! I'd rather get oral sex than anything.

*Janet, 32, waitress*

When I'm teased or tickled.

*Maggie, 22, hairdresser*

A man who knows what he wants and asks me for it up front is a real turn-on for me. I like a man who takes charge and leads the show. Then I can concentrate on what I need to get off, and that makes me wilder. It turns into a snowball effect and just keeps building and building into a rampage of orgasms.

*Martha, 31, school bus driver*

Intelligence turns me on. Brains. Know-how. Plain old-fashioned smarts. Dumb is really just dumb. It isn't a challenge. It isn't ad-

mirable. Stupid is just plain ugly. Give me a man with something between his ears any day. Take all those dumb, pouting, egotistical idiots
and throw them back in the melting pot.

*Sara, 22, model*

Spankings. Not the painful, gut-wrenching kind that would remind
me of getting sent to the principal's office, but soft, playful spankings.
Just enough to make my bottom feel a little bit buzzed makes me
horny and wet. Is that weird? I guess if it turns us on, who cares,
right?

*Betty, 31, clock repair*

## 10. WHAT DRIVES YOU AWAY?

Body odor. Bad breath. People who don't take the time to take care of
their personal hygiene.

*Stacey, 28, bartender*

Jealousy. I don't have time for a jealous man who has a problem understanding who he is and where he is going. I won't stick around long
enough for this to become my problem.

*Diane, 30, teacher*

A pig. A messy pig who needs a maid, not a girlfriend. I'd like to go
into my boyfriend's apartment just once and find it clean. I'd like to
smell something besides dirty socks.

*Tonya, 28, data processor*

Wives. And the men who are married to them but still trying to carry
on with a string of mistresses.

*Deana, 40, probate attorney*

As strange as it may sound, a really attractive guy will drive me away.
Maybe I've just had too much bad luck with good-looking men.
Maybe it is my own insecurity, but whenever I'm with a really drop-

dead gorgeous guy, I feel like the entire world is trying to take him away from me. And I am an attractive woman. I'm not ugly. Men hit on me all the time. It just seems like attractiveness attracts the wrong kind of people. Handsome men coast on their looks, require a higher maintenance, and even after all the hassle and headaches, ultimately leave you to play with a new, younger, or different model. Maybe we should change our definition of "handsome." Maybe it really means the overweight guy with no teeth and little hair who wears high-water pants and will simply spend every day of his life loving you with all his heart and soul.

*Margo, 37, financial officer*

Men who act like little boys and want to call me Mommy. I'm serious. For some reason I've met two men who wanted to play these sick bed-time games and call me Mommy. What's this world coming to?

*Stacey, 30, telephone operator*

# chapter two

# *First Sexual Experiences*

11. *Who told you about sex?*
12. *How did you react when you learned about sex?*
13. *Who taught you about sex?*
14. *Describe your first sexual feelings. How old were you?*
15. *When did you lose your virginity (have intercourse fully)?*
16. *Describe your first experience with intercourse—location, feelings, music, time of year, the whole situation.*
17. *Did your first sexual encounter live up to your expectations?*
18. *Did you tell anyone about your first experience with intercourse? If so, who?*

## 11. WHO TOLD YOU ABOUT SEX?

My cousin. Then, after getting it all mixed up, I talked to my grand-mother. My mother never talked about sex and still doesn't. Go figure.

*Lori, 28, paramedic*

My girlfriends. They seemed to know everything about four months before I did. I don't know why I was so far behind, but they always seemed to know things about intercourse, oral sex, anal sex, and more advanced subjects.

*Sally, 41, homemaker*

Both of my parents told me at the same time. I was eleven. It was excruciatingly embarrassing.

*Amanda, 28, writer*

My brothers. They were older, but just as confused as I was. I didn't get it all straightened out until years later.

*Sasha, 21, graphic artist*

My mother's out-of-work boyfriend not only told me about sex, he tried to show me. The slimy son of a bitch decided, once I turned twelve years old, that he was going to make me a woman. Lucky for me I was faster, smaller, and louder. While he tripped over his pant legs with his erection firmly in hand, I ran outside. I screamed my lungs out. Our neighbors heard the racket and called the police. My mother, bless her soul, believed me and immediately pressed charges against him. That happened over thirty years ago, and I am still getting over it.

*Rachel, 43, guidance counselor*

Books, books, and more dirty books. I hid them all over the house from about the second grade on up through high school. I think my mother found one or two through the years and was just too mortified to ask anyone about them.

*Jill, 25, research assistant*

## 12. HOW DID YOU REACT WHEN YOU LEARNED ABOUT SEX?

I was horrified and convinced that I would never do anything like that.

*Susan, 36, advertising agent*

I was surprised at first, but I was also curious.

*Louise, 41, seamstress*

When my parents told me what sex was, I thought they were joking.

*Jenny, 33, cosmetologist*

I took a cold shower and tried to forget the entire matter. It didn't work. It still doesn't.

*Pam, 21, student*

I was thrilled to death to learn what that wet hole down in the bottom of me was good for. I thought I had a birth defect, and my insides were going to leak out.

*Lea, 47, estate planner*

I absolutely could not wait to have it done to me. I'm still that way today. I like everything and can never seem to get enough if I have the right lover.

*Anita, 38, office manager*

## 13. WHO TAUGHT YOU ABOUT SEX?

My high school sweetheart. We sort of experimented together. It was great.

*Jill, 28, painter*

I learned about sex by watching my cats and dogs. Once I realized that we all had roughly the same kinds of parts, I figured that Little Kitty's pee-pee hole wasn't all that different from my pee-pee hole. The fact that Baby Dog could lick his balls was completely beyond my scope of understanding.

*Connie, 43, promotions director*

My high school sex ed teacher. My parents were way too prudish to talk about it.

*Holly, 43, medical assistant*

My older sister used to let me hide out in the living room when she was making out with Ronnie, who later became her husband. She was sixteen, and I was thirteen. Looking back, I guess it probably sounds perverted, but I loved to sit hidden in the closet and watch the "forbidden" behavior going on right in front of me. Most of the time they just made out and felt each other up. But as their relationship progressed, they went a little further each time. I think my sister liked having me in the closet as her backup insurance. Over the course of a typically hot Georgia summer, their romance intensified, and soon I was watching all kinds of things. I saw my first erection, my first ejaculation (on Mama's favorite floral cushion), and I saw the total thrill of pleasure come over my sister's face when Ronnie performed oral sex on her the first time. My memory might be failing me, but I think my sister looked me right in the eye and groaned when she climaxed in his mouth.

*Donna, 61, florist*

I read books and magazines and watched lots of TV. Then when I wanted to check it out and see if the information was correct, I dragged this neighbor boy to the clubhouse in the backyard and told him to take off his clothes, we were going to do an experiment. He started laughing and then looked like he was going to cry. But I saved his tears by taking off my clothes. His eyes popped open really wide, and his mouth hung open. Then he went screaming and running away. My first affirmation that my information from the other sources was pretty correct was trade school. Can you believe I waited that long? I can't.

*Henrietta, 49, seamstress*

## 14. DESCRIBE YOUR FIRST SEXUAL FEELINGS. HOW OLD WERE YOU?

I was probably four or five years old. I was riding my tricycle, and I remember getting very excited and anxious in my crotch. I can remember it like it was yesterday, and I'm fifty years old. It was the first time I can remember being aware that I could have good feelings down there just from the friction of rubbing my female parts against something. I've been rubbing up against things ever since.

*Marge, 50, nurse*

My brother and I were swimming in the lake when he pulled my swimsuit bottom off and threw it onshore. I was seven and he was six. I was so embarrassed. I retaliated by ripping his shorts off. His little penis was standing straight out from his body. I was amazed. I grabbed it in my hand and refused to let go. He started screaming, and Mom saw what was going on from the shore. She ran right out into the water and gave us both the spanking to end all spankings. At that moment I subconsciously learned how to get a male's attention. I had my brother's undivided attention when I held his penis firmly in my fists. This knowledge has come in handy over the years.

*Sue, 22, student*

I was twelve and my girlfriend had just turned thirteen. We were having a pajama party and talking about boys, boys, boys—which boy we loved the most and how we would kiss our boyfriends like they did on soap operas. I told Susie that I was afraid a boy would laugh at me when I tried to kiss him. She told me she'd teach me all I needed to know about kissing. And she proceeded to teach me everything. She planted a big juicy kiss on my lips and said for the rest of the night her name was Joey. I learned how it felt to have my breasts fondled and kissed. That night I learned how to French kiss. I learned how it felt to have three fingers put up my vagina. I learned how it felt to have my pussy licked. It was my one and only lesbian encounter, and after about thirty years of healthy heterosexual relationships, I have no urge to be with a woman again.

*Diane, 46, teacher*

My first sexual experience came when I saw the Beatles in their first movie *A Hard Day's Night.* My mother had finally allowed me to go to the movies alone with two of my girlfriends, and it was such a thrill to be out of the house without my irritating little brother bugging me. Mama had given me enough money to buy a soda and some popcorn, and I was just the happiest girl alive. We sat right in the very front row in a theater filled with kids just like us. When the lights went down and the music started, Sara, my best friend in the entire world, started screaming. Julie, my other best friend in the entire world, started crying, and so did I. John, Paul, George, and Ringo came on the screen, and I spilled my bag of popcorn all over the floor. I also peed in my pants, soaked my seat, and simply had the most intense sexual feeling of my life. I haven't been right since.

*Rebecca, 42, cosmetologist*

I was at my friend's house down the street. His mother was in the kitchen, and he and I were in his bedroom listening to records, and of course the bedroom door was open so that his mother could keep a careful ear. I was in first grade and he was in second. Well, the next thing I knew, he got in my face and kissed me right on the mouth. Then he pointed to his crotch and said, "Look how my thing gets hard when I kiss you." The next thing I knew, I was on my way out the door, no questions or comments, and wondering what happened. My grandmother explained it all to me when she finally stopped laughing enough to talk to me. I thought it was all pretty strange.

*Donna, 45, auto leasing agent*

## 15. WHEN DID YOU LOSE YOUR VIRGINITY (HAVE INTERCOURSE FULLY)?

I was fourteen and he was sixteen. He was my brother's best friend, and we did it in the treehouse out back. We weren't even dating at the time. We were playing around like always when he told me he loved me and he wanted to make me a woman. It took about ten minutes, and I didn't come. I'm not even sure if he broke my hymen, because the next time we did it, it hurt like hell and I bled all over the backseat of his mother's Oldsmobile. We dated for five years, got married, had two kids, and remain together as I write this. I've never been with another man or woman. I often wonder what my life would have been like if I hadn't gone to the treehouse that fateful day.

*Jenny, 34, nutritionist*

I was thirty-six years old, and I bought myself a male escort. He was a god. Bronze. Built like a bodybuilder. I told him that he was my income tax refund present to myself and I wanted him to make me feel beautiful. I told him that I was a virgin, that I wanted to experience everything and that I didn't ever want to see him again. He was an angel. He seduced me. He kissed me, and caressed every part of me. He took me in his mouth and made me tremble. I felt wave after wave of pleasure from his probing tongue. I twitched and came and he swallowed all my juices. Then he gently mounted me in the missionary position and rocked me to an intense orgasm. Afterward he held me gently in his arms and sang me to sleep. When I awoke, he was gone and a note on the pillow said, "Thanks for the honor of being your first."

*Wanda, 40, career consultant*

I was sixteen and had my first high school boyfriend. I kept telling him no until we couldn't wait any longer. It wasn't what I'd expected—it was great!

*Camille, 42, data entry operator*

I was thirteen. I lost my virginity to the boy next door. We used to hide and play sexually a lot. He coerced me into letting him put his penis inside of me. I don't think either of us really knew what sex was, and we weren't sure if we'd done it or not. It was over rather quickly, and it hurt like hell.

*Sharon, 32, marketing representative*

I lost my virginity on my wedding night at the Plaza Hotel in New York City. I was twenty-two years old, and I married my college sweetheart. We had dated all through school, and after graduating, he took a job in the garment industry. I worked as a secretary for a year so we could have money to make a down payment on a house on Long Island. The entire five years we dated, we never had sexual intercourse. We just didn't even think about it. We kissed and hugged and loved each other dearly, but the possibility of sex before marriage didn't exist for us. We waited, and I am glad we did. The night was lovely. The wait made our marriage night mean something. It remains sacred and special. I encouraged my three daughters to wait until they were married also, but I'm pretty sure they didn't. Two are divorced now, and the marriage of the youngest one is nothing to write home about.

*Marybelle, 60, housewife*

At fifteen years old I thought I knew everything and I probably did. No, just kidding. I was an idiot. Sex was so interesting to me. Especially the way it made boys behave or not behave. I loved the way my body got all heated and the way sweat would bead on my soft skin. My thighs would ache, and that funny feeling would start—way down deep inside my vagina. I simply could not wait to start having sex with my high school sweetheart. We had been dating two years and we talked about it a lot before we did it. It was planned, beautiful, and to this day I'm not sorry. The only regret I have is that neither of us were knowledgeable about how to get me to orgasm. I had my first sex at fifteen but my first orgasm at thirty.

*Lisa Ann, 39, lawyer*

## 16. DESCRIBE YOUR FIRST EXPERIENCE WITH INTERCOURSE— LOCATION, FEELINGS, MUSIC, TIME OF YEAR, THE WHOLE SITUATION.

It was after the junior prom, on the football field with a blind date from another school. I remember grass stains on my dress, the smell of sweat, and the taste of very cheap jug wine. I don't remember my date's name, but I do remember falling in love with his penis and cigarettes that night.

*Jean, 41, decorator*

It was a summer night on a country road in the front seat of my boyfriend's Mustang. Aerosmith was playing on the radio, and after three months of heavy petting, I decided to let him have what he wanted. My panties were on the floor, my skirt was hiked up to my armpits, and my lipstick was smeared. I had been stroking my boyfriend's penis, and his pants were all bunched up around his ankles. All of his change had fallen out of his pocket, and hidden among his pocketknife, Certs, and lucky rabbit's foot was a gold-wrapped rubber. I took his fingers gently out of my soaking wet pussy, placed his moist knuckles on the Trojan, and told him it was time to use that thing. Seven minutes later we were falling out the passenger-side door, scrambling around for our clothes. I was no longer a virgin. He had a cramp in his leg, and the people in the Chevy beside us were too busy making their own memories to notice the trickle of blood running down my thigh.

*Doreen, 29, researcher*

I lost my virginity in a ritzy downtown hotel. I was my boyfriend's eighteenth birthday present. He had worked all summer at his father's furniture store and was saving his money to buy a car. I spent my summer working at the local burger stand. We were both going off to different colleges in the fall, and I wanted to give him something to remember me by. I promised him that if he would pick me up in his new car on his birthday, I'd give him a present that would change his life. We dated and teased each other for weeks leading up to the big day. Since his birthday fell on a Saturday that year, my job was somewhat easier. I made reservations at the nicest hotel in town and put them in my aunt Diane's name. The week before his birthday I took the bus downtown and paid cash for the room (all of $22.95 in 1978). It was such an exciting adventure. During that same week, Tony found the car of his dreams, a red 1968 Camero with mag wheels and only about 120,000 miles on it. His birthday arrived, and I was so thrilled when he picked me up in his new pride and joy. My parents stood on the front porch and waved as we roared away. When we were just out of sight of my house, I told him to pull over. I gave him his birthday card. Inside the Charlie Brown cartoon I'd folded the paid receipt for the hotel room. At first he just looked at the receipt and acted like "what's the big deal about this?" Then it finally hit him what I was actually giving him. We flew down the road. I took the receipt up to the counter while he hid in the lobby. He followed me around to the elevators, and I whispered, "Room 625." I went up first and unlocked the door. A few minutes later I heard a timid knock on the door. There stood my beautiful Tony with a noticeable erection in his pants and a silly grin on his face. We tore the room and each other up. He devoured me with his hands, mouth, and penis. After about an hour of hot passion, we put our clothes back on. Since we didn't have any luggage, it was easy to sneak out of the hotel. I still have the souvenir towel I stole that day. I just hope they didn't send a bill for it to my aunt Diane.

*Sandra, 36, teacher*

Springtime is still a memory-booster for me. It was then the most romantic time of my life and is still. The wind blowing across my skin, my boyfriend and I in the backyard of my sister's house, and chiggers—man, did those chiggers hang in there. For weeks I was scratching all those strange places you never think of scratching. Our music was the groaning, moaning sounds of raw passion mixed with the serenading of crickets in the moonlight. On a blanket in the yard, under the stars and under my boyfriend, I fell in love. Since then we have married, raised three wonderful, creative children who, I am proud to say, are all in college and doing well. I loved that fateful destiny-filled day so much and have even managed to reflect fondly upon chiggers.

*Marybeth, 48, mother and volunteer worker*

## 17. DID YOUR FIRST SEXUAL ENCOUNTER LIVE UP TO YOUR EXPECTATIONS?

No, but I knew it would get better, and I was right!

*Amy, 39, bartender*

Yes and no. I never thought it would be good anyway, so yes, it did live up to my expectations. Unfortunately, I was right, and it wasn't very good. It still isn't after three marriages, a dozen affairs, and forty-five years.

*Chris, 45, attorney*

When I discovered the joys of sex, I was fifteen and it was great. The thrill, the danger, the attention, the heat, the emotions, the raging hormones. Sex is one of the greatest pleasures I have in my life. Screw me and give me chocolate and I'm a happy girl.

*Kaye, 27, physical therapist*

I was so frightened, I don't even remember it. We were doing it in a car, at night, at a place where homeless people had been known to jump out of trees onto couples. I was uncomfortable, bloated, and scared.

*Marilyn, 23, cashier*

No, but I'm still hanging in there. It was too hurried, too scary, and I couldn't breathe. He outweighed me by a hundred pounds. He, being a football jock, was big and strong, and I weighed about 95 pounds. But I am a hopeless romantic and optimist. I just can't let go of the dream and don't want to. Somewhere out there in this big beautiful world is my soul mate. Dammit, what's taking him so long?

*Lisa, 30, leasing manager*

## 18. DID YOU TELL ANYONE ABOUT YOUR FIRST EXPERIENCE WITH INTERCOURSE? IF SO, WHO?

I told my girlfriends in the bathroom the next day at school. They thought I was lying.

*Tonya, 24, receptionist*

My secret remained safe for nearly three minutes. I came home from my date and my pesky little sister took one look at me and said, "You look different. What have you been doing?" I burst into tears and ran upstairs.

*Lisa, 37, accountant*

I confessed to my priest and felt much better when it was all over.

*Frieda, 40, attorney*

I didn't tell a soul. There are some things that should be kept a secret.

*Pat, 33, manicurist*

I called my ex-boyfriend and told him that I'd just given a total stranger, a guy I'd met on the beach, the one thing that my ex had been begging me for all summer. He cried, and I didn't care.

*Carolyn, 19, waitress*

I don't think I have ever told anyone to this day. Although that sounds pretty strange to me, too, I just have a hard time talking about sex to anybody. Someday I'd like to get up my nerve and talk dirty like a foul-mouthed sailor just to see what it feels like. I feel pretty safe putting it on paper, but I would like to see what it feels like to say "pussy," "dick," "suck me, please," and so forth out loud.

*Betty Jo, 31, seamstress*

## Bigger Than Life

I've been married to the same man for over fifty years. We've raised our family and even have grandchildren. My husband is the only man I've ever been with or even wanted to be with. Though he is now eighty-one, we still have a strong, loving, and, yes, sexual relationship. I can honestly say that it has gotten better over fifty years of living, experimenting, and talking to each other.

Through the years we have enjoyed regular sexual happiness by simply taking care of each other's needs and listening to each other's wants and desires.

I was a war bride. We married in 1944 while he was stationed in Indiana. He was training to be a medic in the army, and I was a real life Rosie the Riveter in Tennessee. While he learned how to fix broken bones and drive a Jeep ambulance, I shot rivets into bomber wings all day. I was trained as a teacher, graduated with my degree, and had been the only teacher in a one-room country school. I taught thirty kids in all twelve grades in that single building with a coal stove in the center. When the war broke out, I joined the job force for the good of the nation and was assigned my riveting job for the duration. It was a time of ration coupons, little money, hard work, and lines for gasoline.

My husband and I had been dating for a year when he was drafted. Since I knew he was the one true love of my life, and no one knew how long the war was going to last, we decided we would get married as soon as he completed his basic training in Indiana. The weeks passed, and before I was ready for it, my future husband was getting ready to graduate. He had been assigned to duty overseas, in what turned out to be Sicily and the Italian coast. At the time we didn't know if he was going to be sent to the Pacific or Germany. Though I was a grown woman, my mother was giving me a lot of opposition to getting married. It wasn't that she didn't like my future husband. It was the simple fact that she was going to lose me. I wasn't the baby of the family. Of the twelve children, I was the third from the youngest, but I was the only single daughter she had left. She didn't want to let me go. Four of my brothers were already serving their country. Three of my sisters were working in factories just as I was. I was riveting hot metal all day and then coming home to take care of my mother at night. The last thing she wanted to do was see me run off and get married . . . but that is what I decided to do, with or without her permission. There wasn't any money or time for a fancy church wedding. We were only going to have a quick weekend together with his pass. Any more time and they would have thought he had deserted his post and gone AWOL.

We decided to get married by a justice of the peace and have our honeymoon on the train ride from Nashville to Indiana, just before my new husband was to be sent overseas. My best girlfriend from college and my best high school girlfriend were my maids of honor. We had a simple but loving ceremony and exchanged our vows and rings on the courthouse steps. My husband looked so dashing in his army uniform. I had sewn a pretty new dress for myself, and my friends had pooled their savings to buy me a new hat with flowers on the brim. It was a wonderful day.

That evening my girlfriends took us out for our wedding dinner, and we had a fabulous time laughing and talking about the past and the future. It was past midnight before we made it back to my girlfriend's house, where we were going to spend our wedding night. I was a virgin and so was my husband. I had gone out with several boyfriends on dates, and I had been kissed before. But that was as far as it had ever gone. I don't think I was all that unusual. It was a different world in those days. People weren't as casual in relationships. I was raised with strong family values, and nobody I knew would even consider having sexual relations before they were married. I don't think any of my girlfriends had even thought about having sex with their boyfriends without getting a marriage license first. We were nice, respectable girls who just didn't do that sort of thing. So my girlfriends knew that my wedding night was going to be a big night for me. I think they decided to see how long they could keep us out, so my husband would be so tired by the time we made it to the bedroom, he'd just go to sleep. They didn't know my husband.

When we finally made it to the bedroom, I turned out the lights and turned back the covers to go to bed. My husband went to the bathroom to get ready while I changed into my new nightgown, a gift given somewhat reluctantly by my protective mother. Coming from a family of twelve children, with six brothers, I had seen a penis before. And since I grew up on a farm, I had watched the usual barnyard antics. But the sight I was about to see on my wedding night left me speechless. I saw the door to the bathroom slowly creep open. There, standing in the bright glow, was my husband, completely and proudly naked. His erection was overpowering. I swear his penis looked like a ten-foot-long pole. I can honestly say that it took my breath away. Looking back, I believe I was scared to death. Maybe it was the power of the light and the shadows. Maybe it was the time of night, but I soon overcame my fear.

The next morning we boarded the train and headed for his army base. My husband was so affectionate and loving. He kissed me at the train station, right out in public. I was so embarrassed. I just knew everyone was looking at us and talking about what we'd done last night. They could tell from my face that I wasn't a virgin anymore.

That was fifty years ago. My husband still amazes me today. He's always up to something. We still hold hands. We still kiss in public. And yes, his penis, that lovely weapon of manhood, still takes my breath away. Often.

*Camille, 76, retired school librarian*

## Passion and Proclivity

It all started when I was five. My mother and father told me about sex, because I was going to have a new baby brother or sister and I was asking all sorts of questions. You know, those kinds of questions that make Mom and Dad really, really nervous. The kind of questions that make their palms sweat. You know.

Mom and Dad really did the best they could. I was forever the hopelessly inquisitive child. Very candid and forthright. I would put them on the spot much of the time, catch them off guard. They loved me and tried to do their best, and I loved them back.

At six, seven, and eight, I was still asking lots and lots of questions. Some easy, some very hard to answer, such as "Well, Mom, I understand that God is and was and always shall be, and He has always been here from the beginning, but who are God's parents? Where did He come from? What do you mean He just is?" My mother and dad and I would go around and around with these kinds of questions.

The ones that frustrated them the most, though, were about sex. When I started on that subject, you could feel the change in temperature in the room. Really! Mom's poor little face would turn red, and when Dad would break a smile or, heaven forbid, a laugh, the poor woman looked as if she would just die at any moment without further notice.

"Well," she would say, "girls have this little butterfly"—I later figured out that she was referring to the vagina—"and it's a very special butterfly. It doesn't fly around. It stays at home and listens very carefully to its parents. The little butterfly is a precious thing that belongs to good girls."

"Mom, are all butterflies girls?" I, of course, would ask.

"Well, yes, they are," she would reply, and then take another one of those very deep breaths of hers. She would then continue the story, and it was told over and over to me: "Boys are frogs, and they like to eat butterflies. So the butterflies"—curious little girls like me—"need to stay home, close to their parents, in order to be safe."

Needless to say, I figured out the real story, and my mother lived through it all. Thank goodness there were other people in the world I could talk to. I might have stayed confused my whole life if my sexual knowledge had remained solely dependent upon my mother's analysis of sex and these silly little butterflies and frogs.

High school was a great time for me, lots of boys and friends. Most of my friends weren't having sex, but we were sure wearing it out in discussion. The cafeteria seemed to be the favorite spot to engage in sex chat. We'd look at the boys as they walked by and bet on them. Disgusting hussies, we were. How big did we think his penis was? Had he had sex before? What would he be like in bed? Would his lips feel good on our little butterflies? Stuff like that. Great lunch conversation.

The guys never dreamed what we girls were talking about as we hovered close to each other in deep whisperings. They just smiled and nodded their heads as they walked by us, sat down peacefully, ate lunch, and chatted with their buddies.

I think my parents added to my proclivity toward sex in their distant and confused state, with what they thought was a reasonable explanation of the matter. I, of course, knew something was up right off. Whenever parents hem and haw around about something, you can bet you've hit on a subject worth knowing more about. And not from them. Go find a complete stranger sitting on a stool in the town soda shop, and you will come away with more knowledge than you will get from your parents on the subject of sex. At least that was the way it was for me.

My first sex was during my senior year in high school. I'd been dating the same boy for three years, and we decided we couldn't wait any longer. Had to have it, do it, try it, taste it! Now! And so we did. It was unquestionably wonderful. I've never been right since.

Three kids, twenty years of marriage and bliss later, I still enjoy sex more than breathing air. More than eating. More than anything. Probably even more than my husband does, although he does enjoy it too. This is the same boy from high school, the only boy I ever made love to and the only man I ever made love to. Sex was great the first time with him and still is. I never had any interest in trying anyone else, and so I didn't.

I have two morals to my story:

1. If your children are old enough to put together the sentence to ask the question—answer it. No butterflies and frogs or silly similes. Straight answers for straight questions.

2. If it's not broke, don't fix it. If it feels good and you love it, keep it, and keep it safe and warm. Appreciate and take care of what and who you have in your life.

Do it today.

*Mary Jane, 45, advertising executive*

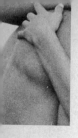

# *Your Sexual Profile*

19. *How many sex partners have you had?*
20. *How often do you have sex?*
21. *How important is sex in your life?*
22. *Are you happy with your sex life?*
23. *What makes your sex life better than other people's?*
24. *If you could change anything about your sex life, what would it be?*
25. *Who do you think has a better sex life than you, and why?*
26. *What special talent makes you wonderful in bed?*
27. *What do you wish you were better at doing sexually?*

## 19. HOW MANY SEX PARTNERS HAVE YOU HAD?

At age thirty, I've only had two. Sometimes I wonder if I missed out on anything.

*Joni, 30, druggist*

I've had 40 or so partners in 20 years of being sexually active. I started having sex when I was 16 and now I'm 36.

*Mildred, 36, cosmetics salesperson*

I have only been with one man. My husband has been all the man I need. We've been together fifty-five years, and I hope God grants us another fifty.

*Katherine, 76, retired*

I haven't had any "partners," because a partner would be someone who would care about my needs and desires. I've had many pricks, dicks, and jerks. I've also had dogs, asses, idiots, and scumbags. So by my count I'm still waiting for my first partner.

*Shirley, 34, salesperson*

I've had three female lovers in my thirty years on earth. My girlfriends have always been there for me when I needed them, and each one remains very important in my life. I wish I hadn't wasted so many years looking for Mr. Right when no man could ever love me the way a woman can.

*Marcie, 30, aerobics instructor*

About fifty, give or take a few, and I still can't get enough. I've been married three times, and each time the divorce was due to a lack of sex. My libido is about as active as they come. And I like to come a lot!

*Jennifer, 46, playwright*

## 20. HOW OFTEN DO YOU HAVE SEX?

Once a year, whether I want it or not.

*Rita, 40, waitress*

I have sex whenever I want it, wherever I want it. It makes me tingle, and I love to tingle.

*Laurie, 24, office assistant*

We make love at the first of the week to start things off on the right note. Usually by Wednesday we find time to squeeze in a quickie, and then we always have sex on Friday night. It's been this way for nineteen years, and it's not going to change if I have anything to say about it. And believe me, I have a lot to say about it.

*Wanda, 45, music teacher*

There used to be a poster saying something about today being the first day of the rest of your life. Well, if this is the first day of my life, I want to spend it fucking. If this is the last day of my life, I want to spend it fucking. I like it. I am good at it. And I really can't think of anything else that I'd rather be doing.

*Melissa, 33, housewife*

Every single night of my married life I've had sex of some variety. Maybe a quickie; maybe a long, hot, sensual two hours of heavy fore-play followed by thrusting, pounding, sweat-dripping, lustful sex; maybe massages and oils and loving, easy sex. We put it in the mar-riage vows to sexually be committed to each other—often. Really we did. And I have to say it was and continues to be the best contractual agreement of my life.

*Jane, 29, lawyer*

## 21. HOW IMPORTANT IS SEX IN YOUR LIFE?

Zip. I'd rather eat, shop, or watch TV than have sex. It's just not that important to me.

*Carla, 29, reporter*

I'd rather fuck than eat. But it depends on what I'm eating and who I'm fucking, or vice versa.

*Ursula, 38, jeweler*

Sex with the person I love is part of what makes me human. It is a very vital part of my being, and I hope to have a sexual experience every day for the next hundred years.

*Margo, 31, medical transcriptionist*

Sex is important to me because it keeps a roof over my head. Love went out of my marriage a long time ago, and the only reason my husband stays is because I am a complete whore in bed for him. We don't talk. We don't go places together. We just sleep together and fuck each other a couple of times a week. He pays all the bills, and I get to live in a nice house and have a new car every couple of years. There are worse ways to live, I guess.

*Nancy, 41, housewife*

I love to be filled up with a hot cock. I like the physical aspects of riding a pulsing, ramming, probing penis. I like the energy, the life force, the sheer power of the sexual act. It is primal and sublime. I used to care about the person behind the cock, but now it is just too much bother. I'll focus on what is important. Names just get in the way.

*Candice, 62, travel agent*

I put sex right up there with breathing. There are many important things in my life, but I can't think of one more vital than my sex life. Someone else can do the dishes, walk the dog, get a nanny to help with the kids, shop, a plumber to fix the toilet, and so forth. But sex is personal and vital to me. I need to be satisfied and often.

*Debbie, 42, executive secretary*

## 22. ARE YOU HAPPY WITH YOUR SEX LIFE?

I can always be happier.

*Eileen, 35, shoe salesperson*

Happy is such a subjective term. I was happy eating hamburger until I discovered filet mignon.

*Rhonda, 22, designer*

I'm responsible for my own happiness, so you can be sure I take the time to please myself. When I'm happy, everyone around me is happy.

*Nancy, 52, hotel manager*

I don't even think about happy anymore. I just try to survive. I don't have the luxury of happiness.

*Vicki, 44, collections agent*

I'm happy when I don't think too much. Intelligence is a gift and a curse. I'm stupid enough to be happy with what I have, but smart enough to realize that I could be doing a whole bunch better.

*Jacklyn, 25, decorator*

My happiness is so important to me. I need to love myself before I can love a man, and I do. I'm now forty and just recently discovered how to love myself. I came to terms with a lot of things that were keeping me from happiness, and from there everything began to unfold like magic. I met the man of my dreams, fell in love, started performing better at work, and had more energy on top of that. My children have noticed the changes, and so have my friends. I love our sex life and can't get too much.

*Johnnie, 40, paralegal*

## 23. WHAT MAKES YOUR SEX LIFE BETTER THAN OTHER PEOPLE'S?

My sex life is better because I work at it. It doesn't come naturally. It is something I care about, so, just like my job, my sex life is something I invest in to make me happy.

*Lindsey, 32, court reporter*

Mine is better because I am better. I'm hot, creative, and I give sex my all. I'm not the prettiest girl in the world, but I'll bet I'm the most satisfying and the most satisfied. Whoever is in bed with me is going to have a great time.

*Rachel, 26, salon manager*

A good sex life is all in your head. When the rest of your life is great, your sex life will be, too. It is part of the total package. If I'm worried about money or my kids or what I'm going to cook for dinner, I can't even deal with getting off. So I put the majority of my effort into making my entire world work, and then the sex takes care of itself.

*Anne, 34, magazine editor*

I was a cheerleader in high school. I could do the splits and cartwheels. I always won awards for my enthusiasm. I was perky and bouncy and full of life. I was just plain bubbly. I still am. I think every man secretly wants his wife to be a cheerleader in life and in the bedroom. I cheer my husband through each and every day of his hardships. I'm always supportive and encouraging. And there have been many nights when I've shown him exciting uses for pompoms. I put my athletic ability to work in the bedroom, where doing the splits takes on a whole new meaning.

*Cindy, 25, real estate salesperson*

I really go out of my way to give special time to myself and my husband. We play together, cook together, read, talk, and take evening walks. We have a great set of locks on the bedroom door, and when we bought this house we did something extra special. We hired a contractor to soundproof our bedroom. Just like a recording studio. When we are making love, I can scream until I turn blue and no one could ever hear me. Not even if they—the children or the neighbors—were standing in the hallway outside the bedroom door. Pretty cool, huh?

*Lettie, 29, librarian*

## 24. IF YOU COULD CHANGE ANYTHING ABOUT YOUR SEX LIFE, WHAT WOULD IT BE?

I'd have one.

*Gloria, 37, accountant*

More partners, more emotions, more sexual adventures. Less concern about what the neighbors think. More time spent on what I like and need.

*Martha, 66, retired government worker*

I'd experiment more with my own pleasure. I wouldn't settle so fast for what my partner wants. I like variety and assortment. I don't listen to the same song over and over. I don't go to see the same movie again and again. So why does society in general, and my husband specifically, think that I should be satisfied with such a plain, same old routine sex life? I feel frustrated and cheated, though I have a perfectly normal life. Maybe I just want to take a walk on the wilder side every decade or so. That doesn't make me bad person does it? That shouldn't be enough to end a marriage of ten years, should it?

*Tammy, 35, stockbroker*

I would figure out how to change my husband's insecurity. He's in therapy, and I appreciate that. If I could speed it up, that would be great. I feel like I'm just marking time and waiting, when we could be doing so much more. His childhood was very cold and businesslike. He's not close to his parents or siblings, and it's hard for me to get really close to him the way I would like to—really best friends as well as lovers. Right now the only time I feel close to him is when we are making love. Then it's right back to the business-feeling relationship. I wish I could have all the time, the loving, unselfishness I feel from him when we are in hot pursuit.

*Yourri, 27, computer analyst*

## 25. WHO DO YOU THINK HAS A BETTER SEX LIFE THAN YOU, AND WHY?

I have a girlfriend who seems to have the most active sex life of anyone I know. She likes to talk about it all the time. Sometimes she actually embarrasses me by being so outspoken. She talks about it like there is no tomorrow!

*Jeanie, 22, secretary*

My boyfriend, because he has the honor of sleeping with me on a regular basis.

*Danielle, 24, editor*

Stupid people have better sex lives because they don't know enough to be upset. They are just happy to get some now and then.

*Jessica, 20, student*

I used to think that rich people, movie stars, and celebrities had better sex lives, more happiness, and easier challenges than I do. But after reading magazines and watching TV for decades, I'm convinced they are just as miserable as the rest of us. You may be a household name, and you may have a glamorous life, but if you can't keep a marriage together after, say, eight or nine tries, you probably aren't a real good role model.

*Veronica, 44, manicurist*

My boyfriend. He cheats and cheats and cheats. I don't like to return evil for evil, but I think he's long overdue. It's my turn. I think I'll fuck everybody in his office first and then tell him to get lost.

*Michelle, 26, secretary*

## 26. WHAT SPECIAL TALENT MAKES YOU WONDERFUL IN BED?

I have great muscle tone and can get in any position. I can also keep up with any man.

*Susan, 24, gym instructor*

My tongue. The men in my life have always talked about my long, wet tongue. I like to start at one end and keep going.

*Jessica, 34, hairstylist*

I have the wettest pussy in the world. I can flood your bed, your mouth, your world. I am the fountain of youth, and all men want to drink from my vessel.

*Veronica, 22, photographer*

I have an incredibly sexy mind. I love to play games, create situations, and act out my fantasies. My lover never knows what to expect, and he likes it that way. I have a whole collection of wigs, toys, lotions, and lingerie to keep my juices and imagination going.

*Charlene, 38, reporter*

Soft skin so smooth you wouldn't believe it. My eyes speak for me, without saying a word, yet when I do speak it is low and soft. My voice is intoxicating. I talk dirty and hot. I choose my words carefully, and every movement is determined and yet effortless and graceful. My touch will melt a man, bring him to his knees to yearn and ache for me.

*Deborah, 39, professional gardener*

## 27. WHAT DO YOU WISH YOU WERE BETTER AT DOING SEXUALLY?

Giving head. I know men love it, and I can surely understand why. I just can't seem to do it without gagging. I wish I could change that. I wish I could do a great job, send my man to the moon, and swallow all that love juice, as he would like for me to do. I just gag.

*Angie, 31, electrician*

I wish I could just let go and enjoy myself. I keep worrying about how I look, what people think, and all that lifetime load of excess guilt. I'd like to just be able to fuck and suck and enjoy sex more.

*Darlene, 27, salesperson*

I'd love to be able to climax during sex, but I never have. Sex with my partner isn't about me; it's all about him. Everything revolves around him—sex, foreplay, you name it. I'm just there to lie on my back and receive. It would be nice to have him focus on me once in a while.

*Whitney, 28, art director*

I wish I was better at saying no. My husband goes through these phases where he likes to have rough sex, anal sex, smelly sex, or whatever the guys at work have told him to try. So he comes home all hot and bothered and wants me to do something intimate with a monkey wrench. And like the faithful, obedient little mouse of a housewife I've become, I always play along. Sometimes I just want to be normal and make love like normal people, without all the theatrics. So I guess I just wish that I was better at saying what I really want to do.

*Tina, 36, dry cleaner*

Relaxing. The ability to completely get out of myself, my inhibitions, feeling self-conscious about my body, my hairdo, all of those things girls and women worry about. How other women do it is beyond me, but I sure wish I could do it. My package is pretty and my mind is rather witty, but I just can't let it all hang out, you know?

*Tabitha, 25, receptionist*

chapter
*four*

# Methods

28. *What is your favorite position?*
29. *What is your partner's favorite position?*
30. *What is your least favorite position?*
31. *What is your partner's least favorite position?*
32. *Which position do you use most often?*
33. *Who is in charge most of the time when it comes to having great sex—you or your partner?*
34. *Can you have an orgasm in more than one position? If so, which ones?*
35. *What is the most unusual position you've ever tried?*

## 28. WHAT IS YOUR FAVORITE POSITION?

Any which way but without! My husband thinks I'm a sex addict because I want to have sex more than once a week.

*Judy, 27, law student*

I like to be on top and leading the show. I can set the pace, control the depth, and ride him till I fall off. Plus, it is great exercise for my buttocks and thighs. I don't have thighs of steel, I have "love legs," and I can crush walnuts between my knees. It is a useful talent.

*Alice, 30, buyer*

I like to be on the bottom with my legs in the air. Maybe I'm old-fashioned, but I think those missionaries had the right idea. I like to kiss and look at my boyfriend while we make love. I like it when the sweat falls from his brow into my mouth. I like the intensity of the contact.

*Mary Beth, 24, manager trainee*

I like to spoon. When we are cuddling on our sides, my husband can easily slide into me, and rock me to sleep. His back doesn't give out, his knees don't hurt, and as long as he stays hard, we can make sweet, gentle love for an hour or more. It isn't so athletic, but it is deeply satisfying.

*Rosie, 33, beautician*

Any position is fine with me. It's the chemistry, the touch of his hand, and the warmth and wetness of his lips that turn me on. I like to be on top, controlling the moment, watching his face, and listening to him moan and groan. I like to grab his chest, hair and all, and ride him. I also like to be completely submissive with him on top, just let go and let him bed me hard, fast, and slow, and go along with anything my man can think of.

*Kim, 42, theft control agent*

## 29. WHAT IS YOUR PARTNER'S FAVORITE POSITION?

My baby likes all different positions—on top, on bottom, upside down. You name it.

*Priscilla, 38, dental hygienist*

My boyfriend's favorite position would have to be doggie-style. He loves the feeling of being totally in control, with me being completely submissive. Men!

*Jeri, 24, musician*

My girlfriend loves to lock herself into a sixty-nine position and put the clamp of love on me for hours. Sometimes I think she is going to drown down there, but she seems to find the energy to keep on going and going and going. When she is in her concentrated sexual mode, she does all the work. All I have to do is flick my tongue every few minutes or so, and she is thrilled.

*Alice, 20, receptionist*

My husband likes the missionary style of sex. Him on top and me underneath. He also likes to turn out all of the lights. No music, no wine, no candles, or any "weird" (as he calls them) positions. I know we're not teenagers, but who ever said that sex should be boring for older folks? I would give anything if he could lighten up.

*Mary, 57, homemaker*

## 30. WHAT IS YOUR LEAST FAVORITE POSITION?

I don't like to be on top. He looks at me so intently that it makes me lose my concentration. Plus, it wears my legs out.

*Nancy, 31, computer programmer*

I hate it when my boyfriend wants to do it from the back. I feel degraded. I don't like staring at the wall, and I don't like being treated like an animal. It makes me feel like an object.

*Traci, 36, maid*

It depends on the guy. The right stud could put me on my head and spin me like a top and I might like it. It's not the position; it's what you do with the position that matters.

*Pamela, 42, detective*

I hate to be smothered, cuddled, and kissed softly. For some reason guys think they have to be gentle and tender with me. I might look like a little china doll, but I won't break. I hate being treated like a precious, delicate butterfly. Lay me down and fuck my brains out. Ram me into tomorrow.

*Ashley, 20, day-care worker*

I don't know any position that my husband and I haven't tried. He's sixty-four, and I'm sixty-two. We've been married for forty years, and I hope I have forty more of him chasing me to the bedroom, taking my clothes off, and pulling me to bed. I think the good Lord knew exactly what He was doing when He created this blissful thing called making love.

*Emma, 62, retired librarian*

## 31. WHAT IS YOUR PARTNER'S LEAST FAVORITE POSITION?

For some reason he doesn't like for me to be on top. I don't think it's really uncomfortable. He just can't cope with having a woman who's in control.

*Megan, 23, aerobics instructor*

My boyfriend doesn't like the missionary position. He's really into experimentation and things like the *Kama-sutra.* We're always trying new positions and new things. He says the missionary style is too boring.

*Katrina, 19, dance student*

My boyfriend doesn't like anything except the missionary position. Every time I try to bring a little variety into the bedroom, he gets upset and calls me "nasty." It is almost like he is afraid that he might like it and somehow that might be wrong. He won't discuss it, and it really makes me mad at times. I guess I'm just supposed to shut up and smile while he grunts and groans himself to sleep on top of me.

*Dorothy, 26, tour director*

Any position where he's not in total control. He's a control freak and always has been. Then again, he's so damn good at everything in the bed, I can't complain too much. Even when I am mad and feel like I hate him, I can't wait to fuck him.

*Patricia, 32, tree surgeon*

## 32. WHICH POSITION DO YOU USE MOST OFTEN?

On my back, looking at the mirror on the ceiling, watching my boyfriend's tight buns shake as he pounds in and out of me.

*April, 25, accounts payable clerk*

Me on my stomach, my husband enters me from behind. What they call doggie-style.

*Rita, 38, waitress*

The position I use most is on my side where my lover enters me from behind and I put my legs back behind his bottom. We just stay connected and gently thrust in and out until we fall asleep.

*Frankie, 44, administrative assistant*

Since I broke up with my boyfriend three months ago, the position I use most is on my back with my legs spread and my fingers rubbing my clitoris till it feels raw. I fantasize about the hunks I see on the soap operas.

*Emily, 19, student*

My man has this thing for positions. Variety is the spice of life, I guess. He says if we use a lot of different positions we won't get bored. I think he keeps himself from getting bored by thinking about everything too much. If it works for him, that's great, but myself, I just love him and love his touch. I could care less about what positions. He doesn't know all of this, of course, and I don't plan on telling him, either.

*Gina, 30, furniture company marketing rep*

## 33. WHO IS IN CHARGE MOST OF THE TIME WHEN IT COMES TO HAVING GREAT SEX—YOU OR YOUR PARTNER?

Me! I always set the mood and go after him like a dog in heat!

*Vivian, 27, nurse*

It's pretty equal for us. Depends on the mood we're in. Sometimes I like to be on top, in control and calling the shots. Other times I like to be submissive and docile. My lover is the same way. It's exciting to try different things.

*Jocelyn, 42, art director*

I let him think he's in charge every time. That is the key to actually being in charge. Power is silent.

*Jo, 43, truck driver*

Our kids actually control our sex lives. Between feeding and changing diapers on our one-year-old, and fights and screaming from our six- and eight-year-olds, we are at their complete mercy. A quiet, free moment is so rare, we wouldn't know what to do with it if we had one.

*Jeri, 30, housewife*

He tells me that he wants me to be in charge, but I don't believe him. When I have started to take over, he looks at me weird. He's sending me mixed messages, and it's confusing. I just don't know why he does that. Men are so weird.

*Tina Lee, 24, waitress*

## 34. CAN YOU HAVE AN ORGASM IN MORE THAN ONE POSITION? IF SO, WHICH ONES?

I can come easily if I'm on top. If I'm on the bottom, I come less frequently. It all depends on the friction between my clitoris and my partner. If we're doing it with him entering me from behind, I don't have an orgasm unless he's touching my clit with his fingers while he's fucking me.

*Loretta, 33, consultant*

I can't have an orgasm in any position. I only come when I masturbate.

*Tricia, 25, graphic artist*

I can come any time in any position. All I need is the right man and a good fucking.

> *Rosie, 31, architect*

The only position we've ever tried that didn't make me come was rear-entry. I hate doing it like that. I feel like a dog.

> *Margaret, 35, classical musician*

Any position that exposes my swollen pink clit or allows my partner access to it is guaranteed to produce a terrific orgasm.

> *Misha, 37, fashion designer*

I used to only be able to come when I was on my stomach and my boyfriend gave it to me from behind. I had a pillow under my clit, and I came all the time in that position. Just in recent years I discovered I can come in various other positions. It was a memorable experience to learn this about myself. I can remember it like it was yesterday, and we're still experimenting. My favorite position now is when I am on my back and my lover is licking my clitoris with a steady rhythm. It's so good when I come; I feel like I leave my body.

> *Henrietta, 41, furniture sales manager*

## 35. WHAT IS THE MOST UNUSUAL POSITION YOU'VE EVER TRIED?

I don't want to get too specific, but it involved a swing, a pair of stirrups, and a hell of a lot of imagination.

> *Ingrid, 40, counselor*

My boyfriend and I once tried to do it with me standing on my head—not a practical idea, but an exciting thought. I almost passed out from the thrill, or maybe because all the blood had rushed to my head. It wasn't a complete disaster, but we've opted for simpler positions since that episode.

> *Patricia, 26, caterer's assistant*

My lover and I use a scissorlike position sometimes. It's hard to get the perfect angle for penetration, but once you find it, it's pure ecstasy.

*Louise, 47, park ranger*

We call it our Spanish Love Dance, which is actually quite a joke, since we are two very pale Minnesota natives, but it really is quite enjoyable. I straddle my husband's waist and lock my legs around him. He backs me up to a wall and thrusts away while standing. He can usually go for about ten minutes before his thighs give out or cramp up. We always leave such wicked stains on the wallpaper.

*Nicole, 33, financial consultant*

My lover, God love him, wanted to make love in the hammock in our backyard. It was a tragedy to say the least. He was on bottom, me on top, and a bird crapped in my hair. I screamed, fell off the hammock, and the neighbors came into their backyard and began shouting, "Who's there?" Scrambling through our backyard on our hands and knees, we made it to the back door without being spotted. I think.

*Gari Ann, 35, fast-food restaurant manager*

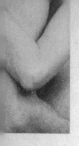

chapter
*five*

# Memorable Experiences

36. *Describe the sexual experience that pushed all your buttons and threw you into a meltdown in record-breaking time.*
37. *Describe the worst sex you've ever had.*
38. *What was your strangest sexual experience?*
39. *What was the messiest sex you've ever had?*
40. *What was your most embarrassing sexual experience?*
41. *Describe the longest sexual encounter you've ever had.*
42. *Describe the shortest sexual encounter you've ever had.*
43. *What was the biggest age difference between you and a lover?*
44. *What was your funniest sexual experience?*

## 36. DESCRIBE THE SEXUAL EXPERIENCE THAT PUSHED ALL YOUR BUTTONS AND THREW YOU INTO A MELTDOWN IN RECORD-BREAKING TIME.

Where do I line up? I don't think I've ever had one.

*Melissa, 23, factory worker*

My boyfriend Paul always satisfies me, but one night was the ultimate highlight in my sexual life. He took me to dinner and then dancing. He was a perfect gentleman—roses, wine, the works. Then on the way home, we stopped at a hotel and made love all night. I think it was his attentiveness to me that made me feel so sexy. It was a night I'll never forget.

*Doris, 28, ticket sales*

John took me out in the middle of a rainstorm one spring night and peeled me like a banana. He used my wet cotton dress as a pillow and laid me down in a pasture of wildflowers. He left his shirt on and only unzipped his pants. We made love with passion and didn't care for a moment how ridiculous we probably looked. The rain felt heavenly. The thunder just added to the excitement. I had sticktights, stems, and mud all over my nude body. He still has grass stains that won't come out after three years of washing.

*Cindy, 35, dairy farmer*

I was standing on a ladder in our kitchen hanging curtains, and my husband approached me quietly from behind. With his hands reaching around my waist, he pulled my shorts down around my ankles, turned me around on the ladder, the curtains falling to the floor. He went down on me as I stood there in total shock. My knees got weak, my legs began trembling, and all I could do was let him take me. It was *the* most exciting, provocative sex we had ever had. My juices were flowing, and my heart was pounding as I had never before experienced. For fifty, that's not too shabby.

*Nadine, 50, office manager*

## 37. DESCRIBE THE WORST SEX YOU'VE EVER HAD.

It would have to be my first time. I was a junior in high school and hopelessly in love with this boy. I thought he was in love with me too, but after we had sex, he dumped me quickly. I couldn't believe how stupid I felt. Not only had I misjudged him, but I had wasted my virginity on someone who cared nothing about me. I'll always regret that mistake.

*Jane, 25, accounting clerk*

I made the mistake of sleeping with my now ex-husband while we were in the middle of our divorce. I've always heard that sex is the last thing to go in a relationship. It was horrible, and it just complicated everything.

*Laura, 33, medical bookkeeper*

The worst sex I ever had was with a new boyfriend. I was mad about him. He was smart, funny, sensitive—everything I'd ever wanted. But he was horribly inexperienced sexually. The first time we made love was a disaster. He had absolutely no idea what to do and became really frustrated when I tried to show him. The sex never got any better and we eventually broke up.

*Natalie, 29, bank teller*

I have small breasts. They aren't ugly, just small. The worst sexual experience I ever had was on a first and last date with a person whose name I've blocked out of my memory. We had flirted for weeks at school, and when he finally did ask me out I was so excited. I bought a pretty blue sweater and a new padded bra to help make a good impression. The dinner was nice. The movie was entertaining. We kissed and held hands and everything seemed to be going fine. On the way home we went to park. After making out for a while, he finally fumbled his way into removing my sweater. He undid my bra and started to fondle my breasts. The jerk was so surprised at their small size that he started laughing. I broke out crying, grabbed my clothes, and jumped out of the car. I want you to know that I walked all the way home, and he didn't even try to follow me. I never spoke to him again, and even though I've since married and go to the same church as he does, I hope he rots in hell.

*Abby, 23, law enforcement officer*

My lover and I tried to have sex after an argument that was unsettled. It just doesn't work that way.

*Pauline, 45, law clerk*

The worst sex is no sex. My body seems to revolt and go into some kind of withdrawal. As preoccupied as that sounds, it's true. I can't think straight, don't want to eat, have trouble sleeping, etc. Fulfilling sex is what keeps me running properly.

*Ann, 41, accountant*

There was this one boyfriend who wanted to give oral sex to me. He said he wanted me to enjoy this "gift" and experience the ecstasy of having an oral orgasm. He described it in such a way that I thought he knew what he was doing. Great, I thought. This is going to be wonderful. Wrong! It was more like being licked by a rabid dog. At least that's how I imagined a rabid dog would feel. Possessed. Not that I've ever been licked by a dog, but it was horrible. I felt so much like he was getting ready to bite me or something, I couldn't relax and I certainly couldn't have an orgasm. I faked it so he would stop.

*Yolanda, 27, video rental clerk*

## 38. WHAT WAS YOUR STRANGEST SEXUAL EXPERIENCE?

Having sex with two men at the same time. It was too bizarre to enjoy.

*Lynn, 31, cashier*

I was really bored with my boyfriend, and I didn't want to have sex with him. I played video games during the ordeal.

*Allison, 24, stockbroker*

My first sexual experience was pretty strange. I thought it would be something that felt good, but it hurt like hell.

*Cindy, 25, photographer's assistant*

The weirdest was when my boyfriend had me dress up like a man and ram a soda bottle in and out of his bottom. He liked it too much.

*Diana, 40, copywriter*

My best girlfriend had me join a threesome one night with her boyfriend. He initially wanted to have sex with me while she watched, but Cathy wasn't too thrilled about that idea. So he entered her doggie-style while she gave me oral, as I videotaped the entire adventure. At the time it felt pretty hot, but watching the tape in the light of day is pretty embarrassing.

*Sandra, 20, waitress*

Watermelon, candy canes, chocolate candy kisses, ice cream, and three men. At one of those cheap motels, not enough towels and funky carpet kind of places, I had one of the strangest and best sexual flings of my life.

*Cathy, 22, receptionist*

## 39. WHAT WAS THE MESSIEST SEX YOU'VE EVER HAD?

The time I was having sex—pretty wild sex—and didn't know I was starting my period. The lights were off, and we were having a great time. We were all over the bed. Right side up and upside down. I think we tried every position possible that night. The next morning when we got out of bed, we both gasped for air and looked at each other. The bed looked like a battlefield with no survivors. When we realized what had happened, we laughed hysterically and burned the sheets.

*Kelly, 25, waitress*

I had sex with my boyfriend out in a field. We had dirt and grass stains everywhere.

*Fran, 30, ski instructor*

My lover and I decided to make human ice cream sundaes once. We used hot chocolate sauce, whipped cream, ice cream, cherries—the whole works. It was sticky and fun.

*Justine, 28, dietitian*

The messiest sex I ever had was the time my boyfriend and I poured a bottle of baby oil on ourselves in an uninflated wading pool. We wanted to be able to slide around on the plastic without leaving stains on the floor. So we were having a good ole slippery time laughing and sliding. I was in the middle of giving him highly lubricated head when the doorbell rang. I looked up to see who was at the door, and at the same moment, he climaxed in my eye. I couldn't see a thing. My parents were at the door. We were both nude, oily, and I had a big old white gob of semen blinding me. It looked like mayonnaise. I couldn't find a towel, and I kept falling down every time I tried to stand up.

*Patty, 24, accountant*

Messy sex is great. I love the juices, body fluids, sweat, heat, and passion of very open sex. No hiding or queasy stomachs. No forbidden places to eat or lick or touch. I completely consume my lover every chance I get. I love the smells of our bodies together. Nothing is forbidden. The messiest sex we had was when he came on my breasts and I urinated on his stomach.

*Wendy, 31, computer operator*

## 40. WHAT WAS YOUR MOST EMBARRASSING SEXUAL EXPERIENCE?

The time I got my long blond hair caught in my boyfriend's zipper and had to get someone to help us. I'm not going to say who it was. I'm still too embarrassed. I'm also not going to tell you what we were doing.

*Jill, 27, interior designer*

I had a bad case of gas one night, and when my lover thrust deep into my warm love nest, I ripped out a fart that could have cracked glass. It was loud, smelly, and totally impossible to ignore. So I started laughing uncontrollably and let two more little farts escape. My boyfriend jumped out of bed, opened a window, and then grabbed the air freshener. Two weeks later, after a big meal of Mexican fajitas, he had the same problem, so revenge was lovely.

*Patty, 23, radio announcer*

I started my period once during the middle of sex with a new lover. The poor guy saw all the blood on his pecker and thought I'd cut him. He freaked out. I thought he overreacted. If I was going to slice off a penis, there would be no doubt about my intentions, and I'd wait until we were finished fucking. Why waste a good hard-on?

*Beth, 33, health spa owner*

My boyfriend's parents walked in on us right in the middle of sex. I could never look them in the eye again. We broke up almost immediately.

*Heather, 28, retail sales*

I guess the most embarrassing time for me happened recently when I ran out of juice while my husband was making love to me. I just went dry. I don't know if he shook all the lubrication out of me when he withdrew his penis each time, or if I was simply dehydrated. I thought I was enjoying the sex, but suddenly I'm all dry inside and my husband is getting rug burns on his pecker. Maybe I'm going through too much stress at work. I must need a new job.

*Samantha, 42, court reporter*

We were sitting in a busy restaurant eating dinner, and after we were through eating I took off one of my shoes and began playing with my husband's penis under the table with my foot. Immediately he got an erection, unzipped his pants so to enable better access, and laid his napkin in his lap over my foot. We were in the back of the restaurant in a booth, but still it was fairly unprotected and we could easily have been caught. In the heat of passion and just as he started coming all over my foot, the waitress started to approach our table to ask if we needed anything. I knew he wasn't going to be able to stop, so I yelled to her before she arrived at the table, "Bring me a hot fudge cake now, and hurry!" I said it like the place might have been on fire. She stopped in her tracks, said, "Sure ma'am," and turned to walk away, looking very confused. That one was too close.

*Teresa, 35, executive secretary*

## 41. DESCRIBE THE LONGEST SEXUAL ENCOUNTER YOU'VE EVER HAD.

It would have to be on our first wedding anniversary. My husband and I rented a hotel room downtown and spent the entire weekend in bed. We didn't even leave the room. We fucked and played the whole time. It was great.

*Jessie, 35, orthodontic assistant*

I once spent an entire evening—about four hours—watching porno movies and masturbating. I slept really well that night.

*Alex, 29, hairstylist*

I was with a guy once who lasted for almost two hours. It was tiring.

*Helen, 40, computer salesperson*

When my husband came back from Vietnam in 1972, we stayed in bed until he simply could not climax anymore. I fucked him, sucked him, and squeezed every last creamy drop out of his testicles. By the time we finished, the sun was coming up and his balls were aching. His knees were shaking, his face was red, and he just looked so completely blissed out. It was a wonderful homecoming.

*Mary, 50, government worker*

Three hours, fifteen minutes. The greatest sex I've ever had. Two men, a hot tub, and candles. Memories still ring in my mind and I can't wait to do it again.

*Joann, 19, advertising agent*

My husband and I sent the children to their grandmother's house for the weekend and locked all the doors to the house. We played music, ate on the floor, had sex in every room, and completely spoiled each other—mind, body, and soul. It was invigorating and relaxing. I learned things about my husband that weekend, and that surprised me. We've been married thirteen years, and I thought I knew every-thing. We're presently thinking about what we will try next.

*Frieda, 47, purchasing agent*

## 42. DESCRIBE THE SHORTEST SEXUAL ENCOUNTER YOU'VE EVER HAD.

The first one I ever had was the shortest. I swear, it lasted less than ten seconds.

*Beth, 25, graduate student*

The shortest sexual experience I ever had was when I was with an older man. I didn't know he was married. We had gotten in bed, and just as he penetrated me, his wife burst through the door. Needless to say, that encounter was pretty short.

*Tina, 40, homemaker*

My boyfriend met me at the door on prom night with a bouquet of flowers and a box of candy. I had on my new pink chiffon party dress. He leaned over to kiss me and climaxed in his pants. It soaked right through his baby-blue trousers and made a dark pink spot on the very center of my dress. We went to the dance anyway and tried to stay in the shadows. Even though most of it dried up before the night ended, every time I look at our prom photo, all I can see is those damn spots on his pants and my dress.

*Leigh, 23, teacher*

My boyfriend came into the bathroom, asked me if I would do some-thing kinky with him, and I said I would. He said, "Will you turn around and just bend over and grab your ankles for me?" I did, and he came in about three strokes. It was kinky to him, and I guess he just couldn't take it. I mean, he couldn't last because he thought it was so good. The part I enjoyed the most wasn't the sex, but just seeing him have so much fun.

*Neida, 26, insurance agent*

## 43. WHAT WAS THE BIGGEST AGE DIFFERENCE BETWEEN YOU AND A LOVER?

I was fifteen and he was thirty-two. He thought I was eighteen, and I thought he was twenty-two. So, mentally, we were only four years apart. But legally he could have gotten eleven months and twenty-nine days.

*Emily, 19, student*

I was forty and he was eighteen. Yes, I seduced the yard boy. He was so cute, and he had been flirting with me for weeks. He had mowed the front yard and part of the side when I brought him a glass of lemonade. I was wearing my tanning suit, and he had on a pair of cutoff blue jeans. He said he wanted me to teach him all about love, so I did. I fucked him and told him to finish mowing the lawn or I wouldn't pay him.

*Faye, 42, housewife*

I was twenty and he was forty. I don't know what I was thinking. We had absolutely nothing in common other than being great in bed together.

*Debbie, 26, driver*

I was eleven and he was thirty-five. I was a schoolgirl and he was Elvis Presley. Though in my mind it was one of the all-time great love stories, in fact, it was just a young girl's dream.

*Joan, 37, banker*

This guy I thought I was in love with, it turned out that he wanted to be my sugar daddy. He was fifty and I was nineteen. I swear he didn't look a day over thirty. Maybe I was just drinking too much wine and having too much fun. I dumped him.

*Tabitha, 24, radio station copywriter*

## 44. WHAT WAS YOUR FUNNIEST SEXUAL EXPERIENCE?

Getting caught by my little sister and then trying to explain to her what my boyfriend and I were doing without morally damaging her for life.

*Kay, 22, lifeguard*

Trying to get drunk—at least relaxed—for my first sexual encounter. Instead, I ended up hugging a toilet. I was as sick as a dog. What a memory!

*Julie, 19, copy girl*

Once, my boyfriend and I were having wild, hot, animal sex in his bed. We had been going crazy for about an hour—lots of foreplay, hot, sweaty sex, different positions. We were both sweating a lot. We changed positions, and he got on top. When our stomachs touched, all of the sweat against our skin made this loud farting noise. It was hysterical. I couldn't help but laugh. Fortunately he had a good sense of humor and thought it was pretty funny, too.

*Sheila, 30, shoe salesperson*

My funniest sexual experience had to be the time my cat jumped on top of my partner during sex. It scared him so much he screamed right out loud during the middle of sex, which was unusual, since he'd never made much noise before. It was a funny experience even though I never would have dreamed a man could lose an erection so quickly.

*Lee, 36, secretary*

In hindsight, my funniest experience was when my lover mistakenly tried to put his penis in my bottom. His aim was a little off, and he thought I was just a little tighter than usual. I kept trying to move him up to the right spot, but he didn't get the hint. I finally told him to get away from my ass and to put it where we both could enjoy it.

*Monica, 22, gas station attendant*

Dinner burning on the stove—someone evidently called the fire department after they saw smoke coming from our kitchen window. My lover and I were upstairs in this really big house, going at it like animals in heat. The fire was easily put out, and as we listened at the stairs we were too embarrassed to come downstairs, so we called our neighbors on the phone and pretended like we heard about the fire from a friend's house down the street. We asked them to tell the firefighters we'd be right there. Then we started to crawl out the upstairs window and lower ourselves with a sheet, just like something in the movies. We thought we had a good plan—to come around the corner of the house as if we had walked from down the street. Our plan backfired when one of the firefighters suddenly came around the house and started shouting that burglars were crawling out of an upstairs window. It was embarrassing and a nightmare trying to explain who we were and what we had been doing. They laughed uncontrollably. To this day we are still good friends with one of them, though, and he and his wife call us the hot tamales.

*Jessica, 30, phone operator*

## Burning Down the House

It was my first summer out of journalism school, and I had taken a job reporting the local news for a century-old weekly newspaper. I had to write obituaries, cover county news, and review an occasional local theatrical presentation of such classics as *The Sound of Music.* The town was quaint, but close enough to a big city that I felt I was at least connected to the real world of news and important writing.

Since this was pre-AIDS and barely post-Watergate, being a cute redheaded investigative reporter for any kind of newspaper was a desirable position.

I was twenty-one, single, paying my own bills, and driving around in a very used but still sporty convertible. Even though the town was one of those where your family would have to have lived for over a hundred years in order to belong, I made friends and met most of the movers and shakers in the community.

The publisher of the paper had been in the business for over fifty years, just like his father and grandfather. He was one of the founding fathers of the state's journalism association and was even honored in the Journalism Hall of Fame. He loved to take cub reporters under his wing and give them the inside lore of days gone by. He knew everyone and had the inside scoop on most local and even a few national politicians. Just when you were sure he was feeding you a line about being at such and such an event or knowing this or that person, he'd pull out a big scrapbook and show pictures of himself smoking a cigar with LBJ or receiving an honor from John F. Kennedy.

I loved working under a deadline, digging up stories, and seeing my byline in the paper each week. I got to work early and always stayed late. Sometimes, when everyone else had given up and gone home, I'd still be pounding away on my trusty Smith Corona. (This was pre-PC and Apple. Type was still set in lead.)

I loved to sneak upstairs to the publisher's office and look at his scrapbook, spin around in his old leather chair, and put my feet up on his ancient wooden desk, the same desk his father and grandfather had used.

I liked being the new kid on the team. I liked the attention, the excitement, and the way it felt to exercise my small but rapidly developing journalistic power.

Then Alexander Reginald IV came home from New England. He was the publisher's golden grandson and was the cockiest, silver spoon–sucking, coupon-clipping asshole I'd ever met. He drove a Porsche Speedster, sported a pretentious goatee, and called himself a photojournalist. His Ivy League accent and tailored shirt basically made me sick.

My dearly loved publisher decided that A.R., or Reggie, was going to be my partner for the summer. He would take pictures and I would write stories. We would be the ace cub reporters and show the community a thing or two about the New Journalism.

It must be true that love and hate are extremely close neighbors, because after an initial week of intense loathing and disgust, I actually grew quite fond of the arrogant little prick. He would capture the scene with his Nikon, and I'd immortalize the moment with my clever phrases. We were a great team.

We went everywhere together, covering the crime scene, the social events, and the community happenings. We became well known for our youthful brashness. I would ask the embarrassing questions at government meetings, and he would snap the outraged reactions on Kodak's best and then splash his revealing portraits across the front page of the paper.

I spent hours in the darkroom with Reggie, developing negatives and making enlargements. While the prints were drying, we'd be fucking like rabbits in the darkroom. I developed an intense passion for the smell of developer. The sight of a safelight's red glow would make me wet. I was on the Pill, and Reggie was always plenty amorous. We fucked ourselves to exhaustion week after week.

With summer coming to an end, Reggie was going back to finish his senior year at Yale. We decided to finish the summer with a bang. After putting in a full day of writing, shooting, developing, and printing, we waited until everyone else had gone home and sneaked into the publisher's office.

Reggie led me over to the grand old publisher's desk, lifted me up, and rolled me back. He hiked my skirt up over my head, threw my red panties on the floor, and sucked my little pink pussy like a man dying of thirst. While Presidents Truman, Eisenhower, Kennedy, and Johnson watched intently from the walls, my Ivy League lover sucked me to a screaming climax.

As Reggie entered me and proceeded to fuck the screaming headlines right out of me, I must have lost control a little bit. As he was grinding in and out of me, I smelled smoke. Was I hot enough to be on fire? In my passion, I'd pushed the antique brass banker's lamp up against a stack of old newspaper clippings and set them on fire. The room filled with smoke as my lover hurriedly jerked his pants back on.

I called the fire department and fanned out the flames. By the time the fire engine arrived, the damage had been contained with the only casualty being a framed picture of the publisher with Jackie Kennedy. The fire chief said it looked like faulty wiring had caused the fire, and I dutifully reported the story as fact in the next edition of the paper. Reggie's photo of the smoke-filled office and the burned image of Jackie Kennedy was picked up by the wire services and published around the world as a political comment on the changing times.

My beloved publisher died a few years after that summer's fire. Reggie is currently working on his big political novel after twenty years of covering the Washington political scene, and I'm a somewhat noted features writer for a national daily newspaper. I also produce an occasional documentary for one of the nation's broadcasting networks.

But I still find time to close my office door every now and then, and let my photojournalist husband impale me on my desk with a hot passion that reminds me of Camelot and fire engines.

*Lucinda, 40, reporter*

## Class Reunion

I'd had twenty years to worry about this stupid event. Twenty years of avoiding the issue, not thinking about the night, coming up with excuses not to go. I didn't really care about any of those people. I didn't like them that much the first time around.

Who was I kidding? My twentieth high school anniversary was coming up, and I was scared out of my mind. I'd missed my tenth reunion because no one had my address in Ohio. But after moving back home three years ago I'd made the mistake of getting back in touch with some of my old high school pals. The ominous invitation to the ceremonies arrived a full six weeks before the event, and to make matters worse, two of my childhood girlfriends had called me to make sure I'd received my invitation.

I hadn't reached my goals in life yet. I wasn't a millionaire. I wasn't internationally known. I was just a basic mom trying to keep my head above water and my kids in line.

My business partner and I were struggling with starting a new business, and things were starting to pay off. But there just weren't a lot of extra hours or dollars to go around for such things as dinner tickets to a stupid class reunion.

My business partner is a year older than me, and he had attended his own twentieth class reunion last year. He saw my invitation on the desk about a week before the event and just wouldn't stop bugging me about going. I wasn't dating anyone at the time, and just didn't want to go. Period. End of discussion. Shut up and go bother someone else.

He said that the only reason he went to his was because his old high school honey had called him up the day of the reunion and told him in no uncertain terms that he was going to be her date. He said that he too originally hated the idea, but really, really, really had a great time at his reunion.

I told him I didn't have anyone to go with. He told me he'd take me. He had just ended a two-year relationship and thought it would be nice to meet some new women close to his own age.

I told him I didn't have anything to wear. He gave me his credit card. I told him I wouldn't be able to find a baby-sitter. He told me to sell the kids and invest the profits in a new stereo system.

The day of the reunion arrived. They had an informal picnic at the park on Saturday before the big dance that night. With great reluctance, I found my tightest pair of blue jeans, wore a simple blouse, and took my kids in my trusty ole sedan down to the festivities. My business partner couldn't make it to the picnic. I was on my own.

And you know what? It wasn't so horrible. I saw a bunch of old friends, caught up on twenty years of gossip, and generally had an okay time. But this was just the picnic. The dinner was going to be a whole other can of worms. People would be dressed to kill. Alcohol would be flowing, speeches would be made, and everybody would be giving me the third degree. Why would I put myself through such torture?

My business partner had a surprise waiting for me. When I pulled into the driveway, there was my business partner in a black tux. He was holding a bouquet of red roses, and standing beside a jet-black 1974 (the year of my high school graduation) Corvette.

He told me to hurry up and change into my black silk gown before the Corvette turned back into a pumpkin.

We made our entrance at the country club where the dinner was being held. I wanted everyone to see our grand entrance, and they did.

I felt great. I looked great. My business partner was charming, witty. I was playing the part of the successful single superwoman to the hilt.

I saw several old boyfriends. They had aged, some better than others. Some were married, some were divorced.

The one thing everybody noticed most about me was the fact that my waist-length black hair was now gone. My hair was my trademark in high school. For some strange reason, I'd decided to whack it all off a couple of months before the reunion. I don't know if it was a subconscious desire to have another good excuse for not going or what. Most people assumed that I'd cut my hair short decades ago.

Instead of having a live band, the organizing committee had chosen a DJ and a karaoke system. We all roared while the football team sang "Leader of the Pack." The student council president slaughtered "Born to Be Wild." I was really having a good time, drinking, laughing, talking. My partner made small talk and explained that he wasn't one of them, but had actually attended our archrival high school in a nearby town. One woman swore she remembered him from chemistry class, but she was simply drunk. Though my partner didn't seem to notice her obvious character flaws, I did.

Since everyone remembered me from choir, I made several trips to the spotlight. My voice was strong. The words to the songs were right in front of me on the video screen, so I sang everything everyone asked for. I did everything from Patsy Cline's "Crazy" to old Beatles and Carpenters songs. I loved being in the spotlight. I became the ultimate torch singer with my slinky silk dress and my glass of champagne. I must have performed over twenty songs. It was really a wonderful experience.

The drunk woman who claimed she knew my business partner dragged him out on the dance floor and did the dirtiest dance I'd seen in ages. She was all over him like a wet mop. The cheap floozy was laughing much too loud, and spilling wine all over my partner's tux. Naturally, she tried to wipe the wet spot off with her tongue.

I decided it was time to get off the stage and let someone else sing. I rescued my partner from Bad News Brenda, and after having a few more glasses of champagne, I asked him to dance.

The next song was James Taylor's "You've Got a Friend," one of my favorites. I hugged my partner tightly, flashed a drop-dead glare at Brenda, and danced. We both started singing along with the lyrics, even doing harmony. We were good. No, we were fabulous! We danced and we sang and we laughed, and we spun around and around.

It was truly magical. I kissed my business partner in his ear and giggled seductively at his every comment. The crowd became simple background noise, and I saw my business partner in a whole new light.

We danced until they physically unplugged the sound system. We were joined at the waist, inseparable. I was Cinderella and he was Prince Charming. It felt great.

My former boyfriends had somehow managed to leave without saying good-bye. Oh, well, maybe I'd see them in another ten years.

On a perfect moonlit night in the deserted parking lot of a stuffy country club, I found my reunion on the hood of a jet-black 1974 Corvette.

*Sue, 38, advertising executive*

chapter
*six*

# Men

45. *What type of man turns you on?*
46. *What type of man turns you off?*
47. *What do you think men need most from a woman?*
48. *What do men seem to want most from a woman?*
49. *What do women need most from a man?*
50. *What do women want most from a man?*
51. *What do you envy most about men?*
52. *What do you envy least about men?*

## 45. WHAT TYPE OF MAN TURNS YOU ON?

A well-built, tanned man with a nice butt.

*Pam, 40, ad salesperson*

Any man with a good personality, a nice smile, and pretty
eyes.

*Tonya, 26, receptionist*

A man who is ready and willing.

*Danielle, 22, telemarketing specialist*

An intelligent man with a wonderful sense of humor. A great laugh
makes me wet.

*Wendy, 34, paralegal*

A man with an accent from someplace other than Brooklyn or New Jersey.

*Shirley, 20, hairdresser*

One that wears leather loafers, khakis, and an attitude.

*Melinda, 35, secretary*

I like men that know what they want and have a clue as to how they are going to get it. Smoke is cheap. I like fine men and finer things.

*Liz, 51, furniture restorer*

## 46. WHAT TYPE OF MAN TURNS YOU OFF?

A fat one. Gross!

*Katy, 20, clerical assistant*

One who is arrogant, snobby, and full of himself.

*Linda, 36, customer service representative*

Any man who acts like a baby is a real turn-off. I don't like immature, jealous, or insecure men. There's nothing worse than a jealous guy with no self-confidence.

*Katherine, 25, medical student*

A smooth talker who likes to touch everyone. I hate guys who have all the answers and tell the most amazing stories. I always want to count my fingers after I shake their hands to see if anything is missing.

*Julie, 40, seamstress*

Blue-collar workers with grime and grit under their fingernails. My father was a mechanic, and he always came home with filthy hands. I know there is nothing wrong with honest labor, but I want a man with smooth hands and nice fingernails. I want to be able to look forward to his touch.

*Jasmine, 19, student*

Skinny men are a turn-off. Small, narrow, weak-looking shoulders, skinny legs, and no butt. I like muscles and meat.

*Chrissy, 29, paper manufacturer*

Bullheaded, opinionated men who don't listen. Men who can't share bother me, too. I like a man to be a gentleman, not a little boy sucking his thumb. That's what mother's tits were for, when he was an infant. But not pigheaded either.

*Katrina, 23, restaurant salesperson*

## 47. WHAT DO YOU THINK MEN NEED MOST FROM A WOMAN?

I don't have a clue! More sex and colder beer?

*Teresa, 41, bank teller*

Men need a woman to be wet, ready, and silent unless spoken to.

*Joann, 24, dancer*

Men need what women need: love, devotion, friendship, and a good slap on the behind every once in a while to keep them in line.

*Shirley, 55, seamstress*

They need to be fucked hard, sucked to a climax, and then told how wonderful they are every night.

*Marty, 40, marketing representative*

Men need to be slapped silly. Maybe it would knock a little sense into their good-for-nothing heads. They do such damn fool things all the time.

*Maggie, 53, housecleaner*

Slaves.

*Priscilla, 35, homemaker*

Soft hands caressing their body, whispers of "come love me" in the night, and warm lips on their love organ.

*Veranda, 49, truck driver*

## 48. WHAT DO MEN SEEM TO WANT MOST FROM A WOMAN?

The ability to be unconditionally sexy. Total freedom from inhibition. A wild kitten in bed, a lady at the PTA meeting, and a good mother all rolled into one neat package.

*Mia, 28, housewife*

I think they really like it when women can be sexually spontaneous. The less planning and the less structured, the better.

*Toni, 31, nurse*

Approval. Acceptance. Loyalty. Less talk. More sex. Don't fish better than they do.

*Gina, 39, teacher*

I think men want women who have big boobs, a huge sex drive, and no opinion about anything.

*Sarah, 30, personnel director*

Men want a woman who will suck their dick every night and tell them how wonderful they taste.

*Janice, 45, interior decorator*

Men will never tell you this, but they actually want a woman to be their best friend. They want to be able to share their secrets, build trust, explore their feelings with women, but they are afraid of what the other guys would think. I really believe that men are little pussy cats inside. Behind every big bully of a man there quivers an insecure little boy. If women would just take care of that little boy, their love lives would improve immensely.

*Betty, 33, social worker*

Unconditional love. Emotional support and a best friend. A soul mate. A woman they can do a variety of things with: take walks in the park, play golf or a hand of cards, go sky-diving, or just sit beside each other with a couple of good books. The ability to do everything and nothing together.

*Norma, 55, auto worker*

## 49. WHAT DO WOMEN NEED MOST FROM A MAN?

A man who is secure with who he is, not needing another mother but needing a partner, lover, and friend. A man who knows how to be a friend and enjoy a woman as a whole person and not just as a vehicle for sexual pleasure.

*Ruth, 28, financial advisor*

Money, love, and new clothes.

*Mary, 18, student*

Gentle love hugs, open signs of affection, and a warm, deep soul kiss in the morning before I go to work.

*Amy, 32, social worker*

Women need a man who is secure, confident, trustworthy, and dependable.

*Sue Ann, 40, office manager*

I don't know about all women, but I need a man who loves me unconditionally and wholly.

*Greta, 38, photojournalist*

I need a man who won't leave me when I gain a few pounds or add a new wrinkle. I want someone to grow old with, not someone who makes me feel old.

*Sonya, 47, business owner*

Security, kindness, and a best friend. A real life-partner. My husband and I do almost everything together, and we've been married for forty-one years.

*Ruby, 63, retired office manager*

Men's needs are really no different from women's—the things they need the most, anyway. Patience, a true and honest friend, and forgiveness when they make a mistake. They need to know the world is not going to stop if they make a mistake.

*Claudia, 69, homemaker*

## 50. WHAT DO WOMEN WANT MOST FROM A MAN?

Honesty. Fidelity. Women want monogamous relationships.

*Joni, 28, fashion buyer*

Women want men to listen. Really listen. Slow down and listen. Not just pretend to listen.

*Wanda, 33, marketing consultant*

Women want to be right as often as possible. We feel so pressured to be competitive.

*Roberta, 25, teaching assistant*

We want to feel truly appreciated.

*Dorinda, 45, office manager*

I want to be fucked until I run out of liquid. I want to be ridden hard and put up wet. I want to be fucked till I pee on myself.

*Michelle, 24, librarian*

I want a man who knows how to make love to a woman. A slow hand, warm and deep kissing. Knowing how to take every part of my body and make it tingle and squirm will keep my attention and devoted love. Some men just don't get it. They go too fast and hard, it's over too quickly, and then they act like they've really done something fabulous. Men aren't the only creatures who need good sex in order to stay monogamous and happy with one person.

*Kate, 34, postal worker*

## 51. WHAT DO YOU ENVY MOST ABOUT MEN?

Being able to pee anywhere, any time. Must be nice.

*Gerry, 40, therapist*

Men are lucky not to get a period every month. What I wouldn't give not to have to go through that.

*Lori, 22, unemployed*

I envy men because they don't have to shave their legs. They can be ready to go anywhere in ten minutes.

*Ramona, 27, financial manager*

Since I am a gay woman, I guess the thing I most envy about a man is his ability to approach attractive women and take them home at night. Most of the women I desire would be repulsed by the idea of having sex with me or any woman. So even though I'm smart, attractive, and great company, I will always lose out to the ugly, dumb jock simply because he has a penis.

*Linda, 24, graphic artist*

I am a heterosexual woman, but I would really, really like to be a man for at least one month. I think the children would listen to me better, I would get more respect at work, and mostly I would love to feel what it's like to have an organ driving, pumping in and out of a woman. Then they just wipe the thing off and go on to the next thing. It sounds great to me. Have dick, will travel.

*Mona, 40, quilt manufacturer*

## 52. WHAT DO YOU ENVY LEAST ABOUT MEN?

Being so stupid and clueless.

*Jenny, 33, technician*

Being faced with the difficult task of having to find a woman who will put up with them.

*Kathy, 35, medical transcriptionist*

Having to conform to society's macho standards.

*Rebecca, 45, anthropologist*

The thing I least envy about men is how society expects them to foot most of the bills for modern civilization. Expectations on men to provide, lead, and inspire are so much higher than they are for women. I can think of nothing more terrifying than to be a white male under twenty-one with little or no education and even less natural ability. The pressures on him to succeed must be crippling.

*Jennifer, 19, philosophy major*

I would not want to be the average man. I do not envy selfish, arrogant, stubborn men. I would envy a monogamous, unselfish man with good character. I would envy being able to get ready more easily, and their wardrobe seems a breeze compared to a woman's. And it takes them about two minutes—tops—to put their hairdo together.

*Vivian, 49, beauty operator*

### Bless His Heart (and Kick His Ass)

He's just quirky, you know. He can't help it. That's the way he is, and I know it. He's a good man at heart and means well, but I want to kick his ass at least three or four times a week. Men!

In the beginning, when we first met, I thought he was so unique, so funny, and so wonderfully different. Well, he's different enough, and although he is still funny and unique, compared to other men I know, I get so irritated at some of his traits that I want to throw my hands up in the air and say, "Out of here, you idiot, you're driving me crazy!"

Procrastination is one of his traits. He'll know something is coming down the pike, some deadline or appointment, and invariably wait to the absolute last nanosecond to address it and then behave as if the world, the entire world, is in flames, as if this beast is biting him in the ass. I think about him having a stroke, or giving me one. I usually try to stay out of his way when he's in that mode. Lie low. Do something else. Steer clear, go shopping, out with friends, go to Africa—something, anything, just get the hell out of his way.

Then, when the crisis he created is over, I want to kick his ass. I want to kick it for all the confusion and stress he caused. All of the uneccessary frustration he put on the whole household. I want to wrap him up in a big brown box and send him to Guam. But I love him.

Love is unlike any other feeling in the world. The opposite of love is indifference. I am never able to be indifferent about him. If I love him, and I do, he can get to me. Make me angry, make me passionate, he can push all sorts of buttons, and alarms go off, and I want to kick his ass, blah, blah, blah.

I honestly don't want to control him or change him from the person he is. I just want him to be more responsible. More timely, courteous, and caring of other people's schedules. A little voice inside me says, "Well, you don't have to live with him," but I do. I love him. I'm devoted to him. I'm in this for life, and I knew it from the start.

I wish I could get his nose out of the books and his hands off the remote. My husband stays behind in everything he is supposed to be doing or taking care of, because he's a man. I know that sounds prejudiced, but so be it. Most men I know who are my age are terrible procrastinators. Why is that? Hell, I don't know. That's just the way it is.

Maybe it's God's little joke on the women of the world who have to live with these boys. Maybe God is thinking it will keep us on our toes. Who knows?

I'll give you an example of one irritating difference between men and women. A difference that irritates us, not them—by any stretch of the imagination!

It was Christmas Eve in 1992. Stanley was supposed to have done his shopping, and I had done mine. I did all of the grocery shopping for Christmas dinner and all the shopping for everything else around the house, things I knew we would need through the holidays. He only had to buy presents for our children, his mother and father, and me. I shopped for everything else.

We had agreed long ago, when we were first married, that he should share in the shopping for the children and he should buy gifts for his parents. That made sense to us; he knew his parents better than I did.

Well, over the years, my tummy has cringed at holidays, wondering if he forgot—or bought and lost the gifts. Sometimes he has purchased gifts ahead of time and put them away for safekeeping. Well they're still safe. No one—and I mean no one, to this day—knows where they are. That's Stanley. But I love him wildly. I can't help myself.

He forgets to shower until the last second before everyone else is ready to go. He loses his car keys. He checks out at the store and comes home without the bags. He leaves all the lights on, the TV on, the doors unlocked, and falls asleep on the couch with the remote (his best friend) in his hand.

When I need something from him, I have to organize him first. When I want to have sex, I have to orchestrate and organize that. But I have to say, once we get going, once I get him thinking about sex and ready for it, he's an absolute animal. He's passionate, warm, voracious, and just plain good at it. I cannot imagine life without Stanley. I cannot imagine sex without Stanley. I most definitely cannot imagine my life without sex, either. And good sex. Sex like we have. Okay, enough about that, or I'll have to stop my story and go find his ass.

To continue about Christmas, Stanley—you guessed it—forgot to buy his share of the presents. On Christmas Eve I found myself running around like an insane person, trying to make up for lost time and duties. Of course, Stanley was at my side, helping all he could. He was carrying packages, helping me look, and gazing at all of the weird people in the malls. He dropped me off at the front door of every store. He parked the car for me. He is a loving man. I just want to kick his ass because he is so disorganized. Everything could have been done on time and ahead of time. But it wasn't.

I jumped in there and helped with his list, and everything turned out all right. We had a great Christmas dinner, all the family gathered around, and just after dinner we went Christmas caroling. It was a day full of love and just the right amount of Christmas spirit.

When we had said good night to all of those we love and adore, Stanley turned into that other creature I love so much. He had remembered to buy some new candles for our bedroom. He had written a poem for me and bought me a beautiful diamond necklace. He made love to me as if it were our first time, and I felt desirable, pretty, and loved. I cannot imagine my life without him. I love him. He is my best friend. I just want to kick his ass sometimes. Maybe I'll do it tomorrow.

*Loretta, 55, homemaker*

# chapter seven

# *Body Parts*

53. *What do you love about a penis?*
54. *What do you not like about a penis?*
55. *What do you love about a vagina?*
56. *What do you not like about a vagina?*
57. *Do you think women's breasts play an important role in great sex?*
58. *What do you consider the most attractive part of the male anatomy?*
59. *What do you consider the least attractive part of the male anatomy?*
60. *What do you consider the most attractive part of the female anatomy?*
61. *What do you consider the least attractive part of the female anatomy?*
62. *Do the length and width of a penis matter?*
63. *Where is your sexual hot spot?*

## 53. WHAT DO YOU LOVE ABOUT A PENIS?

I like the way the veins bulge out.

*Monique, 26, reporter*

I love the hardness and the power and then marvel at the way it turns into limp spaghetti so soon.

*Rita, 30, systems analyst*

The way it fills me up and gets my attention.

*Shawna, 25, makeup stylist*

My boyfriend is uncircumcised, and I love to play with his hooded wonder. I like to get the little connecting flap of skin between the head and the foreskin and suck it really hard.

*Dawn, 34, clerk*

I love the way it totally controls my man's mind. If I can get his penis to pay attention with a quick squeeze and maybe a little lick, I can have anything—and I do mean anything—I want. His mind just shuts down, and his penis makes all the important decisions. His brain wants to spend a night out with the boys playing cards. His penis wants to spend the night in me. Guess who wins?

*Bonita, 23, textile worker*

Being able to whip it out and it's ready! I like seeing it grow and then fall into this tiny little soft thing. I like the power men have over a woman.

*Catherine, 42, painter*

I love the truth in a penis. Men can't lie or fake an erection. It's the one and only thing they cannot lie about!

*Elizabeth, 47, secretary*

## 54. WHAT DO YOU NOT LIKE ABOUT A PENIS?

I hate the smell of a dirty one.

*Erin, 19, student*

The way having a penis or not controls a person's destiny.

*Madeline, 42, gardener*

I don't like the fact that a good dick is hard to find or that a hard dick usually belongs to an even bigger prick.

*Suzi, 33, cashier*

I don't like how a penis can hurt me. When I'm not in the mood and my boyfriend won't take no for an answer, I hate the way he forces himself in me and has his way with me. I hate the way my body responds to his dick even when my mind doesn't want him. After three or four sharp, dry thrusts, my body gushes moisture and I can't turn back.

*Lindsey, 20, bartender*

I think a penis is scary. It always seems ready to explode. It looks like a big earthworm, and I have always hated icky things. Why didn't God make the male sperm producer more attractive? In nature, some species have such amazing sexual organs. Bright colors, swollen glands, interesting shapes. Why must human reproductive parts look like something to hide in a mound of manure?

*Candice, 23, zoological groundskeeper*

The way a hard one controls me. Especially if the man attached to it is worthless. A really good fuck is hard to walk away from.

*Sissy, 32, telecommunications*

## 55. WHAT DO YOU LOVE ABOUT A VAGINA?

That I have one.

*Ronnie, 38, teacher*

The mysteriousness of it.

*Claire, 34, data processor*

I like the way it looks like a flower and is such a secret place.

*Denise, 28, floral designer*

I love everything about it. Especially the clitoris. It's so hidden and sensitive. I love it when my husband touches it lightly or licks and sucks on it. I can feel it swelling up and peeking out between my lips. It's such a wonderful feeling.

*Jody, 29, bank teller*

I love the way it smells after sex. I like the secretions, the juices, the musk, the way it takes a beating and keeps on ticking, and panting for more. I like that I can be ready for sex any time and not have to worry about getting an erection. I like that I can outlast a dozen men and still beg for more.

*Sharon, 24, physical therapist*

The secrecy of it. Men don't know what you are feeling until they touch it. Then the cat's out of the bag.

*Janet, 41, dentist*

## 56. WHAT DO YOU NOT LIKE ABOUT A VAGINA?

The way it bleeds once a month and makes your life a living hell.

*Jennifer, 19, college student*

All of that nasty pubic hair. It's gross.

*Corinne, 35, artist*

The smell. How disgusting!

*Maggie, 37, weight control counselor*

The fact that you have to get a mirror to see inside yourself. How many little girls have had the horror of thinking a part of them had been cut off when they saw their little brother's penis?

*Constance, 23, medical technician*

I don't like the way I get horny and wet and it throbs with an aching kind of feeling and my husband is at work. I can masturbate but it's not the same.

*Reba, 51, homemaker*

## 57. DO YOU THINK WOMEN'S BREASTS PLAY AN IMPORTANT ROLE IN GREAT SEX?

To men they do, but in more of a visual way. To women, they do if she has sensitive breasts. I have very sensitive breasts and love to involve them in great sex. I particularly like it when a man licks my nipples a lot.

*Nicole, 26, songwriter*

Tits are all most men want. If they could put their penises inside a nipple, they'd be in heaven. A vagina is just a place to hold their genitals while their eyes, hands, and mouths consume our breasts.

*Connie, 29, bartender*

To me, absolutely. My nipples are very sensitive and highly erogenous. I love for my partner to suck on them before we make love. I'd almost rather have him lick my nipples than my clit.

*Sandi, 37, property manager*

I think they definitely do, although sometimes men are cautious to express it too much. If the woman has small breasts, I think men are afraid she will be self-conscious if he pays too much attention to them.

*Barbara, 28, dancer*

Sure they do! That's why they coined the phrase "breast man."

*Leann, 31, ticket seller*

Yes! And the bigger the better.

*Lois, 32, social worker*

My girlfriend loves to be rough with my firm nipples. She likes to have me go braless. She likes to pinch my nipples in public places. She loves to devote hours and hours to consuming my breasts. I used to think men were bad. She is just as obsessed with breasts. Loving tits is universal.

*Eve, 22, jewelry salesperson*

You bet they do. There is something attached between my breasts and my clit. When my husband licks my tits, I swear I can feel it in my vagina. I start getting wet and ready to be taken immediately.

*Patty, 22, word processor*

## 58. WHAT DO YOU CONSIDER THE MOST ATTRACTIVE PART OF THE MALE ANATOMY?

Big, strong, sexy hands.

*Lindy, 30, supply clerk*

The sexiest part of a man's body is definitely a nice tight butt.

*Suzanne, 33, telemarketer*

Eyes are the most attractive part of any man.

*Georgette, 37, paramedic*

A good personality is the sexiest thing a man can possess. The ability to make conversation, the compassion to care about others. Those are the important things. A nice tight ass doesn't hurt either.

*Lydia, 33, computer programmer*

His penis, of course. I like other parts of a man's body, but let's face it, his penis is the organ that takes care of my needs.

*Stacey, 24, cocktail waitress*

I'm a leg woman. I love sexy, strong legs on a man. I love them even more if they are very hairy. I like to run my hands up and down my husband's legs and thighs.

*Wilma, 43, telephone sales clerk*

## 59. WHAT DO YOU CONSIDER THE LEAST ATTRACTIVE PART OF THE MALE ANATOMY?

The penis, of course. It's a good thing it's good for something, but it certainly is an ugly thing.

*Agnes, 31, licensed practical nurse*

I think penises and testicles are pretty much a tie for the honor of being least attractive. I think that's why men keep them covered up.

*Judith, 40, travel agent*

An Adam's apple is my least favorite part. I'm not sure what it does, but it sure looks stupid. Why are some men's so big? I just want to hit them with a sledgehammer.

*Deedee, 20, student*

Men with no butt. A lot of men seem to have the problem of no butt. Why do women have the butt department cornered?

*Stephanie, 21, grocery store clerk*

I hate men who walk cocky. I like confident men, but when they strut they look stupid. They remind me of roosters.

*Jody, 39, computer repair technician*

## 60. WHAT DO YOU CONSIDER THE MOST ATTRACTIVE PART OF THE FEMALE ANATOMY?

Breasts. Definitely breasts. They're beautiful.

*Jeanette, 37, delivery driver*

If they're nice, a pretty set of long, shapely legs would have to be the most attractive part of a woman's body.

*Cheri, 25, personnel advisor*

The most attractive part of most women's bodies is a pretty neck and soft, smooth shoulders and backs.

*Freida, 34, typesetting supervisor*

Pretty eyes and dainty eyelashes make the difference between a pretty girl and a gorgeous woman.

*Rhonda, 24, make-up artist*

Luscious lips and a wet, open mouth can turn the girl next door into a purring sex kitten. It is simply makeup and attitude. A little of both can work miracles.

*Gloria, 40, elementary school principal*

Tiny hands and feet. I think men like that a lot, and face it—it doesn't really matter what we women think is attractive. It's all about what the men like.

*Heather, 21, shoe salesperson*

Really tight, warm, and accessible pussies.

*Trish, 24, typist*

## 61. WHAT DO YOU CONSIDER THE LEAST ATTRACTIVE PART OF THE FEMALE ANATOMY?

The female body is wholly beautiful. It's an exquisite thing.

*Vera, 35, stage manager*

I think the vagina is a little short on aesthetic value, but I'm sure others will disagree with me.

*Maggie, 27, proofreader*

The least attractive part of a woman has to be stretch marks. They look so disgusting and seem so cruel. Isn't it enough that a woman has to go through childbirth? Why must she be burdened with stretch marks for the rest of her life?

*Katie, 33, housewife*

Too much butt and heavy thighs. I think they call them saddlebags.
Why is it men don't have the same problems?

*Yori, 21, student*

A sagging vagina. That thing has got to be tight or your man will be
looking for another one. Those damn men are so picky.

*Betti, 45, nurse*

## 62. DO THE LENGTH AND WIDTH OF A PENIS MATTER?

I prefer a wide penis. A long one can sometimes be painful if the man
is really endowed. But width seems to do it for me. I like a penis to be
very hard and wide enough to cause me to stretch. That really takes me
over the top.

*Lainie, 42, jeweler*

A short-dicked man has to have a great personality or lots of money
just to survive.

*Sandra, 29, baker*

Size certainly matters to me. I can feel the difference. Bigger is better.
Longer is better. Thicker is better. I like to be filled up with a hard
penis that goes all the way up to my stomach.

*Ashley, 28, sportswriter*

No way. All that matters is having a partner who cares about you. The
rest takes care of itself.

*Stacy, 22, student*

I hate men, but I do love the shape of a penis. I have a very realistic
rubber dildo that really does the job for me. It is thick, long, and
glows in the dark. It even has some warts molded onto the surface for
extra friction.

*Dottie, 38, contractor*

I have to be honest and say yes, it matters. Sexually speaking, a long, wide penis makes a difference, and I'd be lying if I said it didn't. I would like to say that it is not the most important thing. I'd rather have a man who treats me like a lady, is monogamous, and has a great sense of humor. Making me laugh is very important. Then we can love each other and laugh about his tiny little thing together. Or maybe not.

*Tonya, 29, marketing rep*

Not really, if he knows how to love a woman emotionally and mentally and if he treats her well in general.

*Mary, 55, department store salesperson*

## 63. WHERE IS YOUR SEXUAL HOT SPOT?

I've heard there is such a thing, and I wish to hell I could find it.

*Cora, 45, personnel director*

The man who knows how to kiss the back of my neck owns my body.

*Jasmine, 23, exotic dancer*

I would sooner lose my left arm than hurt my clit. It is the center of my emotions. Love my clitoris first, love my mind second.

*Pauline, 28, lawn specialist*

The soles of my feet have always been a hot spot for me. I love a man who can give a good foot massage.

*Cyndi, 30, telephone operator*

My belly button is quite an erogenous zone. I love having my belly button tickled, licked, and kissed.

*Delia, 29, chemical engineer*

When my boyfriend is French-kissing me, he sometimes sucks my tongue into his mouth and won't let go. The harder I try to pull it out, the tighter he grips me. For some reason this really turns me on.

*Jenny, 19, convenience store clerk*

My g-spot is certainly my hot spot. When my boyfriend performs oral sex on me, he probes my insides with first one, then two fingers. When my juices start flowing, he puts a variety of different pressures on the upper part of my love canal. The sensation is overwhelming. The faster his tongue and fingers dart around, the harder I climax.

*Lisa, 41, flight instructor*

It really, really turns me on when a man has a great voice. A deep, sexy voice turns me on. Eyes are good, too. The way a man watches me and speaks to me with his gaze really gets me hot for him.

*Eileen, 36, nurse's aide*

## Cute Cheeks

I love my husband's mind, his ability to provide for our needs, and all the other things a wife is supposed to love. But if the truth be known, the thing I love most about my husband is his butt. I worship my husband's tight little ass. We have been married for ten years, have two lovely children and a mortgage we can live with. We have a vigorous sex life. I love to fuck, suck, and come. But nothing gives me as much pleasure as caressing, nibbling, kissing, and leaving suck marks on my love's bottom. I love everything about his ass—the texture, the color, the curves, the dips, the dark recesses, the hairiness.

Most of our love sessions begin and end with my face, tongue, and lips buried in his firm ass. I love to hold his cheeks in my hands and work them like fresh bread dough. I love to flick and dart my probing tongue in and out of his tight anus. I love to force my pointed pressure into his forbidden chamber. I can lick for hours. I can make him cry like a baby.

If I focus enough attention on my baby's butt, I can get anything and everything I want. I can go shopping, wreck the car, and burn dinner, but as long as I give his buns the attention they need, I'm the queen of his heart.

I don't have to worry about any other woman taking my place because I keep my man happy and firmly squirming in my mouth. Maybe other women's marriages would be in a little better shape if they'd start paying attention to their lovers.

I buy tight work pants and jeans for my husband. I like for him to leave his underwear at home. When he bends over I want to see smooth, tight fabric stretching over his fine backside. I enjoy showing him off in public, and I love knowing that after a hot, sweaty day out in the world, when we are alone and in for the night, his cute cheeks are mine and mine alone.

*Melissa, 36, computer programmer*

# chapter eight

# *Masturbation*

64. *Do you masturbate?*

65. *How do you masturbate?*

66. *Where do you masturbate?*

67. *How often do you masturbate?*

68. *What do you think about when you masturbate?*

69. *Do you feel comfortable when you masturbate, or do you feel as if you are doing something naughty?*

70. *Do you consider masturbation an important part of your sex life?*

71. *Have you ever masturbated in front of your partner? Did it have an effect? Describe it.*

## 64. DO YOU MASTURBATE?

I do. At least once every day.

*Edie, 28, home health aide*

I have made myself come every day for over twenty years. I discovered my clit when I was thirteen years old, and once I learned how it worked, I never stopped. I don't smoke, drink, or do drugs. But I do know how to make myself climax. It has been the one constant in my life. I've been through two marriages. I love men. I love people. But only I can make myself come. I always find time to take care of my sexual needs. The old joke about my hand being my best friend is true. I love the way I make myself feel.

*Millie, 33, photo lab technician*

My fingers are my best friends. Why else do I keep my fingernails so smooth and closely clipped?

*Jenny, 42, claims adjuster*

I would rather fuck a dead man than play with myself. I like being pleasured by someone else. I like the shared passion, the mutual lust.

*Susie, 18, cashier*

Only if I have to. I would much rather be with a man than masturbate. I can't imagine wanting to masturbate. I need to do it sometimes, but only because I have no one to be with.

*Brenda, 22, cook*

## 65. HOW DO YOU MASTURBATE?

I like to lie in the bathtub and let water run down over my clitoris. Feeling the slight pressure of the water on my clit and letting the water run over my hot slit is one of the most intense sexual feelings I've ever experienced.

*Heather, 29, sales representative*

I rub my clit and dip my finger into my tight hole to get enough hot moisture to send my clit throbbing.

*Katy, 32, real estate developer*

I masturbate in several ways. Sometimes I stroke myself. Other times I actually put objects—beer bottles, hairbrushes, my fingers—inside me.

*Mandy, 33, software developer*

I put my fingers on my pussy and start rubbing. It comes to me very naturally. I can do it in the car on my way to work. I can do it at lunch. It isn't complicated. It just feels good.

*Janet, 26, medical transcriptionist*

I put a long candle in my vagina. Holding my legs together so that it won't slip out, I lie on my tummy and wiggle my ass so that it feels like I'm being fucked. With my hand on my clit, I imagine being licked. It's kind of a physical and mental process.

*Orlinda, 24, clock repair technician*

I can sit in a chair and squeeze my thighs together a certain way and make myself come. The wonderful thing is the fact that I can do it anywhere, anytime. The hard part is not screaming. I have to remember when I am in public.

*Wendy, 38, receptionist*

## 66. WHERE DO YOU MASTURBATE?

I usually masturbate in the shower or the tub. Water is so sexual and can really heighten my pleasure.

*Darlene, 27, claims examiner*

I masturbate in bed, on the floor—anywhere.

*Terri, 21, ad salesperson*

Sometimes I masturbate while I'm driving my car. I've narrowly escaped several accidents while masturbating. I think part of the appeal is the danger and the fact that it is considered forbidden.

*Carlette, 45, housewife*

You name the place and I've probably done it. I keep a mental list and add new locations to it weekly. Keep your eyes open and you just might catch me in action someday.

*May, 28, lab technician*

I do it in front of the bathroom mirror so that I can see my body and my face. I love the expression on my face when I start to come. Coming is so powerful and I love the way it just takes over.

*Connie, 52, teacher*

## 67. HOW OFTEN DO YOU MASTURBATE?

Every time I get a chance!

*Julie, 22, college student*

I masturbate at least once or twice a day. Maybe more if I'm feeling particularly horny. It only takes a few minutes, and it always feels great, so I don't see anything wrong with it.

*Paulette, 43, housekeeper*

I try to masturbate once every morning as soon as I get up. It's a good way to start off the day.

*Carmen, 38, cook*

I just stopped smoking, so I seem to be masturbating about every hour on the hour. I need to keep my hands busy. If I was a little more agile and able to bend my neck more, I might be able to do something about my oral fixation too.

*Ruby, 25, physical education teacher*

Maybe once a month. I don't like to do it if I can have the real thing. I am much happier if I can have a man pouring himself all over my body. I really like a man to come on me, on my breasts or on my face.

*Debra, 47, stenographer*

## 68. WHAT DO YOU THINK ABOUT WHEN YOU MASTURBATE?

Being with other women. Going down on a woman. A woman going down on me. I've never been with a woman. I'd like to try it. Someday maybe I'll get the nerve and find the right woman.

*Margie, 38, driver*

I think about a dozen men making love to me on a swinging hammock. They run out of steam and I keep begging for more.

*Callie, 41, supervisor*

I dream about riding a beautiful horse naked with my long hair flowing in the summer breeze. The bulging flesh of the mighty steed makes my pussy ooze.

*Jolene, 23, receptionist*

My husband and I have a wonderful sex life, and I love to go down on him. When I have to masturbate, I think about sucking him. That does it for me every single time.

*Frankie, 47, tobacco farmer*

I know I should think about a big, sexy hunk nailing me to the floor, but I dream about having all my bills paid. I think I've been a working single mother just a little bit too long.

*Felicia, 30, dental assistant*

## 69. DO YOU FEEL COMFORTABLE WHEN YOU MASTURBATE, OR DO YOU FEEL AS IF YOU'RE DOING SOMETHING NAUGHTY?

Naughty? Are you kidding?

*Terry, 21, hotel desk clerk*

No. But, I wouldn't want to get caught doing it.

*Jo, 31, volunteer worker*

The feeling of doing something naughty makes me come quicker. I like to jerk off in public. I like knowing that the scents of my arousal are going in my co-workers' nostrils every day. It makes me wetter knowing I could get caught.

*Belinda, 23, receptionist*

I masturbate so much my arm goes to sleep and I get calluses on my fingers. So maybe I'm just a little too comfortable with the whole matter. Can you get carpal tunnel syndrome from too much masturbating?

*Trudie, 36, cosmetician*

I love to masturbate, and I don't think there is anything naughty about it. With AIDS and all the other ailments in the world today, what could be safer?

*Sonnie, 27, meat packager*

I'm afraid to do anything but masturbate until I get married. There's just too many things that can go wrong. My boyfriend and I masturbate together, and we have found a lot of foreplay-type things we can do to please each other without ever having intercourse. It's great and it's safe.

*Tammy, 19, jewelry salesperson*

## 70. DO YOU CONSIDER MASTURBATION AN IMPORTANT PART OF YOUR SEX LIFE?

Yes. Particularly if it's the only thing I have at the time. I can't just go out and pick up some strange man in order to get some.

*Cindy, 24, teacher*

These days masturbation is my sex life. I kind of like it that way. I always satisfy myself, I don't cheat on myself, and I know what I like, which is more than I can say for any relationship I've ever had.

*Evelyn, 40, car rental agent*

Masturbation is absolutely the best way to get comfortable with your body and explore what makes you feel good, what makes you feel great, and what doesn't. It's important for a woman to know what she needs sexually. I would encourage everyone to try it.

*Roberta, 34, researcher*

Is breathing important to you?

*Jo, 27, office worker*

I believe masturbation is a waste of time and energy. I'd rather paint or cook or work in the garden.

*Juanita, 47, florist*

I'd rather be fucked and sucked and licked and kissed long and hard by a starving man, but masturbation is faithful, steady, always there anytime you need it, and you don't have to worry about anyone else. It has its advantages.

*Wanda, 45, interior decorator*

## 71. HAVE YOU EVER MASTURBATED IN FRONT OF YOUR PARTNER? DID IT HAVE AN EFFECT? DESCRIBE IT.

Yes. The first time was by accident. I was rubbing my clitoris while he was licking my breasts. Suddenly and unexpectedly I started climaxing. He rose up for a second and looked at me and then, with this great big smile on his face, began to lick my breasts and my neck and everything else in sight. It was amazing how excited he became. As I was finishing, he gently went down on me to lap it up. I highly recommend it for anyone. It was great.

*Hope, 22, legal secretary*

My boyfriend loves it. Especially when the lights are on.

*Fran, 34, restaurant manager*

No way. I think he'd be offended if he thought he didn't satisfy me enough, so I would never masturbate in front of him.

*Victoria, 25, graduate student*

I love to masturbate in front of my husband. He goes wild when he sees me touching myself. I wish I could persuade him to masturbate in front of me. I think it would be a real turn-on.

*Marie, 40, housewife*

My man loves to watch me do anything sexually. A perfect evening for him is watching me take a bubble bath and masturbate. Then he helps me out of the tub, takes me to bed, and goes down on my clitoris for a while. He says he loves to feel how hard my clitoris becomes after I have climaxed. Then he gets on top of me and thrusts in and out of me real hard. His penis is not that big, but he sure knows how to work it.

I love to see him get really steamed up, and if watching me masturbate does it for him, so be it.

*Jessica, 29, pizzeria manager*

## Subway Secrets

I used to hate the hour-long commute on the subway to and from work each day. I never knew what to do with all the time. If I lived in Manhattan, I could get to work or home in about fifteen minutes. But who wants to live in a closet with a fold-up bed and a scenic view of a dumpster?

I'm a career woman with a high-pressure job in advertising. I'm creative, athletic, and good at what I do. But I made a conscious choice to live in a town with trees and lakes and families. I pay as much rent in Connecticut for a house with a yard, a garage, and neighbors as I would for a one-room efficiency in the city.

I'm single, thirtyish, and attractive. I work hard, make good money, hope to move up or out in the near future. Until then I find myself faced with a two-hour train ride each workday, and there is nothing I can do about it.

So I masturbate during the train ride. I stopped reading books. I gave up eating bagels and carryout. I don't knit or sew. I bury my fingers in my pussy. I plunge and poke my inner lips. I rub my clit until it is raw. I soak my panties and come with great ease and frequency.

I like to get on a car that is crowded with other passengers. I find a seat where I can see everyone entering the train. I like to be seen by those getting on. I stare intently into people's eyes. I focus and concentrate on making eye contact. I want them to know that I'm aware of them and acknowledge their existence. I breathe deeply. I part my lips. I look serene, content, and in control. The fact that I make eye contact usually startles most of the passengers. They have no idea of my sexual actions. They're just freaked out that I'm staring at them. People usually go out of their way not to make eye contact in this part of the country. So when I make contact and stare, half of the riders turn away and withdraw. Then, of the half who keep looking at me, maybe one or two will actually look at me long enough to realize what I'm doing with my hands.

I'm not subtle, but I'm not obnoxious. I don't seek out conversation. I don't flirt. I'm just serious about giving myself pleasure. I don't tease. I look as many women in the eye as I do men. I look at attractive men and women. I look at plain, nondescript people. I stare into the eyes of everyday, unglamorous working commuters.

I don't fantasize about having sex with any of the people on the train. I don't pretend anything. I just look deep into strangers' eyes and rub my moist private parts. I make myself tingle. I make myself hot and wet and musky. I change my rhythm, alternate my strokes, move my fingers around my labia, and massage my clitoris. I make my nerves tingle. I make my thighs twitch. And I love the way I make myself feel.

*Andrea, 33, advertising executive*

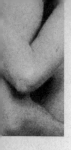

# chapter nine

# Oral Sex

72. *Do you like giving oral sex? Under what circumstances?*
73. *Do you like receiving oral sex? Under what circumstances?*
74. *Do you like to give and get at the same time (69)?*
75. *What do you like best about giving oral sex?*
76. *What do you like best about getting oral sex?*
77. *Where do you like the semen to be placed—in your vagina, on your chest, in your mouth, or not anywhere?*
78. *Is it important to your mate that you swallow?*
79. *Do you swallow?*

## 72. DO YOU LIKE GIVING ORAL SEX? UNDER WHAT CIRCUMSTANCES?

I love oral sex. I love giving head in weird places. Public places. I like the power, knowing he's trying to keep it together, but can't. One time, when we were in a theater, he hollered out loud, and people turned around in their seats to see what was going on. He just kept on coming, and I think he enjoyed knowing people were looking and probably knew what was happening. It was great. Everyone should try it.

*Nina, 46, insurance examiner*

I like to drink wine and suck my boyfriend. When he is right to the point of coming in my mouth, I pull away and let his sperm flow into my glass. Then I swirl the special elixir around in my goblet and gulp it down.

*Joan, 26, community organizer*

No. I choke. I wish I could learn to do it. My boyfriend is dying for it.

*Carol, 24, student*

I like to use oral sex as my power play. It is my favorite reward for good behavior. It is intimate. It is powerful. And it doesn't mess up my makeup if I put the right pressure on his penis with my hand. Three minutes of concentrated effort makes my husband putty in my hands and mouth.

*Brandie, 30, personnel director*

I don't think oral sex was intended to be a part of sex. It just doesn't seem normal. Friends have told me if I ever tried it I would love it, especially the response from my husband. I like the way my husband is now, so why risk it?

*Martha, 59, lawyer*

## 73. DO YOU LIKE RECEIVING ORAL SEX? UNDER WHAT CIRCUMSTANCES?

You better believe it. I can't imagine a woman in her right mind saying she doesn't like it. Nothing compares to it. Having a warm, wet tongue slide all over my vagina relaxes me at first. Then the pleasure quickly turns to a heated passion. I orgasm so completely—it's wonderful. I wouldn't want to live without it.

*Dedra, 26, store manager*

I like to have my pussy sucked any time. I don't care who does it, as long as the person knows what to do. There are many ways to heaven. One way is through my pussy. If pleasure is the goal, oral sex is one of the best routes to that destination.

*Jody, 40, telephone operator*

I'm always afraid of how I will taste and smell. My boyfriend wants to go down on me everywhere, anytime. I want to be squeaky clean. He doesn't care. I actually think he prefers me to be funky, sweaty, and smelly.

*Elaine, 18, college freshman*

I absolutely love to have oral sex under any circumstances. I love to give and receive. Nothing compares to the pleasure I get from oral sex. The gentleman does need to know what he is doing, but if he does know, he can own my body.

*Carol, 45, stockbroker*

## 74. DO YOU LIKE TO GIVE AND GET AT THE SAME TIME (69)?

No. I find it hard to concentrate and do a good job pleasing my partner. I get so distracted. You can't give and get at the same time.

*Randi, 23, factory worker*

I love locking ourselves into a circle of love. My juices flow into his mouth, his juices flow into my mouth. It is a circle of sex. I like the dance. I like the instant reward. I like the pacing. I like the heat.

*Irene, 33, college professor*

Sometimes I get so excited that I bite my boyfriend's penis, and that puts an immediate pause in the action. Can I help it if I grit my teeth when I lose control?

*Rita, 19, factory worker*

My husband does, but I don't. I like to be able to fully concentrate when I am going down on him. I also like to see his face, and if he's doing me at the same time, I can't.

*Jannie, 48, hotel manager*

## 75. WHAT DO YOU LIKE BEST ABOUT GIVING ORAL SEX?

Being able to please my man.

*Rhonda, 38, housewife*

I like the way my lover's penis fills my mouth. I love to flick my tongue up and down the length of his penis and run my tongue in circles around the head.

*Kathy, 28, modeling instructor*

I love it when my husband comes in my mouth. It's so personal and so intimate.

*Rona, 45, optician*

I like the physical act of swallowing. I like the gulping, the sensation of receiving nourishment. I like to feel like I am being fed a most personal appetizer.

*Annie, 29, store manager*

The smells and watching his penis swell. I really, honestly love the smell of my boyfriend's penis.

*Amanda, 22, secretary*

## 76. WHAT DO YOU LIKE BEST ABOUT GETTING ORAL SEX?

Having my lover concentrate completely on one thing—pleasing me.

*Greta, 40, fitness trainer*

I like the way it feels when my partner runs his tongue lightly over my clit. When he gently licks the lips of my pussy. When he lets his tongue dart in and out of my hole. Oral sex is heaven.

*Peggy, 50, housewife*

Everything about getting oral sex is wonderful. The feeling, the intimacy. Oral sex is the best form of sex.

*Renee, 27, branch store manager*

The tongue, definitely the tongue.

*Millie, 24, horse trainer*

Receiving, not having to think or do anything but receive. He tells me to lie down and enjoy. And I do. He totally takes over, and my body responds to him in every way. He should teach this stuff.

*Dinah Lee, 32, tire repair store clerk*

## 77. WHERE DO YOU LIKE THE SEMEN TO BE PLACED—IN YOUR VAGINA, ON YOUR CHEST, IN YOUR MOUTH, OR NOT ANYWHERE?

Everywhere. I love it.

*Penny, 37, administrator*

Semen doesn't bother me and doesn't turn me on either. I can take it or leave it.

*Jackie, 56, garment worker*

I think it is sticky and gross. It makes me gag. It smells like bleach and looks like pus. I don't want the nasty stuff anywhere near me. Period.

*Charley, 18, student*

I love it when my lover comes all over my breasts and my stomach. It turns me on to watch it spurt out of his stiff penis.

*Jackie, 40, car rental agent*

Actually I think it is erotic to have him come on me—my tummy, my chest, et cetera. The trouble is that I'm allergic to the stuff. It makes my skin break out instantly. Go figure.

*Ula, 21, music store clerk*

## 78. IS IT IMPORTANT TO YOUR MATE THAT YOU SWALLOW?

I don't know. Sometimes I don't think it is, and then other times he teases and makes comments that make me wonder about it. Sometimes I wish I could figure it out.

*Billie Jo, 20, secretary*

Yes, it is the one thing that gives me complete control over my man. Will I or won't I? He never knows until the very last second, and it certainly keeps him on his toes.

*Heidi, 35, cake decorator*

Of course it is. He is, after all, a man.

*Sharon, 32, events coordinator*

It's plenty important to him, but not important enough to make me sick. I'd never do that.

*Suzi, 34, illustrator*

He's never, ever mentioned it, and I haven't asked him. I assume it is not important to him. He certainly talks about everything else with me, and I think he would have said so if it were a big issue. Me personally, I don't like it. It's hard to keep from choking and takes away the sensuous mood I'm in.

*Lena, 46, hardware store clerk*

## 79. DO YOU SWALLOW?

Not if I can help it.

*Polly, 46, police officer*

No. I worry about eating stuff that wasn't meant to be eaten. I wonder if it's healthy.

*Brenda, 20, cook*

Yes, I do. I love it. And what's more important, he loves it. When he sees me swallowing and lapping up his come, it makes him crazy. He really gets off on it. The more I take, the more he gives me.

*Maggie, 31, medical aide*

No. I like it all over my body, though. I like my boyfriend to shoot it on my breasts, my bottom, and my pubic hair. He likes doing it that way and doesn't seem to care that I don't want to swallow it.

*Shannon, 34, city official*

I like to let his sperm flow into my mouth, then I swish it around and blow bubbles with it. It is really an amazing thing to think about. Millions of little potential human beings forming a floating air bubble with air from my lungs and juice from my mouth. It is surreal.

*Marian, 23, graduate student*

You are what you eat. I do not swallow sperm.

*Dottie, 27, dentist*

## Tastes Familiar

Though it first happened over twenty years ago, I can still remember the salty forbidden taste of my lover's (now my husband's) semen on my tongue. And I will always look forward to our annual vacations in New Orleans.

We were both students at Tulane in the seventies. I had just transferred from Connecticut the previous quarter and had met this really great guy at a frat party. We had been dating hot and heavy for three months, and we truly loved exploring our young bodies and our exploding sexuality. I loved to suck him to a climax on a daily basis. Unlike some of my girlfriends, I loved swallowing—no, gulping—the creamy stuff. It was wonderful.

My first Mardi Gras was coming up, and I had heard all the stories about endless parties, wild orgies, and massive hangovers. I was eating my share of King cakes, killing hurricanes with ease, and building a collection of Mardi Gras beads.

My boyfriend's frat was having a costume party in celebration of Bacchus, the Roman god of wine and, quite possibly, sex. Everyone had spent weeks assembling elaborate masks, capes, and headdresses. No one was supposed to be able to recognize anyone else at the party. It would be a night for unknown identities. On this night you could be anyone you wanted to be. I decided to dress as Cleopatra with an exotic mask I'd put together from peacock feathers.

The day finally arrived. I was so excited. My excitement died when my boyfriend told me he had to make a quick trip home to see about a family matter. (It turned out that he was going home to borrow money for my engagement ring, but I didn't have a clue about that.)

My roommates convinced me that since I had spent so much time on my costume, it would be a shame to miss the party. They dressed up like whores, which wasn't a real big stretch for either of them, and we went to the party, determined to get rip-roaring drunk, which we did. We drank ourselves silly. We danced and flirted and laughed so much our faces hurt. A tall guy wearing a black Zorro mask and a vampire cape had been giving me the eye all night. He'd bring me drinks and nibble on my neck. He'd sweep up behind me, throw his cape over my head, and tickle me. I was just drunk enough to think his stupid antics were sexy. I ignored him most of the night and danced with at least twenty guys. But around two in the morning I found myself out on the wrought-iron balcony of our French Quarter party hotel making out with this guy. We hadn't actually said a word. Anyway, blame it on the booze, the heat, my raging hormones, or the fact that my boyfriend had stood me up, but I decided to give this masked stranger the best blow job of his life. I tore his pants down to his ankles. I held his penis firmly in both hands and sucked him hard. I pumped, licked, almost choked. He was so big, hard, and excited. When he came, he gushed. I smacked, swallowed, and basically drank him whole. Right before I passed out, I remember thinking how familiar he tasted.

I awoke in the morning all cuddled in my new lover's arms. His pants were still down at his ankles, his cape was draped over the balcony, and his mask had slipped down below his chin. When I saw him in daylight my heart stopped. I'd seduced my boyfriend! He had made it back to the party after all!

We married later that year. I figured the party incident was a sign. Even when I thought I was seducing a total stranger, he turned out to be my boyfriend. He never suspected that I was too drunk to know it was his pecker I blew on that balcony. I'll never tell him any different.

*Nancy, 46, decorator*

# *Orgasm*

80. *Are you orgasmic?*
81. *Do you experience multiple orgasms? How often?*
82. *How long does it take you to climax during intercourse?*
83. *How long does it take your partner to climax during
    intercourse?*
84. *How often do you climax when you have sex?*
85. *How often does your mate climax?*

## 80. ARE YOU ORGASMIC?

I was not orgasmic until my twenty-fifth year in this world. I never
knew what I was missing!

> *Sonya, 32, teacher*

I am very orgasmic. In fact, if my partner cannot get me over the edge,
so to speak, I do it myself. That usually doesn't bother my partners. In
fact, they seem to like to watch me.

> *Fran, 41, systems analyst*

I come when my lover comes, even if I'm not ready. It's my duty as a
woman to time my pleasure to coincide with his.

> *Joan, 37, literary agent*

It comes and goes. Sometimes I explode like Roman candles. Other
times I can't come for the life of me. It has to do with everything from

my job to the weather to what I ate. It is such a fragile system of checks and balances, I've basically given up trying to predict them. When they come, I come.

*Bobbie, 36, bank teller*

It took me a long time to figure out what an orgasm was and how to have one. It was the best thing I've ever known and remains the best.

*Carrie, 34, teacher*

## 81. DO YOU EXPERIENCE MULTIPLE ORGASMS? HOW OFTEN?

Sometimes. Always once, often twice. I have wondered what it would be like to have five or six. Someone tell me. Please!

*Renee, 19, student*

I come like a water faucet stuck on full flow. I scream, twitch, and explode like a firecracker. Life is good when I'm coming. It certainly doesn't suck. Sucking is another subject altogether.

*Georgia, 21, flight attendant*

No. It's hard enough to come once, let alone more than that. I can't even imagine.

*Jane, 21, ad sales*

When I'm in the start of a new relationship I can come just thinking about him. Then reality sets in, routines develop, and my climaxes take a lot more work. Then I have to play tricks with my mind. Does that make me a mind fucker?

*Angela, 24, musician*

My mind wants to come five or six times, but my body can only come once a day. I don't understand it, that's just the way it is.

*Karnie, 37, dispatcher*

## 82. HOW LONG DOES IT TAKE YOU TO CLIMAX DURING INTERCOURSE?

It depends entirely on the guy and the position.

> *Tosha, 27, assistant manager*

Sometimes I can come pretty quickly. Sometimes it takes longer. Sometimes I don't come at all.

> *Beverly, 37, real estate agent*

As long as I want it to.

> *Anita, 40, assembly-line leader*

If we've engaged in a lot of foreplay and I'm really hot and wet, it sure doesn't take long.

> *Rose, 30, computer salesperson*

I don't come at all. I act. I fake it. I scream and cry and scratch, and don't feel a thing. I don't want to admit there is a problem, so I continue my little charade. I've done it for years. Why stop now?

> *Judith, 48, internal revenue agent*

Not very long, but we've been at this a long time. We've got experience on our side. And my husband is very perceptive and loving.

> *Martha, 72, retired postal worker*

## 83. HOW LONG DOES IT TAKE YOUR PARTNER TO CLIMAX DURING INTERCOURSE?

Never, ever long enough!

> *Maura, 40, lawyer*

If I've been giving him head beforehand or if he's been drinking, it can take forever. He can go and go and go.

> *Celeste, 30, career adviser*

On a good night, half an hour. On a bad night, five minutes.

> *Helen, 36, postal worker*

It depends on how horny he is, and if a football game is about to begin.

> *Lori, 22, swimming instructor*

It depends on the mental process. If we've been romancing each other mentally beforehand, he has to work hard at controlling himself or it's way too quick. He's gotten much better over the years at doing that. I love the mental foreplay, though, and wouldn't want to live without it, even if it meant he couldn't last as long.

> *Holly, 38, banker*

## 84. HOW OFTEN DO YOU CLIMAX WHEN YOU HAVE SEX?

I come every time I can.

> *Morgan, 34, art teacher*

I don't think I've ever climaxed. If I have, it wasn't a big enough deal for me to notice, so I guess I've never climaxed. Tell me what I'm missing. I'd really like to know.

> *Melanie, 30, housewife*

I work at making myself come, so I have an orgasm every time I have sex.

> *Angel, 24, hairdresser*

I don't allow myself to climax during intercourse. I only climax from masturbation because I don't want anyone else to have that much power over me. I don't want some egotistical prick to be able to brag about how he made me quiver. I'm a cold fish in bed, and that is my choice.

> *Bette, 37, real estate agent*

In the beginning I was so concerned about my boyfriend that I didn't care whether I came or not. Then one night I told him I wanted him to really take care of me. I wanted to have lots of foreplay, touching, and kissing, and I wanted to see him undress. I was totally satisfied at the end of our sex, and the interesting part was that he enjoyed it more than ever before. I didn't realize that he would be turned on by me wanting more out of our sex life. Men are so hard to read sometimes. I'm glad I changed my attitude.

*Patricia, 25, radio disc jockey*

## 85. HOW OFTEN DOES YOUR MATE CLIMAX?

Every time I want him to.

*Pat, 50, x-ray technician*

He comes every time we have sex. That's what sex means to him. No climax, no sex. He is strictly interested in emissions. Lord help him and me when he encounters his first bout of impotence. It won't be a pretty scene.

*Alene, 45, cafeteria cook*

Just about every time. It's a pretty rare occurrence when he doesn't.

*Tina, 23, sales associate*

My boyfriend only climaxes once, regardless of how long our lovemaking lasts. Every time he gets right to the point of orgasm, I make him stop and force the sperm back down. He can build it up right to the point of exploding four or five times a session. After I am satisfied with the number of my climaxes, and only then, I work him back up into a state of frenzy. He pops his cork and fills me up with thick, creamy spunk. His balls ache, and I love the pain it causes him.

*Lydia, 27, program director*

Every time we have sex. I'm the one who doesn't climax every time.

*Ruby, 64, housewife*

## Nowhere

To this day my mother thinks I got my husband because I was a nice girl. She taught me from a very early age what a lady should look like, talk like, walk like, and dress like. My father is a man's man, still a gentleman, and my mother, needless to say, is the perfect lady. I do love my mother and believe in the values she taught me. But being a nice girl had nothing to do with getting married.

Love was a big part of why I decided to get married. Sex—no, great sex—was what bound us to each other forever. We have the most spontaneous and exciting sex life of anyone I know. When my husband and I were in high school, everyone knew we adored each other. We were the perfect couple. All of our friends knew we would always be together: they thought they knew why.

The first time I knew we were truly made for each other was on a September afternoon after school. My mother and father had decided that now that I was a junior in high school, I could ride in the car with my boyfriend to and from school. The ride to school that morning went just as my parents thought it would—fine. But the ride home that afternoon would be planted like an oak tree in our minds.

The ride to my house from school normally took about twenty minutes. We left the school parking lot, and he began to talk to me. He asked me about the homecoming dance that was coming up. When I didn't answer him, he looked over at me and his eyes opened wider than I have ever seen them to this day. I had carefully slid my skirt up over my thighs while he was talking. My legs were golden brown from the summer sun. My white lacy panties glistened next to my warm brown skin. I was hot. I was wet. I felt wild! I slipped my right hand into my panties, laid my head back, and started to wiggle. I was wetter than I had ever imagined I could be. I was dripping. His hands were on the steering wheel and mine were inside me. He had to fight to keep his eyes on the road. I was fighting to keep from screaming in ecstasy. I didn't want to come yet. That would surely have driven him right off the road. Besides, I didn't want this to end.

Seeing me masturbate was driving him wild. I knew he was a safe driver and would not lose control and kill both of us. I loved the tension on his face from the agony of not being able to reach me. He could only watch and listen. I loved having that kind of power over his body without touching him, only looking at him and touching myself. I was in control now, and I loved every powerful, sensual minute. I was getting to the edge, and he knew it. He grabbed himself through his jeans with his right hand and said, "Oh, my God, I can't stand it. I love it. I love you. I don't know what got into you today, but I hope you never change. I'm so hard I can't believe it. I never knew I could swell up this big and this hard!"

Then he took a turn away from the direction to my house. I knew I had achieved my goal. I had wiggled and moaned and dripped all that he could stand, and now I was going to get my reward!

He pulled off onto a dirt road and headed for a large green pasture out in the middle of nowhere. Nowhere became the most memorable and exciting place I have ever been. The land was green and cool, and the September breeze was crisp and just right. It couldn't have been more perfect.

As soon as he stopped his Chevy at the edge of the woods, I jumped out of the car. My skirt was up over my hips, my pretty red blouse unbuttoned and blowing in the breeze, and my thighs dripping wet. I bent over slightly, leaning on the car door, pulled off my panties, and tossed them in his lap. With my skirt still pulled over my thighs, I ran for the nearest tree. My back toward him, I bent over and grabbed my ankles! I thought I might faint. I felt intoxicated from the excitement.

His car door flew open, and he grabbed his zipper and pulled at his jeans while running toward me. He couldn't seem to get out of them fast enough for either one of us. I felt like a wild animal in the woods, waiting for him to reach me, waiting to be driven out of my mind. He got me. He held me tight and rode me hard. I was completely his to do with as he wished. I was taken by this stud of a boy, and he wasn't letting go. His hands were all over me. He was all over me. I was still bent over, and he had complete control of me from behind.

Then as suddenly as he had entered me, with that overwhelming thrust, he stopped. He pulled out and began teasing me with tiny inches of his love. Then I felt him pull completely away from me. No part of him was touching me, and just as I straightened up and turned around, he dropped to his knees and began licking me with his warm, wet tongue. I went out of my mind! Facing him as he licked my body like an ice-cream cone was almost more than my knees could handle.

This was the first time I'd climaxed from oral sex, and there I was, standing under an oak tree in the middle of nowhere. I screamed. I gasped for breath. He grabbed the backs of my legs and, with his face buried between my thighs, took me to a place I knew I would want to go again. I loved it. It was heaven. Just when I thought he was going to let go, he turned me around and thrust himself back into me from behind. We were both screaming. He was coming, and I was still coming. With love all over us and nature all around us, we lay there in the pasture and smiled.

Then, after gathering up our clothes and heading for the car, he opened my door and we went home. To this day we have the greatest sex life! He is always a gentleman and I am always a lady—when we want to be. Thank God for nowhere.

*Dianne, 25, college student*

# Before and After Sex

86. *Can you have great sex without foreplay?*
87. *What is perfect foreplay?*
88. *How long should foreplay last?*
89. *Should women be as focused on foreplay toward men as men should be toward women?*
90. *What type of foreplay drives you wild?*
91. *What type of foreplay drives your partner wild?*
92. *How do you feel after sex—turned on, sleepy, hungry, refreshed?*
93. *What do you like to do after sex?*

## 86. CAN YOU HAVE GREAT SEX WITHOUT FOREPLAY?

Yes. Sometimes nothing can replace a quick, little bit rough roll in the hay.

*Rhonda, 27, singer*

If I'm in the right mood, I don't need any foreplay. I have plenty of natural moisture most of the time anyway. I always have an itch that needs some attention.

*Odessa, 29, instructor*

Sure. You can have great sex by yourself. It's not like you have to have foreplay before you masturbate.

*Wanda, 40, cartoonist*

Foreplay is absolutely imperative. It's a common misconception among men that women can reach orgasm simply through intercourse. In actuality, women need foreplay, whether it is kissing, cuddling, oral sex, or touching. I think most women have difficulty climaxing without foreplay. For me, foreplay is an emotional turn-on. It feels good when my husband is attentive to my needs and cares enough to take the time to give me pleasure before sex.

*Susan, 44, physician*

Absolutely not. If I'm not warmed up before my guy tries to enter me, the sex is horrible. I like to be teased, tickled, and made to feel desirable before he even thinks about putting his penis in me. This girl wants to be loved first, and fucked second.

*Karen, 34, housewife*

Foreplay is sex. The rest is fucking.

*Sally, 37, paralegal*

## 87. WHAT IS PERFECT FOREPLAY?

Willingly done. No cell phones. No beepers. No deadlines.

*Jamie, 32, executive director*

Perfect foreplay is a slow hand, an easy touch, and a lot of time to relax, tingle, and say, "Hello, my love."

*Leagh, 33, designer*

A fabulous dinner, teasing and flirting in public, followed by a couple of glasses of wine, and then slow, soothing strokes of love and tongue.

*Mona, 28, gardener*

Oral sex. Lots and lots of oral sex. It drives me wild.

*Lynn, 35, pianist*

Perfect foreplay for me is when my husband turns off the television and focuses all of his attention on me.

*Dena, 35, antiques dealer*

He took me in his arms with a hold that told me he would be there for me whenever I needed him. Then he gently led me to the sofa and sat me down. Never taking his eyes from mine he took off my blouse very slowly, and while he was touching my breasts he told me about the things he was going to do to me. In very detailed and descriptive words he told me how I would feel after he did those things to me. He was right and always is. I love the way he takes my mind and then my body.

*Donna, 40, bank teller*

## 88. HOW LONG SHOULD FOREPLAY LAST?

As long as possible.

*Sherrie, 28, graduate student*

Foreplay is a form of personal expression. It doesn't have to be quick or take a long time. It can last however long you want it to last.

*Lillian, 42, florist*

Until both me and my partner are ready to explode.

*Josephine, 30, waitress*

It should last until neither one of us can stand not joining our bodies together. He should be hard as a rock, and I should be moist as chocolate pudding.

*Dolly, 23, graduate student*

At least twenty minutes. I know everything these days is hurried, but wonderful lovemaking shouldn't be. It's well worth the time for men to give their women those twenty minutes or so. The sex will be much better, and she will be more attentive to his needs if she doesn't feel cheated or rushed.

*Mattie, 45, psychologist*

## 89. SHOULD WOMEN BE AS FOCUSED ON FOREPLAY TOWARD MEN AS MEN SHOULD BE TOWARD WOMEN?

Definitely. Although men are more visual, I think. Maybe the foreplay doesn't mean the same thing for men. Maybe they would rather have a little modeling or a striptease? My husband loves it. The kind of foreplay he gives me is different from what I give him, though.

*Carolyn, 30, teacher*

I don't think men care about foreplay. Foreplay for most men is spitting on their hands and grabbing their dicks. If they are hard, you had better be wet.

*Bonnie, 21, delivery driver*

If you ever want to have a satisfying relationship, everything should be equal—or at least close to equal.

*Kim, 29, accountant*

I don't really care if men have sufficient foreplay. I know what I want, and a man is just the tool I use to get it.

*Dawn, 27, tollbooth operator*

Men don't need foreplay to come. They need foreplay given to them so that they can learn about what women need. Kind of a show-me-don't-tell-me theory.

*Elaine, 51, doctor*

## 90. WHAT TYPE OF FOREPLAY DRIVES YOU WILD?

I don't care what kind of foreplay I get as long as I get it!

*Ruth, 34, bank teller*

Oral sex before sex is great.

*Florence, 40, cocktail waitress*

I like for my husband to suck on my tits, lick my nipples, kiss his way to my belly button, flick his tongue on my clit, and put his fingers inside me.

*Rosie, 43, craftsperson*

I love soft, sincere touches. I love for my man to look deep into my eyes and tell me how much he loves me. I like to be relaxed. I like to feel that what we are doing at that moment is the most important thing in his entire world. Knowing he wants me makes me wetter than any secret technique or proven pickup line.

*Christie, 23, ladies' clothing salesperson*

Sexy music, pinching lightly on my breasts, and working his way down to oral sex. I don't think men know what power they could have over women if they learned more about oral sex. If they were really good at that, they could pretty much have anything they wanted from a woman.

*Amy, 28, sleep therapist*

I like to be taken like a wild animal in the woods. Rough biting, licking and wrestling during sex drives me wild.

*Tammy, 21, student teacher*

## 91. WHAT TYPE OF FOREPLAY DRIVES YOUR PARTNER WILD?

He loves for me to give him head before we fuck. Sometimes he likes it when I suck his nipples, kiss his stomach, and bite him lightly on the butt.

*Andrea, 20, retail salesperson*

My boyfriend likes to perform oral sex on me before we have sex. He really gets off on it, and he's really good at it.

*Ginger, 30, tailor*

Foreplay? Are you kidding? It's hard enough to find the time to have sex.

> *Delilah, 39, painter*

My lover goes nuts when I do a striptease for him in the living room. I taunt him slowly, and casually drop my blouse, my skirt, my panties, around the couch. Sometimes I even use the remote on my clit. We haven't seen the eleven o'clock news in months.

> *Sarah, 26, telecommunications specialist*

Spontaneous, unpredictable foreplay. He loves not knowing what I might do next. The more outlandish the better. He's very straight and serious at his job, has lots of responsibilities and pressures. When he comes home, he likes me to be in control and he doesn't want to even be able to guess what I'm going to do to him. Hey, it works for us.

> *Sophie, 42, anesthesiologist*

## 92. HOW DO YOU FEEL AFTER SEX—TURNED ON, SLEEPY, HUNGRY, REFRESHED?

I'm usually worn out, pissed off, and frustrated.

> *Lou, 51, short-order cook*

I'm usually lying in a puddle of love juices, with my nerves pinging endlessly while my clit throbs in the dark.

> *Carlene, 29, genealogical researcher*

I'm usually hungry, horny, and hung over.

> *Marie, 40, nurse*

I usually feel safe, loved, and thirsty.

> *Amber, 20, model*

I usually feel as if someone rammed a telephone pole up my vagina.

> *Belinda, 34, short-order cook*

I keep a towel beside our bed so that after sex we can wipe away the sweat and juices if they're all over the place. We can hardly move, much less get up, because we really give it our all.

*Vivian, 36, auto plant worker*

## 93. WHAT DO YOU LIKE TO DO AFTER SEX?

Sleep! My husband is a real sex machine. When we have sex, we're going to have sex for at least an hour. Hard, fast, passionate, animalistic sex. We're going to sweat and give each other one hell of a workout.

*Mary Ann, 40, deli clerk*

I think it's incredibly sexy to take a shower together after we make love. Sometimes we get so aroused while we're showering together that we wind up doing it again anyway.

*Janet, 28, receptionist*

I usually get up, take a shower, get dressed, and go to work. Now, how can you have a bad day when you start it off like that?

*Jasmine, 28, cashier*

I'm usually so frustrated after my so-called sex session that I finish the job myself with my hand. While he snores and sleeps, I have a fantasy trip and make myself climax a couple of times before I finally nod off.

*Cora, 44, registered ER nurse*

I like to eat a pint of ice cream. Good sex and good ice cream just seem to go together. The more calories, the more sex I need to take those pounds off. So it is a delicious cycle of sweat and cream.

*Mattie, 23, physical therapist*

We like to lie in the bed next to each other and talk, but while we're talking, we're holding each other and feeling each other's skin. Sometimes we eat nice cold fresh fruit.

*Frankie, 19, music student*

## Harmony

He started romancing me the moment we met. We could communicate so easily, something I wasn't used to. It had been a long time since I had dated anyone, and I was more than a little excited about this man.

Everything with him was so effortless. He was in control, and yet I felt perfectly safe with him. I knew we were going to be lovers and more the minute I met him. And I was right.

He is all man—very strong, and very masculine. He is highly intelligent and justifiably confident. A gentleman, a lover, and a friend.

Before we make love he is attentive, kind, sensual. He moves slowly around the room lighting candles. He will ask me if I am comfortable, if I would like something to drink, and he gets it without hesitation.

He plays me like fine music. I yearn for him to touch me. I ache inside for him to enter my body and give me all of his love.

After we make love he is even more attentive, if that is possible. We talk and we listen to soft music echoing in the background. We discuss anything and everything. I love the company of this man. I don't feel pressured, hurried, or self-conscious when I am with him. I don't feel like we are through after we finish making love. The time we have together after making love is as beautiful as the time that precedes it.

He helps me dress, just as he helps me undress. Never have I experienced that before.

I hope I live long enough to enjoy this forever.

*Jeanette, 38, paralegal*

# Sex Talk

94. *Do you like to talk dirty?*
95. *What do you say when you are talking dirty?*
96. *Do you like your mate to talk dirty?*
97. *What does your mate say to make you hot?*
98. *Do you make noise during sex?*
99. *Do you like your mate to make noise during sex?*
100. *Are you a screamer?*

## 94. DO YOU LIKE TO TALK DIRTY?

Hell, yes. The raunchier the better. I shed my polite little ways and become a foul-mouthed whore. I sound like the possessed little girl from *The Exorcist,* and I love it. So does my husband.

*Abby, 34, certified public accountant*

No. I'm way too inhibited to ever talk dirty. It's embarrassing.

*Joan, 36, housekeeper*

Slut talk is fun and turns my boyfriend on in a hurry. I say things like "Come fuck me, baby. I need your dick in me right now. Fuck me until I beg you to stop. Come on, baby, fuck me hard." He says things like "Be my little whore, baby. Be my little fucking whore. Lick my balls and stick your finger in your pussy and tell me when it's wet enough to deserve my big hard dick." I absolutely love talking trash and hearing it in bed.

*Carol Ann, 23, computer operator*

Talking dirty I think would be great fun. I get wet when I hear it in a movie. I'm just too damn scared to do it.

*Alisha Marie, 41, claims adjuster*

## 95. WHAT DO YOU SAY WHEN YOU ARE TALKING DIRTY?

I like to say nasty things in different languages. I have a T-shirt that has forty different ways to say "Fuck you," and I love to work those phrases into my love talk. Somehow when you whisper filthy things in Swedish, it sounds so much nicer.

*Carol, 25, research assistant*

I talk about fucking and sucking. I tell my husband to put his big hairy root up my hot twat and to fuck me hard, hard, hard. I swear and scream and squeal.

*Dinah, 38, auditor*

I like to be really graphic and tell my boyfriend how good it feels when he thrusts his long, hard penis into my tight, tiny hole.

*Shelly, 29, project coordinator*

I tell my boyfriend that I love to lick the shaft of his penis and feel it pulsate and grow in my mouth while I'm giving him head. I tell him how much I like the feeling when he's just about ready to come and his penis stiffens up and thrusts and pumps come down my throat. You get the idea.

*Jessie, 20, student*

I tell my girlfriend how I want her juicy pussy to moan for my hot, needy tongue. I degrade her, talk about how no man would have her. I tell her how lucky she is to be my slave and how she needs to make me happy. Then we both usually start giggling and just shut up and have great sex.

*Cheryl, 42, events planner*

I like to boss him around. He loves it, too. I tell him exactly where to lick, what to suck, and how to fuck me. The more details, the better he likes it.

*Anna, 45, auto salesperson*

## 96. DO YOU LIKE YOUR MATE TO TALK DIRTY?

Sometimes it really turns me on when my lover tells me in explicit detail how he wants to fuck me. Other times it doesn't. It just depends on what mood I'm in. Do I want to have my brains fucked out? Or do I want him to make sweet, passionate love to me? It just depends.

*Ann, 30, leasing consultant*

It makes me incredibly hot and wet when my husband tells me he's going to plunge his hard, throbbing dick into my juicy, waiting pussy and pound in and out of me till I come at least five times. Who wouldn't be turned on by that?

*Betsy, 43, lab technician*

Yes! It makes me feel sexy and hot.

*Rosa, 35, caterer*

I sell used cars for a living, so I hear enough talk in one day to last most people a year. I don't like my lover to talk when he could be using his tongue for much more important tasks. Show me you love me, don't talk about what you are going to do to me.

*Francis, 38, auto resale specialist*

Sometimes. If I've had a good day and we're not on the outs with each other, I love it. If we've been fighting or arguing, then I don't like it. Somehow it seems to work on me wrong if we're not right with each other.

*Nadine, 26, social worker*

## 97. WHAT DOES YOUR MATE SAY TO MAKE YOU HOT?

He whispers in my ear and tells me that he loves me.

*Allison, 26, hotel manager*

She talks about how much she loves the taste of my pussy and how she wants to swallow every drop I can give her.

*Karen, 28, career adviser*

My husband tells me he is going to buy me something sexy and edible.

*Leslie, 34, chef*

He describes every move he is making in explicit detail.

*Bernice, 41, seamstress*

My boyfriend doesn't even have to talk to make me hot. All he has to do is give me one of his sexy looks, and I melt all over the floor.

*Leanne, 32, bartender*

All he does is touch me and start talking about what he is going to do to me and I'm halfway to the moon. Just the sound of his voice makes me tremble with ecstasy. His hands are big and strong; his touch is warm. He knows my body better than I do. His voice is resonant and sexy and I love it.

*Irlene, 49, hotel caterer*

## 98. DO YOU MAKE NOISE DURING SEX?

If I'm faking an orgasm, I really turn it on. Usually, though, I don't make a whole lot of noise.

*Kathy, 36, police officer*

Yes, always. I make lots of noises—moans, groans, sighs, gasps. Sometimes I even talk. My husband loves it.

*Brenda, 40, airport screener*

Sometimes I really get into it and scream and yell and beg my boyfriend to fuck me harder and harder. I'd never talk like that in any other situation, but sometimes, when we're making love, I turn into a foul-mouthed, insatiable woman. It's a great release.

*Victoria, 23, retail salesperson*

If I do, it's an accident!

*Jackie, 28, housekeeper*

My husband actually gets offended if I don't make noise during sex. It is almost as if my making noise lets him know that I'm into it. He's the kind of guy who needs to be reassured that he's doing everything right. I never made noises during sex before he came along, but I almost feel that I have to now. It's not even that I'm faking. It's just important to me that he knows I enjoy it.

*Rita, 44, business owner*

I pant and gasp and scream. I just can't help it. My sex life is very important to me, and I don't try to hide anything. I think he likes it, but if he didn't I wouldn't be able to stop. It's just me.

*JoAnna, 38, picture frame shop owner*

## 99. DO YOU LIKE YOUR MATE TO MAKE NOISE DURING SEX?

I hate it when my lover snaps gum during sex. I'd rather he chewed on something else, like me. But don't bite.

*Kelly, 28, sales clerk*

When my lover comes, he groans and groans, and it does turn me on. I like the emotion, the power. I guess it is primal.

*Teresa, 40, housewife*

Yes! Definitely. There's a real kick in knowing that my lover is enjoying sex as much as I am.

*Ruth, 37, literary agent*

No. He always sounds as if he's faking when he makes noise or talks during sex. It's like he's just doing it because he thinks I want him to do it. It's giving me a complex.

*Misty, 22, secretary*

I would love it, but he doesn't. I don't even know if he's holding back or if he just has no interest in talking or screaming. Sometimes when he does groan, it scares me because I wasn't expecting it. It's almost like someone else snuck into the room. Weird, huh?

*Tamitha, 24, grocery checker*

## 100. ARE YOU A SCREAMER?

I can be, given the right situation.

*Joan, 37, housecleaner*

I'm more than a screamer; I'm a howler. The noisier, the better. I love to let out my inhibitions and scream to high heaven right before I climax. My lover has come to expect it from me after all these years. It's a good thing we live on a farm.

*Bridget, 39, farmer*

No. I'm not a screamer. The walls are too thin. I sure don't want all my neighbors to know when I'm about to have an orgasm. I like to whisper in my husband's ear and tell him how much I love him and how good he makes me feel when I'm about to come.

*Toni, 36, factory worker*

I would love the privilege of being able to scream. We have too many children and not enough rooms to get them farther away from us. The bedrooms are all on the same hall. I think contractors should give the parents more privacy when building houses. Get the kids' rooms away—far away—from the master bedroom.

*Heather, 29, homemaker*

## Is It Live?

I recently put a little spice into my lover's business life and added immensely to his stud-at-large reputation. Fred is a nice but somewhat conservative financial adviser. He makes a good living finding investments for rich people.

He is quite good at spotting trends, finding new opportunities, and discovering diamonds in the rough when it comes to undervalued stocks. He is a voracious reader, always searching for new ventures before they become common knowledge. He reads everything from obscure scientific journals to small-town newspapers looking for tips about up-and-coming businesses.

He uses a pocket micro–tape recorder to capture thoughts, ideas, phone numbers, and leads to follow up on. He will fill up a tape every day or so and then have his secretary transcribe the ramblings to hard copy.

Last week I found an old tape and made my own special recording. I made a sex tape of me talking and moaning and screaming with smacking, licking, and purring sounds. I talked like a sailor. I yelled "Fuck me, fuck me!" I made animal noises. I grunted like a woman in heat. I had a great time.

Fred's secretary got such a charge out of the whole thing that she made a duplicate and shared it with the secretarial pool. The tapes were the hot item of discussion around the office for about a week, until one of the other advisers got caught having sex with his secretary in the copy room. Talk about one-upmanship!

*Sandy, 37, travel agent*

chapter
*thirteen*

# Sex Toys

101. *Have you ever used sex toys?*
102. *Describe some of your sex toys and your experiences with them.*
103. *What lotions do you use?*
104. *What creams and edible playthings do you use?*
105. *What is the craziest or wildest sex toy you have ever heard about?*
106. *What is the wildest sex toy you have ever used?*
107. *Have you ever had a bad experience with a sex toy?*

## 101. HAVE YOU EVER USED SEX TOYS?

Absolutely. Any woman who doesn't own a vibrator is missing out!

*Roberta, 44, property maintenance technician*

Never. Sex between us is heavenly. We don't need inanimate objects.

*Glenda, 34, public relations agent*

I've always wanted to try a vibrator or some sort of wild sex toy, but I can't imagine going somewhere and buying one. I've seen those mail-order ads and have been tempted to order from them, but what would the mailman think? I'd love to try something, but I'd be mortified if anyone knew about it.

*Nicole, 26, photojournalist*

I used to date this really wild, crazy guy who liked experimenting with all sorts of sex toys. He once brought home a dildo, and we had some serious fun with that. We tried all sorts of different things— French ticklers, vibrators, fancy condoms. There was never a dull moment in our sex life.

*Jessica, 25, teacher*

I don't need to use any sex toys. I am a sex toy.

*Trudy, 18, waitress*

We've tried everything known to mankind, I guess. Food, vibrators, candle wax, coffee grounds, the telephone, stuffed animals, and this funny doorbell ringer, to name a few.

*Gwendilynn, 37, advertising agent*

## 102. DESCRIBE SOME OF YOUR SEX TOYS AND YOUR EXPERIENCES WITH THEM.

My husband and I had reached a dull period sexually, so I decided to buy something that could spice up our sex life. I found a huge two-headed dildo and brought it home. He was hesitant about trying it, but agreed that we needed something different and agreed to try it out. We put one end in each of us and spent the entire night fucking each other with this dildo. At one point, I turned him over on his stomach and gently placed this huge dildo up his ass. I kept shoving it deeper and deeper until he moaned and come spurted out of his cock all over the sheets. After that, he put it inside me and brought me to an incredible orgasm. Then we put the love toy aside and had the most magnificent sex we've ever had in our lives together.

*Lynn, 35, housewife*

Dildos aren't for every girl. I guess you will think this answer is weird, but I'm a natural kind of girl. I like to buy a fresh, hard, good-sized cucumber at the grocery. I wash it, smooth down the little bumps on the outside of it, and jump in bed. It never says "Not tonight"; a good hard cucumber is always ready when you are. I rub on it as well as insert it in my warm, wet vagina. When I'm masturbating with my veggies and get ready to climax, I shove that cucumber in me just right and go to town. Nothing beats it for a great quickie. Sometimes I let my husband watch. He loves that.

P.S. Ladies, be sure you keep the cucumber in a special place in the refrigerator, not to be mixed up with supper. Also, the other great thing about this love partner is that when it starts to go soft, you just throw it away and get a new one!

*Debi, 37, musician*

The guys at work gave my husband a gag present when I had to go into the hospital last year for some corrective surgery. It was called a pocket pussy, and it was this cheap, ugly little plastic replica of a woman's reproductive part. Now whenever I'm not in the mood or I'm just plain cranky, I dig this ridiculous thing out of the dresser and tell my husband to go play with his toy.

*Paula, 42, factory worker*

I had one of the best orgasms of my life while my boyfriend was licking whipped cream from my boobs.

*Beatrice, 45, child-care worker*

## 103. WHAT LOTIONS DO YOU USE?

I love it when my boyfriend puts strawberry love oil on my clitoris and sucks me to heaven. He brought this stuff home after a road trip, and it has truly changed my life. When he first pours the oil on my pussy it feels cold. Then it rapidly warms up. When he gently blows on the oil and my body, the stuff heats up like an athletic muscle cream. Soon it is on fire and so am I. My boyfriend teases me with his tongue and then devours me, licking up every drop. I swear by it. I only wish it came in gallon jugs instead of those little bitty bottles.

*Delores, 26, researcher*

My lover really enjoys it when I use a nice scented hand lotion to coat his penis. He undresses and gets into the bed. I put a few squirts of the lotion in my hands, rub them together, and then coat his penis with the cream. I work slow and steady and squeeze his penis while caressing his testicles. I rub it into his skin and then lightly lick the tip of his magnificent hard-on. The rest of the night is ours to enjoy. This has been my secret technique for ten years, and it never fails.

*Jill, 37, personnel manager*

Sometimes we use baby oil to make penetration a little easier, but never any sort of sex lotion.

*Teresa, 25, bookkeeper*

We like to use things like whipped cream, ice cream, and hot fudge sauce. The messier the better.

*Claudia, 40, physical therapist*

The only lotion my husband has ever heard of is spit, and he uses a lot of it wherever he can put it.

*Sandra, 33, food management*

We have to use lotions. I guess that's one of the things that comes with getting older. We still have a great sex life, but we do have lots of various kinds of lotions. Cherry-flavored is my favorite.

*Emma Louise, 68, homemaker*

## 104. WHAT CREAMS AND EDIBLE PLAYTHINGS DO YOU USE?

I love it when my boyfriend puts ranch dressing on my pussy and sucks me.

*Shauna, 20, student*

Virgin olive oil makes life and love so much more enjoyable. It has so many uses and tastes so good.

*Kathleen, 35, computer salesperson*

One fad that has never left my bedroom is edible underwear. I love the power that comes from ripping my lover's G-string off and swallowing the licorice string. I like to tie her up with licorice and torture her with my tongue.

*Roxanne, 37, landscape designer*

Berries are our favorite sexual edible. We like blueberries and black-berries best, though they do tend to stain your dentures and under-wear.

*Barbara, 66, retired postal worker*

Nothing beats vegetables. They're hard and good for you.

*Vivian, 58, seamstress*

## 105. WHAT IS THE CRAZIEST OR WILDEST SEX TOY YOU HAVE EVER HEARD ABOUT?

The wildest toy I've ever seen was a pair of nipple pinchers. They looked like something from a horror movie.

*Eloise, 51, painter*

The automatic vibrating plastic vagina with a fur-lined opening was about the dumbest thing I've ever seen. The companion pocket pecker was pretty dumb also.

*Maria, 37, waitress*

The battery-powered water gun shaped like an Uzi with a purple plastic pecker on the end took my breath away at an adult bookstore.

*Lois, 22, baby-sitter*

The total head-to-toe black leather body shroud with functioning anal opening doesn't seem like the typical Mother's Day present.

*Gina, 34, budget analyst*

I think my husband is the wildest sex toy I've ever known. Seriously. He's really, really wacko.

*Catherine, 32, antique furniture repairperson*

One day my boyfriend brought home this cassette tape that had moans and groans on it. The whole tape was sounds of people having sex. It was so funny we rolled all over the place laughing instead of having sex.

*Rebecca, 20, student*

## 106. WHAT IS THE WILDEST SEX TOY YOU HAVE EVER USED?

A Pez candy dispenser shaped like a duck.

*Deanna, 26, modeling student*

My girlfriend once bought a three-foot-long hot pink double dildo as a joke for a straight friend's wedding shower. We started playing with the thing and one thing led to another, and you know, it just didn't seem right to give a used three-foot-long double dildo covered with K-Y jelly to a friend. So we kept it and named it Barney.

*Suzanne, 29, cosmetician*

We tried those ben-wa balls like they sell in the back of dirty magazines. We never could figure out exactly how they were supposed to work.

*Laurie, 28, weight management counselor*

The wildest sex toy we ever actually used was my daughter's abandoned plastic baby pacifier. I inserted it in my husband's butt one night in a moment of wine-induced playfulness. It certainly got his attention.

*Mary, 33, secretary*

We were at a party just for the girls one night. All of the goody-goodies had gone home early, and just us wild ones were left. We called up an escort service and ordered five men for the ten of us. We had lots of condoms and creams for protection and lots to drink—strawberry daiquiris, I think. Anyway, I would have to give the award to those boys. They were fabulous sex toys, and I'll never forget it. We never told anybody.

*Lolitta, 39, ice-cream company worker*

## 107. HAVE YOU EVER HAD A BAD EXPERIENCE WITH A SEX TOY?

I had a bad experience with a sex toy. I got shocked. This vibrator-type toy shocked me while my husband had it shoved way up in my vagina. I don't know how it happened and I'm sure it was dangerous, but it actually didn't feel bad. We laughed a lot at that one.

*Patty, 30, fast-food industry worker*

My boyfriend and I once used one of the weird textured things he's supposed to put on the end of his penis. It slipped off while we were having sex. When he pulled his penis out of me, it was gone! I'm squeamish about touching the inside of my pussy, so he had to put his fingers up inside me to get it out. Now, that was fun!

*Marjorie, 28, law student*

One time I was playing around with a wine bottle and it got stuck! It had created some sort of a vacuum and would not come out. I was nearly hysterical, thinking I'd have to go to a doctor to get it out. Finally I had to break off the end of it to get it to come out. What a horrible experience.

*Randi, 26, clothing manufacturer*

My worst experience with a sex toy is simply the fact that my girl-friend prefers her dildo to my finger. Since I am often out of town on business, I bought my honey an elegant little vibrating dildo for those long lonely nights when I'm away. I thought she'd use it to please herself when I called home from my equally lonely hotel rooms. After four months of phone play, my baby is almost addicted to her electric toy. She simply loves the feelings it sends through her body. Now she insists that I use the vibrator on her when we make love. I'm somewhat insulted and maybe even a little bit hurt.

*Myra, 38, consultant*

The only sex toy I've ever used is a vibrator, and I can't imagine having a bad day with that dream thing. My vibrator is my best friend.

*Hillary, 48, nurse*

## Shower Rod Attachment

My boyfriend recently introduced me to a new form of exquisite torture. It all began one night when we were playing around in the bedroom. He works as a security guard for a large automobile factory. He wears a uniform and carries a pair of handcuffs on his belt. I've always kidded around about using those cuffs on him—until one night.

We had both had a hard day at work. I'm a waitress at a local meat-and-three diner and I had almost run myself ragged taking care of customers. He had been working long hours putting in a new security system for the plant. We both flopped down on the bed and just lay there for a few minutes collecting our thoughts. My boyfriend started getting a little frisky, tickling me, kissing my neck, and I admit, it was having its effect on me. But I needed to take a hot shower and get into some comfortable shorts. My uniform smelled like fried chicken and hush puppies, and I wanted to remove my makeup and relax. So I jumped up and headed for the bathroom. I was really enjoying my relaxation. I soaped every part of me and just let the water's massaging power take over.

When I heard the door open, I felt a cool rush of air cross my nipples. My boyfriend said he had a surprise for me. I closed my eyes and put my hand out through the shower curtain. (I thought maybe the surprise was the engagement ring I'd been hinting at for months.) I felt something cold snap around my wrists! *Bam. Bang. Pop.* Suddenly my arm was straight up in the air and I was dangling, handcuffed to the shower rod. My boyfriend was nude except for his security hat. Water was dripping all over the floor, and I was basically too surprised to talk. He scooped me up in his arms and started kissing me. I still had bath soap all over my body, but he didn't care. He kissed, he sucked, he probed. The carpet was soaked and I was beside myself with passion.

With my arm dangling from the shower rod, my lover entered the shower and entered me from behind. It was wonderful. It made my knees shake. I felt explosive inside. Alive. On fire. The water splashed. The waves of passion overwhelmed me. He was forceful and dominating and yet sweet and gentle.

We probably looked completely ridiculous, but it was certainly the best sex we'd had in weeks. After he had taken full advantage of the situation, he got out of the shower, calmly put on his boxers, and left me dangling in the shower. It was only after I'd regained my senses that I realized he had never fastened the handcuff on the shower rod. I could have freed myself at any time! While I don't recommend tying people up against their will, I have discovered that a little restraint goes a long way toward a great sex life.

*Denise, 26, waitress*

# Erotic Films and Photographs

108. *Do you like to read pornographic magazines?*
109. *Do pictures of naked men turn you on?*
110. *Do pictures of naked women turn you on?*
111. *Do you like to read erotic literature?*
112. *Would you pose nude? Under what circumstances?*
113. *Have you ever posed nude? If so, describe the experience.*
114. *Have you ever watched hard-core porno movies by yourself? With your mate? With your girlfriends? With anyone? Did you enjoy them?*
115. *Would you like to star in a pornographic film?*
116. *Have you ever made a sexual home video?*

## 108. DO YOU LIKE TO READ PORNOGRAPHIC MAGAZINES?

Yes. The nastier the better.

*Marlissa, 34, project coordinator*

No, not really. It doesn't give me any kind of thrill.

*Jan, 35, clerk*

I love to sneak copies of my boyfriend's dirty magazines. I don't think he has any idea that I like them as much as I do.

*Glenda, 37, flight attendant*

I'm not sure why, but yes, I do, I do, I do. They make me hot like I'm on fire. Not the pictures so much, but the reading. Those words of ecstasy flowing across the page make my hands sweat and my sexual organs swell and pulsate. I can't imagine being without pornographic literature to read.

*Dominique, 26, dry cleaner*

Reading pornographic books and magazines is a part of my daily life. If I can curl up on the sofa with a good book about sex and play with myself, I'm in heaven. I love good music in the background and no phone ringing, just my erotic literature and my thoughts. I do it daily.

*Stacey, 49, medical secretary*

## 109. DO PICTURES OF NAKED MEN TURN YOU ON?

Hell, yes! I love to look at pictures of naked men and fantasize about what it would feel like if they were ramming their cocks into me. I love to masturbate while looking at them.

*Doris, 23, telemarketer*

I love pictures of naked men. If I could put them up at work I would. Men have always had their girlie books and titty calendars. I love hunks, Chippendales, Fabio, Topaz Man, and all those guys in those underwear commercials. I like to look and dream. It gives me pleasure.

*Shirley, 22, receptionist*

I am a graphic artist, and I work on computers all day long. I know most people think only men download dirty pictures from the Internet, but you'd be surprised. I love to find hunks on-line and manipulate their images with my own personal photos. I've spent hours creating masterpieces of nude erect male bodies with added-on head shots of my co-workers. My fantasy man has the body of Mel Gibson, the penis of a Greek stallion, and the face of Bobby over in accounting. I keep an eight-by-ten color ink-jet print in my filing cabinet for inspiration.

*Joan, 30, imaging specialist*

I think there is something seriously wrong with men and women who enjoy pictures of naked people they don't know and never will know. Why that turns some people on, I'll never understand. I think they're sick.

*Heidi, 22, hardware clerk*

## 110. DO PICTURES OF NAKED WOMEN TURN YOU ON?

Pictures of naked women don't bother me, but they don't really get me hot, either. The same is true of pictures of naked men. I'm just not into it.

*Penny, 38, zookeeper*

Surprisingly, they do. I love to see a picture of a busty woman, legs spread, exposing her entire pussy. I'm not a lesbian and never fantasize about other women, but for some reason a picture of a beautiful naked woman drives me wild.

*Cynthia, 24, musician*

No. If I want to see an attractive naked woman, all I have to do is take off my clothes and stand in front of a mirror.

*Jen, 28, copy editor*

I would not have thought so, but they do. I never understood how men could get any pleasure from just looking at sexy magazine pictures of naked women instead of being with a woman. I thought they maybe just couldn't get a date. Not true. Erotic pictures get my mind whirling, and sex is greater than ever.

*Maria, 26, hairdresser*

Since women's fashion magazines are filled with nude women selling everything from perfume to stereos to underwear, I've seen my share of naked women. I guess I'm supposed to like them. I'm not sure why publications aimed at women feature such ads. You don't see nude male models selling chain saws or sandals in science or automotive magazines written for men.

*Sherry, 34, driving instructor*

When I was growing up, men always had girlie photos, and I liked to look at them. I liked to compare their bodies with mine. It gave me an idea of what the men liked and what I could work toward. If you ask men what they like, they tell you one thing. If you watch what gets their attention, you might see something else. At least in my day that was true.

*Betty, 56, retired social worker*

## 111. DO YOU LIKE TO READ EROTIC LITERATURE?

I like to read erotica written by women. I subscribe to several publications that specialize in female porn by female writers, and it really turns me on. I've read male-produced porno, but the stuff from women seems more sensitive and yet sometimes even nastier. I'm not sure if sensitive and nasty go together, but I do know what I like.

*Rachel, 25, research assistant*

Sure I do! I like to read hot, sexy scenes that would never happen in my real life. It's a great form of escape and can induce some wonderfully satisfying sexual fantasies.

*Jackie, 36, doctor*

Hot, smutty romance novels are the best! I like the really, really graphic ones.

*Tammy, 29, salesclerk*

I like some erotic literature, but only the well-written stuff. Some romance novels use such strange terms to describe sex and sex organs. It's not erotic; it's just plain funny.

*April, 22, student*

I like to read stories about bondage and spanking. I like to know every little detail of the clothing and the rituals. I'm not sure if my interest in reading about these topics indicates a desire to actually be spanked or if I just like reading about it. For the time being, I'm content to let my mind experience the pain, instead of feeling the sensations on my backside.

*Abby, 20, pre-med student*

Well-written erotic literature is well worth my time. It sends my imagination on a hand-guided trip, and when I return, I feel very womanly. Ideas for sexual pleasure and tidbits for the sexual imagination cannot be overlooked as valuable and informative. Any help to keep your man interested is a good thing.

*Katherine, 50, veterinarian*

## 112. WOULD YOU POSE NUDE? UNDER WHAT CIRCUMSTANCES?

No. Never. Not for all the money in the world. I could never feel good about myself if I did.

*Bobbie, 45, secretary*

If the price was right, I'd do it in a heartbeat.

*Polly, 39, writer*

I would pose nude if I trusted the photographer or I was real drunk. So if I ever see a guy holding a camera in a bar during happy hour, watch out!

*Frannie, 22, bartender*

If it was done artistically and didn't look like a medical autopsy photo, I might go for it.

         *Susan, 26, medical assistant*

If I could turn back time, I'd pose nude for my husband. He asked me to let him take some revealing photos of me thirty years, three children, and seven grandchildren ago. I was too modest. I was being silly. Now it is too late, and I wish I'd made him happy. Gravity is a vicious force.

         *Connie, 63, systems analyst*

If I could lose another twenty pounds or so I'd love to pose nude. My husband gets really turned on by nude photos. He has asked me to do it many times, but I just can't do it until I lose more weight.

         *Sammie, 29, insurance clerk*

I would pose nude with the right lighting, sexy props, and the right mood. Sometimes I get in these really aroused moods and want to do things with my boyfriend that normally I wouldn't be caught dead doing. I don't know what makes these moods come and go, but he and I both enjoy them. I think I'll try it soon and give him the photos for his birthday.

         *Corrie, 32, martial arts instructor*

## 113. HAVE YOU EVER POSED NUDE? IF SO, DESCRIBE THE EXPERIENCE.

Once. I worried about it for years afterward. I kept thinking how awful it would be if that person blackmailed me. I thought about becoming famous and this guy popping up to haunt me. Then I decided I'd been watching too much TV.

         *Connie, 36, travel agent*

No, but it's one of my biggest fantasies. I'd love to spread my legs for the camera and let the cameraman get a shot of my juicy pink lips with my little clit bulging out. I fantasize that the guy taking the pictures gets so hot watching me that he comes right in his pants.

*Darlene, 35, writer*

Yes, that is how I met my husband. I was posing nude for a calendar, and he was the photographer. It was the beginning of the love of my life.

*Donna, 22, model*

My mother took one of those awful baby pictures of me naked on a rug and proudly displayed it to everyone who came to our house. That was enough humiliation for me. I've spent twenty-seven years living it down, and I still cringe whenever she talks about bringing the family album out after holiday dinners.

*Gloria, 27, scientific researcher*

I went to a party. Actually, in all fairness I would have to call it the party of a lifetime. It started as a girls'-night-out party at a friend's house, and no men were allowed. We had drinks, great finger foods, exotic cheeses, wine, chocolates, and the works. When the music was thumping at our brains and the wine was taking hold, we picked up the phone and ordered men from an escort service. They arrived and did these wonderful striptease dances for us. Then we handed them the camera, and we put on their naughty clothes and did a striptease for them. We asked them to take pictures of us so we would have mementos. They did and the pictures turned out great. Our husbands and boyfriends wanted to buy them from us. That's how good they were and how much they liked them. We said no.

*Hazel, 42, funeral director*

## 114. HAVE YOU EVER WATCHED HARD-CORE PORNO MOVIES BY YOURSELF? WITH YOUR MATE? WITH YOUR GIRLFRIENDS? WITH ANYONE? DID YOU ENJOY THEM?

No. Every time I'm stuck at home by myself and really bored, I think about going out and renting some, but I'm too embarrassed to do it. What would happen if I saw somebody I knew or, worse yet, they saw me?

*Glenda, 45, nurse*

Yes, when the women are attractive and willing. I like to see handsome men ramming their magnificent penises into wet pussies.

*Cheri, 23, communications specialist*

I like the really hard-core male porno movies. I like to see attractive, lean, well-hung men sucking and fucking each other. I like the combinations and the roughness of their actions. The fact that there isn't another female to compare myself with only adds to my pleasure.

*Carla, 27, postal worker*

My boyfriend likes to watch lesbian movies while we have sex. It used to bother me, but when I complained, he'd get mad. Then we'd go for weeks without making love. So now I just shut up and go along with his desires. He's not the only one who can fantasize. I just do it with my eyes closed.

*Janice, 37, reporter*

My husband insisted we go to an adult movie theater and watch this really explicit porno movie, just the two of us. There were really strange looking people in there, and they made me so nervous I don't remember seeing much of anything on the screen. There were men sitting with men and people moaning and groaning. I was 6 months pregnant and thought this was the most stupid place in the world I could possibly be. I'm sure the film was bad; I just didn't stay to prove it. After about fifteen minutes of the movie I told my husband to take me home or I was going to walk and take my chances.

*Veronica, 30, computer system designer*

## 115. WOULD YOU LIKE TO STAR IN A PORNOGRAPHIC FILM?

No. That is truly degrading. Can you imagine making a nasty movie and realizing that millions of perverts are sitting at home masturbating and watching you prance around naked? I can't.

*Marna, 29, executive secretary*

I would love to star in a porno flick if I could pick any leading man I wanted. I think it would be fun.

*Kelly, 32, seamstress*

My husband wants me and my next-door neighbor to make a dirty tape for him while he is at work. My girlfriend seems to be willing, but I'm not sure about it. I've never been with a woman, and I'm not sure I want to see my naked butt up close and in color on the TV in our living room.

*Jill, 31, housewife*

With AIDS everywhere, I can't imagine making a porno movie with multiple partners. If I caught anything from someone while making the film, it would be like watching my own suicide over and over.

*Heather, 22, graduate student*

Home videos are, or can be, sexy and erotic with your lover and even your husband, if you have the right kind of husband. I do think that people who want to appear in porno flicks, for strangers to watch them playing with themselves, have to be very sick and twisted, with absolutely no sex life worth having.

*Alissa, 22, marketing rep for hardware company*

## 116. HAVE YOU EVER MADE A SEXUAL HOME VIDEO?

My boyfriend of two years recently bought me a camcorder for Christmas. He said I needed that because I have children and memories are precious. To his surprise and delightful enjoyment, I put it on the tripod in the bedroom. You wouldn't believe how much fun we have had.

*Gladys, 27, court stenographer*

I don't like the idea of having any documentation of myself in a compromising position. Living in fear of someone seeing it isn't erotic.

*Phyllis, 45, attorney*

The thought is exciting. It's something I'd like to try.

*Rebecca, 28, sculptor*

My husband first talked me into doing a tape showing us making love about three years ago. Now we make a new one every month or so. I really like coming up with ideas and fantasies. It has added a new aspect to our sexuality. I think I'm more creative and maybe even more daring. The first time he performed anal sex on me was for the benefit of the camera. The first time I tied him up and spanked his hairy bottom was recorded in full color and stereo sound. I recommend it as a much more intimate adult memory vault. Besides, most photo labs refuse to develop our film if my husband has an erection. And he always has an erection!

*Julie, 31, makeup artist*

Honestly, it was the most exciting thing I have ever done in my life. It was Sunday afternoon, and the weather was cool and breezy. My hair turned out perfect that morning, and I felt sensuous and fit for a king to eat. Eric and I got out the camera equipment and decided to try our hand at doing a home video. I had been pampering myself for weeks—nails, hair, pedicure, drinking lots of water, taking vitamins—the works. I had been going to bed early, too, so I would feel rested and fresh. We did the video in the bedroom, kitchen, and screened-in porch on the back of the house. It was beautiful, erotic, and pleasurable. I don't think I have ever enjoyed anything more. We each have a copy, and when we have to be away from each other, out comes the tape!

*Cleo, 36, calligrapher*

## Overexposed

I'm an M.D., divorced with three teenage children. I had my children while I put my worthless ex-husband through law school. I have a thriving medical practice in a small suburb. I'm respected in the community and have hundreds of friends, supporters, and valued peers. I give my time, money, and energy to my children, my church, and my neighborhood. I've been divorced for over a decade and have built a pretty secure wall around myself. Or so I thought.

I'm fair-skinned, five feet six and have long blond hair, which I keep braided and pinned in a tight bun when I'm on my job. I wear those oh-so-attractive medical uniforms that make everyone look sexless. I wear reading glasses at work, both to see and to increase my authority. The fact that I would seduce a total stranger, take him to a horse barn, and proceed to fuck his brains out is pretty much out of the norm for me. It all started when my daughter Christine came home from school with a coupon for a mother-daughter session from one of those photography studios that provide makeovers and then dress you up in black leather and feathers.

She thought it would be a great way for the two of us to spend some quality time together. Of course she also loved the idea that she would get to look like a model and I would pay the bill. She came back from the mall with sunglasses for us to wear on the day of our appointment. They had asked us to come in with no makeup on, our hair wet and straight, looking as if we were ready for mug shots. I guess the idea was to look horrible before they took the pictures so that anyone, and I do mean anyone, would look better after being dressed up in black leather and a halter top. So there we were, looking like death, wearing our shades and having strangers make us into goddesses. They put us up front in the first two makeup chairs where everyone in the entire mall could see us.

I was chatting away with my hairstylist when I saw this tall man staring at me. He was in his mid forties, about six feet tall, with a good build, dark brown eyes, and brown hair. He was the only male in the entire place, and he wasn't just glancing at me, he was staring a hole through me. Being my usual assertive self, I asked him what he was doing. He informed me that he was Will, my photographer, and he was trying to visualize how he was going to shoot me.

His comment, needless to say, threw me for a loop. "No one is going to shoot me, and certainly not you! Stop staring at me!" It came out with a force that surprised me. The dozen other women in the studio were as amazed as I was. Everything came to a complete stop and the entire mall seemed completely silent, except for my heart beating a thousand beats a second. I felt my face turn crimson, and I heard my daughter let out a tense little giggle and say "Lighten up, Mom." Frannie, my hairdresser, started laughing. Will coughed loudly and the place resumed its normal noisy pace. I was so embarrassed.

After my hair had been poufed and teased, my face painted and contoured, my breasts pushed up into a golden bulletproof bra, I was ready for my photo session. Two hours of primping and getting ready had made me ready for my fifteen-minute photo session with Will.

I apologized for my outburst and told him to shoot away. He was gentle, funny, and professional. He made me dip. He made me pout. He asked for bedroom eyes. He told me to give him the look that melts men. I told him it had been so long since I'd given that look that I wasn't sure what to do. He changed my outfits discreetly. He helped me put on my black leather jacket. He changed my earrings. He wrapped me in blue feathers and laughed when they tickled my nose. He checked my teeth for lipstick and made me smile. The time flew by. Before I knew we had started, it was over and I was back in the dressing room.

My daughter's portraits were fantastic, and though I'm reluctant to admit it, so were mine. Minutes after the photo session all three of us were sitting in front of video monitors inspecting our poses. I wound up purchasing over six hundred dollars' worth of portraits. But I didn't want the moment to end. As weird as it may sound, I was turned on. Being a model for minutes had made me wet, or maybe it was the way Will's hands had caressed my cheek when he put those clip-ons on my ears.

As we were at the cash register I asked Will if he ever did any outside work. I came up with the silly story that I needed some outdoor portraits taken for my mother. Since the studio only provided shots taken inside from the waist up, he assured me that it was not only possible for him to do outside freelance photos, but it was a common request. We made arrangements to meet Sunday for a private photo session in the country.

I fell asleep that night with my hand drenched from the juice of my pussy. I must have climaxed a dozen times from just the thought of what might develop at the next photo session.

I was awake by the crack of dawn and I was on fire. Every nerve in my body was tingling. I hadn't felt this way in years. I imagined Will nuzzling my thighs. I heard his voice urging me to twist and arch. I imagined myself the world's most desirable model with a stable of assistants at my command. We were supposed to meet at the local Golden Arches at ten and begin our adventure. By seven o'clock I was ready—more than ready. My hot morning shower had just turned on the juices. I was refreshed, breathing hard, and my nipples were like rocks. The anticipation was heavenly. I was ready to pose my sweet little ass off for this man.

I knew from our one conversation that Will was single and that he drove a black convertible. I also knew that he made me laugh and that he had a cute little butt. I knew he didn't wear any underwear because there were no lines showing through his trousers when he bent over the camera at the studio. I knew I wanted to run my hand over his bare buttocks and take his throbbing penis deep into my mouth. I loved the feelings that he had awakened in me. I was alive and nervous. It felt like a first date from high school, only this time I knew I was going to get laid or die trying.

I borrowed several of my daughter's cute little minidresses. I dug out my sexy underwear from the storage closet. I found scarves, fishnet stockings, even an old garter belt left over from a long-forgotten lingerie party. Against my better judgment, I opened a bottle of nice white wine I'd buried in the refrigerator, and proceeded to drink a full tumbler of it. It was barely nine o'clock on a beautiful Sunday morning, and I was most certainly getting drunk and planning to get righteously fucked.

I was right on time at the restaurant. While former and current patients played with their children on the plastic playground equipment, I waited for my adventure to begin. I waved to everyone who waved to me, and I enjoyed the wait. I felt the breeze on my face, sang every song on the radio, and counted the seconds. Will arrived fashionably late, but was appropriately apologetic. He was humble, cute, and professional. His hair was a tangled mess from the wind, and his convertible was filled with camera equipment. I told him I'd arranged to use a friend's horse farm and barn for our photo session. He didn't know that I was a doctor. I'd put on the order form at the photo studio to call me at my hospital, and he had assumed I was a nurse.

We left my car at Kiddie Meal Land and had a lovely drive to my farm. The sky was clear. I shared my tumbler of wine, and we had a great time. We even sang along with the radio and he let me smoke one of his big old stinky cigars. If Will thought anything about my overfamiliarity with the farm he didn't say anything. He let the fact that the dogs and cats came right up to me and licked my hands go by without even a raised eyebrow. We carried my clothes, his equipment, and my picnic basket out to the barn. He brought out a CD player, and we began the session.

I posed demurely in my long flowing dress. We played on the hay bales, and I tried on outfit after outfit. It was like childhood in Granny's attic, only I was with a sexy man and I wasn't an innocent little girl anymore. He must have taken a hundred pictures before I decided to make my move. With his telephoto lens he had taken close-ups of my face softly lit by the sun filtering through the roof of the barn. While he worked on capturing the subtle moods on my face, I slowly unbuttoned my blouse and exposed my breasts. He was so tightly focused on my face that he couldn't see my actions until he took his eyes away from the camera.

When he did notice my exposure, I heard a gasp. "Are we still taking photos for your mom?" he asked softly.

"No, these are just for you and me," I purred.

I walked slowly across the hay, taking my blouse down to my waist as I moved. He put his camera on the floor, picked me up, and gently sat me on the hay. He ripped my lace panties off and impaled me on his rock-hard dick. He pounded his manhood into me. He fucked me over and over. His kisses were hot and salty. His thrusts were earthshaking. I was filled with his maleness. I was stretched and made full. After he came the first time, he paused for a couple of seconds at the most. Then he kissed me deeply, wiped the sweat from my nose, and rode me again. I had hay sticking in my back.

I was sure my pussy was turned inside out from the force of our lovemaking. My anus was whimpering in joyful surrender. I was drunk, fucked, and happier than I had been in years. I was alive and in love with him, life, the countryside, and his miraculous manhood. I wanted to scream out loud with joy and sexual abandon. Instead I took his still sticky pecker, coated with my juice, his juice, and our sweat, and I sucked him and sucked him until he exploded deep within my mouth. I laughed and cried and giggled like an idiot as the creamy come filled my mouth and dropped like molten metal on the hay beside us. He sucked my pussy and brought me to three orgasms. He licked my pink little ass. He tickled my inner thighs. He held me tight and hugged me till I had trouble breathing.

He came six times and would have gone once more if he had any juice left. I came over a dozen times myself before we finally ran down to the creek for a session of watery refreshment and cleansing. Later that week when we had the film developed, the last shot turned out to be one of the two of us making love. His bare bottom is toward the camera, my legs are up in the air, and you can see his penis piercing my vagina. The best we can figure out is that one of the cats must have stepped on the shutter button and tripped it while we were making love. Talk about being overexposed!

*Rachel, 39, doctor*

## A Star Is Born

After my divorce became final, I found myself going back to school—me, a thirty-year-old mother of two with a house in the sub-urbs and the family station wagon in the driveway!

My lawyer did a great job. My ex-husband will have to work two jobs every day for the next fifty years just to meet his child-support obligations, but so what? He should have thought about that before he decided to screw Rebecca, his loyal, but stupid secretary. She may be cute and have a tight little ass, but she has no assets, no property, and very little future. And due to a very understanding judge, my ex-hus-band finds himself in pretty much the same situation. I love it.

Since my own business pretty much runs itself, I have plenty of time on my hands. I also have disposable income, fine taste in clothes, and a great sports car. I still have a decent figure, and I'm certainly a sexual creature. My ex-husband will wake up one day and realize what he ain't getting any more of.

So, with all the adjustments in my life, I decided to go back to school at night. This time I was going to take classes in subjects I wanted to learn about. No accounting classes, no Latin, no Western Civilization. I decided to enroll in film school. I signed up for a film production course where I would learn to make my own student video.

I bought a film school T-shirt, a new notebook, and a camcorder. I later found out that the school provided cameras, so I didn't really have to spend that additional thousand dollars for my own equipment. Who knew?

My employees at work threw me a back-to-school party and even bought a five-pound bag of apples to bribe the teacher. They asked me what sorority I planned to pledge.

The first session was very interesting. There were about twenty peo-ple in my class. They ranged in age from fresh out of high school to people in their mid-forties. Some people were budding film directors. Others were bored housewives, something I could relate to.

We were divided into production teams, and I found myself assigned to a crew of three promising film students, one professional still pho-tographer, and one of the bored housewives.

Each of us would be required to make a ten-minute film on any sub-ject we desired. And we would all work on each other's films as part of the crew. I'd be doing sound on one film, designing costumes on an-other. I'd get to be a producer, director, editor, and cinematographer, all in the course of twelve weeks. It sounded like a lot of fun. The teacher told us the course would require hours and hours of outside work. He told us to exchange phone numbers with each other and get started.

Over the next couple of weeks, we worked on a film about card-players, one about sheep ranchers in Montana, and a music video about Mississippi blues bars.

I loved being out on location with all the kids. We would set up our equipment, turn on the lights, and make "art." I learned how to run the camera. I learned how to hold a boom mike just out of sight. I learned I could make bad films as easily as anyone.

Since I had the most free time, I was available to run errands during the day. I'd pick up props, copy scripts, even drive other crew members around. The fact that I had a gold credit card only added to my popu-larity.

Though I was old enough to be some of the crew members' mother, they treated me like one of the gang. I enjoyed their company. Hated their music, but liked their attitude.

I especially liked being around Philip and Alex, two of the full-time students. Both were very emotional and dramatic. Philip was the seri-ous director type. Alex liked to tell jokes and look up my skirt while I held the boom mike. They both seemed to enjoy being around me. They made me remember what it was like to be nineteen, confused, and horny.

Philip had broken up with his girlfriend a few months before, and I'm not sure if Alex had ever even really had a date, much less a steady relationship.

Our relationships grew from friendly joking to blatantly sexual com-ments. The rest of the crew seemed to spend less and less time with us. Or maybe the three of us just found more excuses to get together dur-ing the week. We were spending an enormous amount of time working on scripts, rewrites, and editing.

Since I was the least experienced "kid" on the crew, we decided to complete my film last. We spent weeks working on Alex's homage to Hitchcock and *The Rocky Horror Picture Show.* Philip wrote a piece about cockfighting and the men who raise the cocks for that purpose. The still photographer made a film about door-to-door salesmen.

The only blood spilled during any of these epic sagas was the time Alex tripped over the camera tripod and banged his lip on a light stand Philip was holding. Alex wanted to capture the blood on video and work the footage into his project. He seemed genuinely disappointed that it dried up before he could tape it.

Every time they asked me about my film, I told them I would tell them more about it when I was good and ready. I made suggestive hints about it being the hottest film of the bunch. I told them to expect anything. I told them I was making a "chick film."

With the quarter end in sight, I was running out of time. I had really grown quite fond of Al and Phil. I decided to give them a very personal graduation present.

I called them both on a Tuesday night and asked them to come to my house on Wednesday for a dress rehearsal of my film. Since we had been rehearsing all during the quarter, that alone didn't arouse too much suspicion.

I had copies of the script prepared on the coffee table when they arrived. A bottle of wine was chilled and waiting. My camera was already on the tripod, ready and able. I left a note on the door telling them to come on in and start reading the script. I told them I was preparing for my role and to go on and make themselves comfortable.

About thirty minutes before their arrival I took a lovely bubble bath and drank a few glasses of wine. I was nervous but incredibly turned on. It had been a long time since I'd had a sexual adventure, and I'd never had two young partners at once.

They arrived somewhat early. They read my note and eagerly made their way inside. I wrapped a towel around my dripping body, stuck my head out the doorway, and told them to enjoy themselves.

I told them there was plenty more wine in the refrigerator if they ran out. Alex took my hint.

I put on my see-through nightgown, perfumed my body, and grabbed my wineglass.

Alex looked as if he was going to fall off the couch when I entered the room. Philip just drooled and stammered something inane, like "Nice outfit," or something.

I told the guys to sit down, and we proceeded to give the script a run-through. I'd written parts for all of us, in great detail. I sat on the edge of the sofa with my legs parted and my pubic hair showing through the nightgown. My nipples were hard, and my vagina was moist.

I'd written a script about a lonely housewife who seduces her pool man and yard boy. Though it was highly derivative and certainly a cliché, they didn't seem to notice. They didn't even protest my sexist lines and obvious plodding dialogue. They just wanted to fuck me as soon and as often as possible.

I had the housewife masturbate for the men. When we read that part of the script, everything kind of went improvisational. I only covered about two pages of the script before Alex fell to his knees and started to devour my pussy. Philip just stared in frustration and amazement until I motioned for him to come closer. I unzipped his jeans and inhaled his slim erection. He tasted clean. He was rock-hard. He came after about ten strokes in my mouth. I drank every drop and kept his erection from dying down.

I got up on the couch and directed Philip to enter me from behind, while I took Alex in my mouth and gave him the same oral attention I'd written into the script.

They were both so eager and athletic, it was overwhelming. I loved them both deeply and completely. I was so raw and animalistic. It was salty, sweaty, drunken lust.

I needed to be wild with them. I felt the years slide down my throat when I performed oral sex on them. I felt beautiful and needed. I felt urges I'd forgotten about. It was delicious. I even loved the fact that most of our action had been captured by my camcorder.

When we went to class the final week, my instructor expected my film to be completed. I told him I didn't get mine done. I gave him some line about not having enough time because my kids were sick. He gave me an incomplete and told me to work on it over the summer. You should have seen the way Phil and Alex smiled. It was almost obscene.

*Sandra, 30, businesswoman*

chapter
*fifteen*

# Strip Clubs

117. *Have you ever been to a strip club?*
118. *If you have been to a strip club, what's the wildest thing you've ever seen there?*
119. *Does your mate frequent strip clubs? If so, does it bother you?*
120. *Would you consider working in a strip club?*
121. *Do strip clubs turn you on?*

## 117. HAVE YOU EVER BEEN TO A STRIP CLUB?

I look back on it still to this day and grin and laugh to myself. I had the time of my life that night, though I never expected it. My husband and I have always had a good relationship—good, honest, open communication. He put it to the test the Friday he came home from work and shouted, "Baby, let's do something different!" Of course I agreed to it, not knowing what he was going to say. I never dreamed he would suggest a strip club. I told him I'd try it if he really thought he would enjoy it.

Well, I'm the one who was dripping wet, pushed to a boiling point, hair sticking to the back of my neck, and couldn't wait to get inside the living room of our humble little abode. I ripped off his clothes, accidentally tripped him to the floor, fumbled for the stereo button, and in one sweep, lit a candle and handed him a bottle of wine and two glasses, and commanded, "Pour. And sit back to be tortured some more."

He was going out of his mind as I was coming out of my clothes, ever so lustily, ever so slowly. Imitating what I'd seen that night, like a crash course in Drive-'Em-Wild 101, I danced, I thrusted, I flaunted, I shook my little ass and my aching pink pussy right up in the poor man's face until he couldn't stand it anymore. We had better sex that night than any night I can remember in a long, long time. What a great idea. We will return!

*Betty Jo, 40, court reporter*

I went to a strip club one night with a bunch of girls from work. We went in with sunglasses on, afraid someone would recognize us and think we were a bunch of perverts. After about fifteen minutes we didn't give a damn whether anyone saw us or not. We were shouting, "Go, Girl!" as loud as the men. The girls came out onstage individually and danced one song each. They were all good-looking to drop-dead gorgeous. The music was thumping, and they played great dance tunes. The part that would get me every time was when the girl would slink up to the pole in the center of the stage like it was a real person and slide her you-know-what up and down and all around. It would tear me up every time. She treated that pole like it was alive. The men would yell and break out in a sweat. We had tons of fun, and I would recommend it to anyone for a great night out on the town. Television, move over!

*Alissa Jean, 32, law clerk*

No. I think you have to be pretty immoral to take part in something like that. Sex isn't supposed to be a group activity. It's supposed to be private. I don't approve of strip clubs.

*Nadine, 39, housewife*

I went to a strip club with my boyfriend, Tony, and couldn't believe my eyes. I'd have to be on some pretty heavy-duty drugs to do what those girls do. They have nerves of steel, I guess. Maybe they get used to guys drooling and licking their chops, but I just can't imagine how they do it. I'll have to say it did get me excited and now I understand why Tony likes these places and stops by there for lunch once in a while.

*Billie Jean, 28, internal revenue agent*

## 118. IF YOU HAVE BEEN TO A STRIP CLUB, WHAT'S THE WILDEST THING YOU'VE EVER SEEN THERE?

Yes, I have been to a strip club, and the wildest thing I've seen wasn't on the stage. It was the stupid men trying to pretend like they weren't married or weren't perverts. What a joke!

*Sybil, 30, equipment leasing consultant*

The wildest thing I ever saw in a strip club was when one of the spectators got a little overexcited and tried to touch one of the girls onstage. The security guards jumped on him and threw him out so fast, I couldn't believe it. Now, that was wild.

*Gretchen, 40, computer technician*

Everything about a strip club is pretty wild to me. It's amazing that those girls are able to get up onstage and dance around completely naked and be so comfortable about it.

*Carrie, 26, secretary*

You've probably heard about it, but my husband and I actually witnessed a woman and a donkey in a Mexican strip show. We were on a tour about twenty years ago in a border town on the Texas line. The cabdriver asked if we wanted to see something wild. My husband naturally said that he did, and since I had no intention of being left alone in a foreign country with an ugly cabbie, I went with him.

The place was a broken-down shacklike building. It was filled with tourists seated on sagging fruit boxes. Six young female dancers came out one at a time and did standard striptease numbers, going down to G-strings. The crowd grew restless and started yelling for the donkey. After three or four moderately attractive dancers performed their numbers, this time ending up fully nude, the tattooed bouncer brought a saggy, broken-down, floppy-eared donkey out on the stage. The lights didn't dim. They just flicked off. When they came back on, there was an even saggier stripper standing beside the poor animal. Her name was Juanita, and she must have been at least sixty years old. She was probably fifty pounds overweight, and her makeup looked like it had been shoveled on. She took off her top, and her breasts looked at least seventy years old. They gave a totally new meaning to the term "saggy." She dropped her panties and walked over to the donkey. The donkey was so jaded he didn't even acknowledge her presence. She rubbed up against the animal's side and moaned. The donkey just flicked his tail at the dozen or so horseflies biting his butt. She grabbed his balls and gave them a squeeze. The donkey raised his tail and delivered the most amazing shit right on her panties. The aroma filled the shack and was overwhelming. The dancer cursed the donkey and stormed out. The audience just sat collectively stunned and eventually left in silence.

*Amelia, 55, office manager*

Just being in the strip club was wild for me. However, even wilder was when two of the girls who work there got into an altercation. They didn't have much to grab on one another, so mostly they were biting and pulling hair, until one of the other girls came out of nowhere with an upper cut. I think that's what it's called. It was the craziest and wildest thing I've ever seen anywhere. Two naked women who, just seconds before, were strutting like dainty little maidens on the shiny dance floor for all the people to gaze upon and fantasize about taking them home. Fantasize about having wild erotic sex with them, sleeping with them, and stroking their long, lustrous golden hair. Now it was suddenly up to these men and women patrons to leave the cleared club and go home to try not to think about the hairballs that lay on the floor, along with the blood from their noses and the missing teeth. That was the one and only visit to a strip club for me and I'll tell you it was plenty.

*Clarrisa, 38, farm equipment dealer*

## 119. DOES YOUR MATE FREQUENT STRIP CLUBS? IF SO, DOES IT BOTHER YOU?

My man would never go to one of those places. They are disgusting. What does he want to go look at a used-up piece of pussy for, when he can come home and have me?

*Nell, 30, factory worker*

My husband loves to go to titty bars. He and his friends get together and go about once a week. I don't like that he goes, but there's not much I can say. At least I know where he is. I just have to wonder about what he does there.

*Stephanie, 30, housewife*

My boyfriend and I love to go together. It blows men's minds when I walk in on his arm. You just don't expect to see a woman walking into one of those places. I think strip bars are great. We go as often as possible, watch the dancers, and then go home and fuck each other till the sun comes up. It heightens our sex drive. Every once in a while I'll buy him a couch dance or a table dance. That guarantees that I'll be getting some that night.

*Jamie, 27, security guard*

My husband met me in a nude club. I was the prize. He does not go to nudie bars anymore. He doesn't have to. I give him his own private table dance every night.

*Vanessa, 22, dance instructor*

My female lover and I love to go to titty clubs. We are monogamous with each other, but we like to go watch the other girls, and quite frankly, we like to watch the men make fools of themselves. They are so funny, and it gives us just one more reason why gay is great. I think they should give the men bibs at the door to catch the drool.

*Hassie, 31, court reporter*

## 120. WOULD YOU CONSIDER WORKING IN A STRIP CLUB?

No way. Those women are sluts. And the men who go there are pigs.
*Randi, 32, waitress*

I wouldn't unless I had no alternative and was completely broke.
Working in a strip club ranks right down there with being a hooker. I
don't think either profession is right for me.
*Melissa, 25, advertising manager*

Consider it? Hell, yes! I think it would be great! Selling sex, showing
off your body in front of horny, excited men. I think I'd get a real
charge out of it. I love to run around naked. I have a great body—
huge, perfectly shaped breasts, slender hips, long legs. I'm proud of
my body, and I'd love to be a stripper.
*Jennie, 22, telemarketing supervisor*

I have worked in a strip club. It's degrading. And even if they say they
don't, most of the girls I knew were more than strippers. There was
plenty of prostitution going on there, and the men who knew what to
ask for could get anything they wanted. I didn't like it. I only did it
for the money. It was scary. All those men staring at you. Who knows
if one of them is crazy or could start stalking you? I'd never do it
again.
*Ellen, 30, housewife*

If I could approach it as an art and if no one would know who I was,
I'd love to be an exotic dancer. I just don't want people following me
home or coming up to me in the grocery store. I don't mind showing
my body, it's the intrusion into the rest of my privacy that bothers me.
*Belinda, 25, stock researcher*

If I had a boyfriend or husband who thought working in a strip club
would be okay, I'd get rid of him in a hurry. If I were starving to death
or my children were going to be taken away from me because they

were financially neglected, yes, I'd work in a strip club. But only as a very last resort. A very, very last resort!

*Cindy, 38, optometrist*

## 121. DO STRIP CLUBS TURN YOU ON?

I don't know. I've never been in one.

*Jane, 40, teacher*

Yes and no. It's an uncomfortable environment. It would be too weird to have a group experience like that. After you're gone and you think back to what you saw, that's kind of erotic. But when you're there, it's just too weird to enjoy.

*Lena, 35, photographer*

Yes. Men or women. It doesn't matter. It's hot. It's sexy. And best of all, it's live. I get really turned on at strip shows. I beg my lover to do stripteases for me. What a turn-on. The naked body is beautiful, and I enjoy looking at it.

*Vicki, 26, business consultant*

I went to a lesbian strip club once with a group of gay friends. I was the only straight one in the bunch, and my friends made a point of letting the dancers know it. Those dancers must have seen me as a challenge. They were dancing inches away from my mouth. They touched my face, they blew in my ear. My friends were rolling on the floor with tears in their eyes from laughing. But the joke was on them. I actually had a good time.

*Ella, 22, hairdresser*

I couldn't wait to turn twenty-one so I could go to all of the places I couldn't go before. Strip clubs were one of them. I'll never forget the disappointment I felt when I finally arrived. I thought it would be slinky and beautiful and sexy. It was dark, dirty, and nasty. Nasty is not sexy. Nasty is nasty.

*Marilynne, 22, student*

# chapter sixteen

# *Places*

## 122. WHERE DO YOU LIKE TO MAKE LOVE?

Anywhere. Anytime.

*Robin, 21, student*

I kind of prefer the bedroom. But the kitchen counter is always a nice change.

*Dianne, 32, florist*

I like to do it on the floor. Nothing wrong with a little rug burn every now and then.

*Jenny, 26, greenhouse operator*

I think the best place to make love is definitely in the shower. I love to get in a steamy, hot shower with my lover and go at it. With the water pounding on our naked bodies as we bump and grind, it's ecstasy.

*Tammy, 30, bookseller*

The hallway stairs going up to the second floor are great for sex. The carpet runner protects my knees, and the rail keeps my boyfriend from falling over the side. As long as the neighbors stay away from our front doorway, we are safe and satisfied in suburbia.

*Gayle, 35, travel agent*

I would love to try it on the open road. I'd love to get in a convertible with an Italian love god and fuck him while he was driving. Wind in my hair, sun on my back, and sit right in his lap and do it.

*Clara, 38, recording studio owner*

## 123. HAVE YOU EVER HAD SEX IN A PUBLIC LOCATION?

My lover and I did have sex in a public location. We were in a restaurant. I was making out with my sweetheart under the table with my feet. It sounds crazy, but it was one of the greatest sexual highs we have ever experienced. He still talks about it.

*Michelle, 37, advertising director*

I made love in church with my future husband. While the family was down below praying for my soul, we were up in the balcony making a little future church member. We were lying on top of each other on the back pew while my best friend, Sally, and her boyfriend, John, felt each other up and kept an eye on the minister. I became pregnant that night, married three months later. Now I proudly bring my growing family to church each week for uplifting sermons. That was seven years ago, and I feel my family is truly blessed. Thank God for long-winded sermons and sparsely attended night services.

*Vickie, 25, graphic artist*

My high school boyfriend and I had sex under the bleachers once during a football game. I can't imagine what would have happened if we'd gotten caught!

*Missy, 24, personnel assistant*

My boyfriend and I had sex once in a telephone booth. We were horny, it was raining outside, and the hotel lobby was empty. I was working as the night clerk, and James was just hanging out, killing time. We took a chance, locked the front door, and ran into the phone booth. It wasn't very comfortable. We both were worried about getting caught. The sex probably wasn't as good as I remember it. But at least we tried it, and now I know what it is like. Sometimes different is sexy, sometimes it is just different.

*Tabitha, 24, hotel management*

In my grandmother's backyard my first child was conceived. I had just gotten married, and we thought it would be great fun to sneak out to the backyard in the middle of the night after everyone else had gone to bed. We took a blanket, some cheese and pop and lay under the stars making love. It is to this day one of my most precious memories, and the only bad thing that happened was when we were waking up. My grandfather was looking down on us as he had gone out early to walk the dog. The dog was sniffing my brand-new husband's balls and Granddad was laughing uncontrollably.

*Rollanda, 37, book dealer*

## 124. WHAT PUBLIC LOCATION WOULD YOU LIKE TO TRY? WHY HAVEN'T YOU?

In a public park, right beside the pond, so we can hear the ducks quacking. I think it would be awesome to feel the breeze on my skin and hear the ducks while we're making love. The only reason we haven't is because we're afraid we'll get arrested.

*Rachael, 24, accountant*

I'd like to do it in the middle of downtown on lunch break when hundreds of people come out of their office towers. I'd lie right down in the middle of the sidewalk, hike my dress up, and drag my boyfriend into me. It would be great. Maybe I'll do it on Thursday.

*Cindy, 29, data entry operator*

I've always wanted to do it in an elevator. I think I've been watching too many movies.

*Hope, 25, interpreter*

I think the most romantic place anyone could ever have sex is on the beach late at night. My husband and I just aren't adventuresome enough to try it.

*Lillian, 45, insurance agent*

On the roof of our home. I think it would be a scream to be up on the roof doing it and watching the neighbors mow their yard or work in their garden, never knowing what was taking place next door right overhead. I think we're about to get up the nerve to try it. My husband is afraid I'll scream when I come. He's quite a lover.

*Jenny, 31, dance instructor*

## 125. TELL US A FRIEND'S TALE OF SEX IN A PUBLIC PLACE.

My girlfriend told me about sex on a train. They were in the dome car; they could see the Rocky Mountains and deer running through the fields. It sounded like a combination novel—Louis L'Amour meets Fabio.

*Rebecca, 26, receptionist*

My roommate did it at a bus stop with her girlfriend. She just went down on her while they were waiting for the bus, while about ten people were watching. It was Gay Liberation Day and she wanted to prove a point, which I believe she did. It's a wonder she didn't get arrested.

*Susan, 39, florist*

One of my ex-boyfriends told me he and his girlfriend did it on a football field. But if how he treated me is any indication, he was lying.

*Marsha, 25, free-lance makeup artist*

My best friend had sex with her boyfriend at an outdoor concert. They had a grass pass, which basically gave them a spot on the side of a hill. The concert was an all-day affair. By the time it became dark, they were drunk, horny, sunburned, and bored with the music. They were making out on their blanket when the headline act came on. Since I was sitting right beside them, I can testify that Bob entered Susan from behind. He pumped her for about five minutes, climaxed, and then fell on his side, with his penis oozing sperm. He passed out before the main act's first song was finished.

*Tracy, 20, student*

This guy told me he and his date did it while on a horse. Good grief, I can't imagine that being any fun, or romantic. Painful comes to mind.

*Bobbi Jo, 49, toy store clerk*

## 126. WHAT DO YOU THINK ABOUT SEX OUTDOORS? ANY PERSONAL EXPERIENCES?

I love sex in the woods during the early days of spring. I like to run naked and hide behind the trees, laughing and acting like a wood nymph.

*Shannon, 32, assembly-line worker*

I like to screw on the beach with the waves lapping at my toes. Just keep the sand out of my special places, keep me lubricated, and have at it.

*Heidi, 36, news correspondent*

My boyfriend and I were once caught having sex in a public park at the same time SWAT teams were storming the place, trying to appre-hend an escaped prisoner. We were in some bushes making love when I looked up and saw a commando dressed in military fatigues pointing a rifle at my head. I almost died. I screamed and fell off my lover. He jumped up and covered his genitals. Five gunmen stood around our bush with their guns pointed at our heads. It was only when their commanding officer arrived on the scene and told them to put away their rifles that I realized I had peed on myself. At least they didn't take us in. And they did capture that prisoner about a quarter of a mile away from our bush later that day.

*Lucy, 29, pharmacist*

Stay out of the poison ivy, watch out for fire ants and bees, and keep downwind of bears and park rangers. Those are my rules for outdoor sex.

*Suzy, 19, waitress*

My lover and I went out for a lovely dinner and then to a drive-in movie. They still have those places if you look hard to find them. We did it in the car with the top down and people on both sides of us. At first we were shy and wondered if they would get out of their cars to go rat on us. Instead, they started doing the same thing. It was great. It was like an orgy but in three different cars. I don't remember what the movie was.

*Sheila, 47, stress management counselor*

## 127. AUTOMOBILE SEX? DRIVING DOWN THE ROAD OR PARKED?

I love to suck my husband off while we ride down the interstate. He puts the Buick on cruise control, activates the radar detector, and gives me that look. I unzip his pants, release his penis from its confines, and suck away. I hike my dress up over my hips and let him watch my squirming ass wiggle in the bucket seat. I suck him slow and steady while pumping his shaft with both my hands. It certainly makes commuting much more pleasant.

*Shelly, 29, restaurant manager*

Most of America was made in the backseats of cars. I think Henry Ford is actually the father of this nation. All George Washington did was chop down a cherry tree. Ford gave men a way to get that cherry before it became a tree.

*Ruth, 35, screenwriter*

I love to go parking. The whole ritual still excites me after fifteen years of marriage. It keeps me young and makes my husband horny. I just wish they had more drive-ins showing bad monster-movie triple features. A videotape just can't compare to a three-story-tall Godzilla on a summer night at the Sunset Drive-In.

*Marla, 28, server*

Give me a three-hour ride in a limo. It beats a hotel room anytime. The feel of leather seats, the free booze in the refrigerator, the gentle swaying of the car, the rough bumps of the highway—it all adds up to a romantic experience. The chauffeur will look the other way if you want him to, or stare at you the whole time if you desire it. I love to play in a limo in the middle of the evening rush hour. The thrill of being watched and the constant change of scenery are just fantastic. For less than the price of a hotel room, any girl can have the ride of her lifetime.

*Holly, 34, fashion designer*

My boyfriend and I did something we thought was really original. Erotic, too. He parked in the carport, and I got on the windshield. I pulled my cute little summer dress up and took off my panties. Then I sat on the windshield and rubbed and wiggled my privates and gave him a private show. He had a wonderful view, and it excited him more than I can tell you. I was pretty hot myself. I could see his face, and I could also see him stroking his penis. When we were to the boiling point he got out of the car and fucked me on the hood. We plan to keep this one on our sexual menu.

*Leslie, 46, pet shop owner*

## Sex between Superman's Legs

I always thought Metropolis was an imaginary place, like Shangri-la and Oz, but I was wrong. The home of Superman is a very real place, and, as I recently discovered, a very memorable place to make love. Located at the southernmost tip of Illinois, the town is about three hundred miles and fifty years away from Chicago. This quaint little town is friendly, clean, and definitely slower paced than the Windy City.

I'd recently moved to Chicago to work for a large, prestigious law firm as a legal assistant. I'd toured the lake area of Illinois, seen the museums, Greek Town, and Second City, and had been to the top of the Sears Tower twice. After a few months of the big city I was ready to get out in the country and see Middle America. I convinced my boyfriend, a fellow legal assistant, to take a weekend getaway down through Lincoln country. It would be an adventure, I told him. He yawned. I didn't want to fly to New York City for a weekend of theater, fine dining, and shopping on Park Avenue. I wanted to go to the country. I wanted to see life on a smaller level. I wanted to feel the earth between my toes. I wanted to smell fresh-cut hay. I wanted to go to a place where people said "Howdy!" to each other and actually smiled once in a while. How about a weekend retreat to the home of Superman? *That* he might like to see! Turns out he was a big Superman fan in his childhood.

We planned a pleasant picnic lunch, a leisurely trip down the backbone of America. When we entered Metropolis, the first thing we saw was a huge billboard welcoming us to the home of Superman. It was painted in the style of a 1930s billboard, the kind motorcycle officers used to hide behind in old black-and-white movie classics. We stopped the car and took pictures of each other standing under Superman. Everything in town was related to Superman—the drugstore, the flower shop, even the antique mall had a Superman connection. But the item that most fascinated my boyfriend was right in the center of the town square. Right in front of the quaint old historical courthouse, right where most cities would have a monument to their Civil War heroes, Metropolis featured a bigger-than-life full-color three-dimensional statue—no less than a living shrine to Superman! He was amazing. He was so big. So bold. So strong.

The statue had a strange effect on my boyfriend. The billboard had been great, but this statue was something else! We parked the car and slowly approached the statue. Cars were zipping all around us, but my boyfriend was oblivious to them. The police station was located right next to the courthouse, and patrol cars were pulling in and out with increasing regularity. He didn't seem to care. He ignored traffic. He jaywalked, jumped over the crowd-control maze of fences, and hugged Superman's leg. He looked me straight in the eye and simply said he was going to fuck me right between Superman's legs!

It was still daylight on a Saturday afternoon in the quaint little river town, and my legal-assistant boyfriend was willing to risk it all to ram his pecker deep inside me in a town square while a dozen policemen worked only yards away! It made perfect sense to me, but it was still daylight and we would have to come back later.

We posed for a few pictures and even found a nice local couple to take our picture together with each of us smiling and holding on to Superman. We decided to have a nice dinner at the local family eating establishment on Main Street. Most of the customers were senior citizens who appeared to know everyone else in the place. We were obviously the new kids in town. People were friendly. It was charming. The waitresses were fast and friendly. We ate till we were stuffed and then shared a piece of fresh-baked apple pie. We planned our adventure. I would go upstairs to the rest room and take off my panties. We decided rear-entry was probably the most efficient position for our escapade.

I was in the turn-of-the-century bathroom upstairs pulling off my underwear when our waitress came in. When she walked in, I had my dress hiked up, my panties off, and was getting ready to put them in my purse. "You planning to go make love on Superman, honey?"

Turning three thousand shades of red all at once, I weakly nodded my head and squeaked out an inaudible yes. She laughed and told me to make sure it was real dark and to do it real quick on the side of the statue that was hidden from the police station's view. "You'll have about five or six minutes before a car comes around the square and hits your lover's shiny butt with its headlights." Later I realized that she hadn't even used the bathroom herself. Had she been sent to deliver that specific message for my benefit? After going back down to my boyfriend with my satin panties safe in my purse, I gave the waitress a five-dollar tip and carefully walked from our table to the door. I swear every couple in that place knew what we were going to do! They were all smiling just a little bit too much.

Anyway, she was wrong. We had a good seven minutes before we were busted!

*Jessica, 22, legal assistant*

# chapter seventeen

# Voyeurism, Exhibitionism, and Group Sex

128. *Are you an exhibitionist?*

129. *Have you ever knowingly had sex with your partner in front of anyone else? Describe the experience. Did you like it?*

130. *Have you ever been caught having sex?*

131. *Are you a voyeur?*

132. *Have you ever watched another couple have sex?*

133. *Have you ever had multiple partners or attended an orgy?*

134. *Have you ever fantasized about a threesome with another man?*

135. *Have you ever fantasized about a threesome with another woman?*

## 128. ARE YOU AN EXHIBITIONIST?

I love to show my body off to total strangers. I wear sexy clothes, have a sexy body, and like to make people happy. When I know people are looking at me, it makes me bold and wet.

*Carrie, 28, designer*

No way! Some things should be kept private.

*Lou, 40, housewife*

I'm proud of my body, but I don't want anyone to see it other than my boyfriend. I'm not into showing it off, but looking? That's another story altogether.

*Ellie, 43, newspaper columnist*

I like to wear clothes that show off my lines and leave little to the imagination. Though I'm totally covered, my skintight dresses proudly accent my nipples and pubic area. I keep my bush trimmed and my body firm. I get a thrill out of being completely covered from head to toe, and yet one look shows all I have to offer.

*Joni, 20, model*

I wish I could do the things that run through my head. In my mind I am an exhibitionist. I love to see men watching me, wishing they could fuck me. Wishing they could take me home or to a wild, exotic place and have their way with me. In reality, I am always clothed and thinking about bigger and better things. Someday maybe I'll actually do something really erotic and exciting. Never know.

*Rebecca, 34, graphic designer*

## 129. HAVE YOU EVER KNOWINGLY HAD SEX WITH YOUR PARTNER IN FRONT OF ANYONE ELSE? DESCRIBE THE EXPERIENCE. DID YOU LIKE IT?

When I was in college, my boyfriend—now my husband—and I had sex in my dorm while my roommate watched. He thought I was doing it to be kinky, but I was actually doing it so my roommate could see what power I had over my man. She had been making none-too-subtle hints about how she could have any man she wanted, insinuating that the only reason my boyfriend was still mine was because she had chosen to leave him alone. I wanted her to see with her own eyes the power I had over my lover. While she watched from her side of the room, I put on the show of my sexual life up to that moment. I was a lust-driven animal. I dominated. I thrust my hips. I fucked with every bit of energy I could muster. I was a sex maniac. My boyfriend was in heaven. My roommate left the room in a huff, and she never said another word about taking my man away from me.

*Josie, 35, stockbroker*

Yes! It was exciting. It was my husband, me, my best friend, and her husband. We had a foursome. It was terrific once we overcame our embarrassment.

*Grace, 45, realtor*

No. And I don't intend to.

*Anna, 32, housewife*

Every time I doubled-dated with my best friend, we ended up listening to and watching each other have sex. We always went parking together, and we always had sex with our boyfriends, who later became our husbands. There was no such thing as privacy in a parked car. We all heard every smack, groan, moan, and even fart. We belched, sang songs, zipped and unzipped our clothes.

Looking back after fifteen years, it seems strange that we thought nothing about being so intimate just inches apart from each other. We still live in the same town, and go bowling together every couple of weeks. Maybe we should get our teenager to baby-sit with the four other kids while we old farts go out and have sex in the Ford Taurus for old times' sake!

*Suzanne, 31, physician's assistant*

Now this was a great idea. My husband and I have a great marriage, but we had been talking about doing something a little kinky. There's this friend of his that I found sexually attractive, and his wife is good-looking, too. We recently asked them to join us. They said they just didn't feel like they could get into that, but they would love to watch us. We all got in the living room and turned the lights down low, put on soft, sexy music, and brought out some wine for everyone. They sat on the sofa, and we got on a blanket on the floor. My husband gave the performance of a lifetime. Good old male ego, I guess. It was fabulous. They got so overheated they tore off each other's clothing and fucked like animals. We four have a standing Friday night date every week.

*Paula, 45, boot manufacturer*


## 130. HAVE YOU EVER BEEN CAUGHT HAVING SEX?

A herd of cows once trapped my boyfriend and me in a barn while we were busy doing it. They made such a noise mooing that we had to stop in mid-session before my neighbor came out to see what all the ruckus was about.

*Chrissie, 29, personal shopper*


My two little sisters caught me having sex with my boyfriend once when we were both eighteen. I was supposed to be baby-sitting, and they were supposed to be asleep upstairs. I was trying to be quiet, and my boyfriend was trying to come as quickly as possible. I wasn't doing my job, and they weren't even in their bedrooms. I wasn't remotely quiet, and my boyfriend took forever to get off. Right in mid-stroke on the living room floor, he looked over at the couch, shouted "Oh, shit!" and pointed to my sisters. It was a crash course in human sexuality that most ten- and eleven-year-old girls can only dream about. Ten years later I'm still paying dearly for their silence.

*Camille, 28, promotion director*


My parents caught me having sex in the living room when I was seventeen. They charged my eighteen-year-old boyfriend with statutory rape. He lost his scholarship to a Bible college. I was sent away to live with my aunt in Detroit, and my life was changed forever. My boyfriend refused to have anything to do with me, and after a year of returned letters and denied collect phone calls, I gave up. I never heard from him again. I never forgave my parents.

*Kristy, 30, secretary*

My mother caught my boyfriend tasting me, and I thought I would die. He didn't see her standing behind him at the door, and I was so shocked I couldn't speak or move. She was shocked and just stood there with her mouth open and a face like she'd seen a ghastly ghost. The funny thing was—it seems funny now, but it wasn't then—he kept on licking and fingering and smacking at my pussy while she was still standing there behind him. When he realized she was there, I truly thought he was going to have a stroke. At seventeen that would have been pretty sad. The even funnier thing was, about ten years later my mother asked me how did a guy at seventeen learn how to do that so well? She said I was very fortunate; most men of forty or more never seem to get it right.

*Tara, 30, lifeguard instructor*

## 131. ARE YOU A VOYEUR?

I think I am to a certain extent. I mean, I wouldn't want to be present with another couple getting it on in the same room, but it is exciting to watch people when they don't know you're watching them. I live in a high-rise apartment building. Every once in a while I can look out my window and see someone undressing or see a couple having sex. That's exciting.

*Jacqueline, 30, actress*

I'm not, but I'd love to be if ever given the chance. I fantasize about it all the time. I love pornography, love adult movies, and would really get off on watching other people. That's got to be a kick.

*Shane, 32, academic adviser*

I grew up watching my six sisters make out. I didn't see them have sex, but I did get a thrill watching them kiss and hug their assorted boyfriends. I still like to watch romantic movies. Even as a little bitty girl I never thought it was yucky to see people kissing. I didn't turn away. I wanted to see more.

*Paula, 29, horse trainer*

I might like to watch another couple for about thirty seconds, but then I would have to have some myself. It's very erotic to me to think about watching other people, but I've never tried it.

*Sherry, 21, pawn shop clerk*

## 132. HAVE YOU EVER WATCHED ANOTHER COUPLE HAVE SEX?

Yes. Once when my husband and I were on vacation we stopped at a live sex show. It was horrible. I'd always been mildly intrigued by the thought of watching another couple have sex, but it was an awful experience. It cost too much, it was in a cold, dark basement, and the couple was just disgusting.

*Marilyn, 24, special events planner*

One night I was having a party and had several friends over. We all got completely drunk, and before I knew it, two of my guests were having sex on the living room floor. Everybody really got into it. But afterward we all felt a little embarrassed.

*Tabitha, 30, security officer*

I once saw a hooker give a guy a blow job in an alley. I guess that technically they were a couple, but it sure didn't look like love.

*Rita, 21, clerk*

I caught my father giving my mother oral sex. I was in high school and came home around eleven from a bummer date. My parents obviously weren't expecting me, because when I came in, I heard my mom moaning. The door was open, and my dad's legs were dangling out from under the covers. His head was most definitely buried in my mother's vagina. I didn't disturb them and went straight to my room. Around three o'clock my mom burst in, demanding to know what time I'd snuck in. I told her that when I came in they were too busy to notice me. She gave me a funny look and didn't say anything else. I fell asleep unsure of my feelings about oral sex and my parents' willingness to engage in it.

*Rebecca, 30, nurse*

Once when I lived in a tiny efficiency apartment my mother and dad were spending a week with my new husband and me. It was the first time I had seen them in a year. They were on our bed, and we took the sofa bed, which was right on the other side of the same room. Well, they thought we were asleep and I wished I had been. It was really too weird watching my parents have sex. It looked to me like Dad was pretty good and Mom was loving it.

*Aubrey, 27, clown*

## 133. HAVE YOU EVER HAD MULTIPLE PARTNERS OR ATTENDED AN ORGY?

It sounds like a 1970s joke, but I actually fucked my high school boys' basketball team. While I'm horrified to think about it now, it happened on a Sunday afternoon after the big Saturday night game. In our little farming community, basketball was the prime claim to fame for local athletes. Our school wasn't big enough to field a strong football team, but, boy, oh boy, could those country boys shoot hoops. I worshiped the players and had grown up with most of them from first grade on. I think one of them might have been a second cousin, but big deal. By the time I was a senior I'd already dated four of the five starters, and the fifth one was the cutest one of the bunch.
I brought two six-packs of beer to the informal afternoon practice. They drank and played ball. I drank and flirted. I became the prize if one guy sank a particularly hard shot. It started with kisses, and pretty soon my head was spinning. My panties were up on the basketball goal, and my handsome athletes were lined up to slam-dunk me on their magnificent love poles. It was sloppy and wet, and even though it ruined my reputation for the rest of my senior year, it was probably the best sex I ever had.

*Mindy, 42, insurance salesperson*

I had a foursome with my boyfriend and two of his military buddies. Jerry had been bugging me for weeks to have an orgy. He didn't seem to mind the idea of me fucking other guys as long as he could do it with their girlfriends. So he pitched the idea to his bunk buddies.

They loved it and thought their girlfriends would get into it. They drove to town on a weekend pass and brought their ladies. By the time they had made the sixty-mile trip, everyone was a little high and turned on. We went out to eat, then dancing. One of the girls left her date at the club after he flirted with some other woman. The other girl was getting progressively drunker. When the five of us made it back to my apartment, the guys were ready to go. We all took our clothes off in the bedroom. The other girl tripped taking her panties off and stayed on the floor, passed out. I loved all the attention, and simply fucked my boyfriend right in front of the other two. He looked up and told them to join in, so we all had a big old time. I screwed all three of them and fell asleep in a heap of sweaty, drunk soldier boys. My boyfriend acted cool the next morning, but we broke up about two weeks later. The other guys never called me either. I'm just glad I was on my period and didn't get pregnant.

*Margo, 23, hairdresser*

It all took place in one day. I got my divorce finalized, dressed to kill, went to a bar I'd never been in before on the other side of town, and picked up two handsome men. They had just returned from playing golf and were in a great mood. They were single and available, and they had money. I was a slut that day, and it felt great. I told them exactly what I wanted, and they gladly gave it to me. We had lots of drinks, but we weren't drunk. I told them I didn't want to do this slobbery drunk and not be able to remember it. They laughed and said, "Whatever the lady wants."

We ate a fabulous dinner after leaving the bar and then went to one of those Ed's Beds motels with the mirrors on the ceiling and never enough towels. It was clean enough, and it had great porno movies running. The pornos were already running when we entered the room. I thought that was pretty funny. They stripped for me, danced for me, and took me to sexual taboo heaven. They were my hookers. When the sex was over, I put on my clothes, said thank you and left. Now I know why men like to behave they way they do. It was exhilarating. I was thirty.

*Deborah, 40, community planner*

## 134. HAVE YOU EVER FANTASIZED ABOUT A THREESOME WITH ANOTHER MAN?

Of course! I'd keep them in constant rotation, keeping one in me at all times. I would be selfish and demand that they suck and fuck me until they ached. I'd have petroleum jelly by the bed to keep everything slippery.

*Laura, 25, musician*

One man is too many for me. Why would I want to deal with two insensitive, insecure babies?

*Heather, 28, student teacher*

I'd like to be with two big dumb jocks who only wanted to please me. I would like to go at it animal to animal. No polite manners. No witty small talk. Just grunting, thrusting, ramming, animal moves. One in front and one in back. Fill me up.

*Meredee, 39, contract negotiator*

I have, but not very often. I live with two men, and all three of us—my studs and I—have sex on a regular basis. That keeps me pretty busy. George manages the housework, Tony does all the shopping and cooking, and I manage the money, taxes, and business dealings. We evenly share the bills, and we all three have professional careers. It's the most wonderful living arrangement I can imagine. They are great, normal, heterosexual men, and I feel like the luckiest girl in the world.

*Renee, 35, certified public accountant*

## 135. HAVE YOU EVER FANTASIZED ABOUT A THREESOME WITH ANOTHER WOMAN?

I'd like to clone myself and then have a threesome. I could do twice as much, and I wouldn't be jealous of myself.

*Corey, 21, retail sales associate*

I'd like to have my best girlfriend do me while my boyfriend watched and waited until I finally gave him my nod of approval to join in.

*Angela, 29, lawyer*

Every time I have an orgasm with my boyfriend, I am thinking about women. I don't know why. I think about having sex with women while I'm having sex with men. Especially oral sex and titties. I love women's breasts, and I love the thought of a woman tasting my pussy. I also think about going down on women. These thoughts and fantasies keep me going. I look forward to the experience.

*Christa, 31, picture framer*

## Truckers' Delight

I accidentally discovered an interesting way to pass the hours on a recent road trip. My boyfriend of six months decided to take me on a gambling minivacation to a new floating riverboat casino on the Mississippi. While he had been to Atlantic City, Las Vegas, and the Bahamas on gambling excursions, I'd never touched a slot machine, much less gambled. I was really looking forward to our trip. We planned our getaway, and I decided to dress up for the part of a gambling girl. I bought a bright red slinky blouse that accentuated my cleavage and slipped easily off my shoulders. I had on matching red high heels, black fishnet hose with matching garter belt, and an oh-so-short white skinfitting miniskirt. I put on way too much makeup, super bright red lipstick, and enough blush to look permanently embarrassed. I'd braided my waist-length blond hair into a bun that defied gravity. If I'd had a feather boa, you'd have thought I was a 1930s vintage gangster's sweetie. I looked the part of a cheap, shameless hussy, and I loved it, as did my boyfriend.

When he met me at the door I was chewing bubble gum and swinging my pearl necklace. I looked deliciously slutty, quite a change from my normal attire of white starched uniforms and sensible shoes. Since we only had two hours before departure time, we had to hurry down the interstate; riverboat casinos leave the dock on time, with or without you. Even though my boyfriend would probably have rather called the whole trip off and just played cops and robbers with me in the bedroom, we jumped into his red Italian convertible and zipped off to the Big Muddy.

While my boyfriend drove well above the speed limit, I sipped a Bloody Mary and enjoyed the ride. The sun was bearing down. The skies were clear and blue. Everything was just great. We sang along with the oldies station, screaming out the lyrics to everything. The sun, the vodka, the roar of the sports car—it was all wonderful, relaxing, and somewhat intoxicating.

Suddenly a big semitrailer passed us on the left-hand side. The trucker blasted his horn, blinked his lights, and barreled on down the road. I waved, smiled, and had another sip of my Bloody Mary. A couple of minutes later another big truck blasted by, honked its horn, and blinked its lights. Then another, and another. Now, after six months of riding in my boyfriend's little red convertible, I'd grown accustomed to being noticed with my long blond hair blowing in the breeze, but this was different. These trucks weren't just honking once and zipping on by. They were waving and signaling.

Finally two more big diesels pulled up beside us, one on either side. The three of us were just cruising down the interstate like a convoy. They were both waving and honking, and I smiled and waved back. This was just a little weird. Then I noticed a cool breeze on my nipple. I looked down and my new red blouse had slid down to my waist and my nipples and my breasts were shining in broad daylight.

No wonder they were waving! I must have been the best road show of the day. When my boyfriend saw what was going on, it turned him on so much I thought we were going to run right off the road. His reaction was amazing.

The truckers had obviously been talking to each other on their CB radios. Instead of covering my breasts and ending the show, I proudly cradled them and pinched my nipples till they were hard. One truck driver stayed right beside us for over twenty miles, speeding up and then slowing down to see me. He looked so sad when he finally had to take his exit. He blew me a kiss as he left the interstate.

My boyfriend watched ahead for families in minivans and little old ladies driving twenty miles slower than the speed limit. I didn't want to shock the entire motoring public. Whenever we passed a trucker, I'd yawn, stretch my arms out, and give the sweetest little smile. My sunburned nipples pointed high as I did my best feline moves. I finally took my hair out of its braids and used my golden tresses to cover my breasts like a modern-day Lady Godiva. The experience was totally liberating. I learned a lot that day—how to lose a hundred dollars in a shiny slot machine, how to run through a full parking lot screaming "Stop that boat," and how to make truckers from several states smile and honk their horns.

*Sylvia, 32, medical technician*

# chapter eighteen

# Same-Sex Fantasies and Experiences

136. *Have you ever fantasized about being with another woman?*
137. *Have you ever fantasized about a woman while having sex with a man?*
138. *Has any woman ever tried to seduce you? If so, did it flatter you, or did it make you angry?*
139. *Have you ever made love to another woman?*
140. *Do homosexual men interest you?*
141. *Would you like to see two men having sex with each other?*
142. *Would you like to see two women having sex with each other?*

## 136. HAVE YOU EVER FANTASIZED ABOUT BEING WITH ANOTHER WOMAN?

Many, many, many times. I think the thrill for me is the fantasy. Like many aspects of life, the reality of actually doing it would probably be disappointing. I'd rather imagine the forbidden fruit than try it and be let down.

*Linda, 40, writer*

I fantasize about having hot lesbian sex with a strong black woman. Her dark ebony skin would be such a contrast to my pale pink coloring. I would let her do anything to me, and I'd do anything she asked me.

*Linley, 25, art student*

I had a dream about doing it with my art teacher in college. I dreamed she seduced me and then painted me in body paint. I never pursued this fantasy, but it did keep my mind occupied when I was having trouble visualizing perspectives.

*Joyce, 20, video store clerk*

Every time I go out with my boyfriend and he's into that macho egotistical thing he gets into, I think a lot about being with women instead of him. I'm sick to death of men and I just might cross the bridge.

*Shalena, 28, beautician*

## 137. HAVE YOU EVER FANTASIZED ABOUT A WOMAN WHILE HAVING SEX WITH A MAN?

If I wanted to be with a woman, I'd do it. When I'm with my lover, I'm with the one I want and I don't need to think of anyone else, male or female.

*Mary Ann, 39, loan officer*

Yes, I think about another woman being down around my clitoris, licking me as my lover thrusts his penis deep inside me. Someday it may happen for real.

*Sally, 28, dancer*

In a weird way, I have. I sometimes imagine I'm outside my body looking down on my lover when we are making love. I float around the bed and our bodies, flowing in and out of our openings. I imagine I'm in my vagina and watching his penis enter me. I imagine I'm sperm inside his penis, rushing out to enter my womb.

*Shirley, 42, potter*

My lover is the lover of all time. I simply cannot imagine thinking of anything or anyone else when he is caressing my body. He starts with deep, soft kissing, and at the same time his hands are slithering over my body like silk. He slides down to taste me and I swear I couldn't do it better myself if I could reach that far. No, I think only of him.

*Torrie, 32, clinic secretary*

## 138. HAS ANY WOMAN EVER TRIED TO SEDUCE YOU? IF SO, DID IT FLATTER YOU, OR DID IT MAKE YOU ANGRY?

My best friend tries to seduce me every time she gets drunk. One of these days she'll probably get lucky.

*Melinda, 34, collection agent*

My brother's wife tried to feel me up at our Thanksgiving dinner. It made me feel very strange. On the one hand, I was mad because she was offering to cheat on my brother, and yet it did make me tingle. Maybe it was just so unexpected, or maybe it was a deeply hidden fantasy of mine. I rebuffed her, and nothing has ever been said about it since. But we both know what happened, and sooner or later the subject will come up again. I don't know how I'll react.

*Sharon, 38, social worker*

A total stranger came up to me at the health spa and said she would love to make me come in her mouth. I just laughed at her and kept on shaking my tight buns in her face.

*Lana, 20, operator*

A classy middle-aged woman approached me in the powder room of a nice local restaurant. She told me her husband thought I would make a suitable lover for her while he watched. She looked attractive, intelligent, and spotless. I was so surprised I couldn't talk. I stammered out an embarrassed thank-you and went into the stall to pee. Some other women came in, and when I opened the door, my mystery seducer was gone.

*Pat, 21, x-ray technician*

While I was enrolling in college last fall, a secretary at the school was giving me these strange looks. I couldn't believe it. Later in the week she came by my dorm and asked me out. What's the world coming to?

*Debbie, 18, student*

## 139. HAVE YOU EVER MADE LOVE TO ANOTHER WOMAN?

No. But you can sure bet I'd jump at the chance!

*Melanie, 28, delivery person*

No. I think it's wrong. God didn't plan for that. It isn't right, and I'd never do it.

*Lucille, 51, secretarial director*

Yes. The first time I made love to another woman I was nineteen. I'd always thought I was a lesbian, and that experience convinced me that I was. I had been with men before but had never experienced anything like this. I've always loved women. Sex is a beautiful thing whether you're gay or straight. It doesn't matter.

*Julie, 23, public relations agent*

I like to have sex with women who have never thought of themselves as gay. I like to make them feel bothered, confused, flattered, maybe even guilty. I like to be their first woman. It gives me pleasure to show them how good sex with a female can be. Most of them cry and climax in overwhelming waves of release and joy. Being the first is certainly worth the effort it sometimes takes to seduce a reluctant hetero woman.

*Amy, 32, banker*

Yes and no. I make love to myself all the time because I don't get enough from my boyfriend. A woman besides me, no. But I might throw him out and get one.

*Jean, 58, secretary*

## 140. DO HOMOSEXUAL MEN INTEREST YOU?

Homosexual men are true men, and like all true men they have little room in their lives for women. At least they pretend that they don't need women.

*Judith, 44, interior designer*

I like the challenge of trying to change their minds. I'm egotistical enough to believe that once they taste my pleasures they will never be satisfied with anything less than my purring vagina.

*Ruth Ann, 36, financial consultant*

I could easily fall in love with a gay man. At the risk of sounding stereotypical, the gay men I've known are more sensitive, understanding, and better groomed than straight guys. Gay men seem to have more of the qualities I like in a man. I just wish they could see me as more than a fag hag.

*Cynthia, 25, painter*

Gay men don't interest me sexually, but they make better friends than straight men and even better friends than women.

*Theresa, 50, hospital administrator*

## 141. WOULD YOU LIKE TO SEE TWO MEN HAVING SEX WITH EACH OTHER?

I love to see two men giving each other oral sex. Seeing hard penises sliding in and out of two tight mouths makes me wet. I like the force gay men use when they suck each other. The sheer power of their strokes and the total lack of sensitivity intrigues me. I like the no-nonsense approach they take when they simply focus on ejaculating. Harder, faster, quicker. It is pure sex drive.

*Meredith, 28, soccer coach*

I am repulsed by the thought. I think it's disgusting, sickening, and wrong.

*Sarah, 36, housewife*

I like to watch my best friends, Tony and Steve, make love. They are both quite flamboyant and artistic, and they love to show off for me. There is something about staring directly into the eyes of a handsome man while he is being anally penetrated by another man. It makes me completely aroused. I love sharing their intimate moments.

*Jessica, 24, wardrobe manager*

I can't think of anything more exciting than to watch my husband and another guy having sex. I think I would come just watching. The only thing that might worry me is if he liked it too much and didn't want me anymore.

*Patty, 25, florist*

## 142. WOULD YOU LIKE TO SEE TWO WOMEN HAVING SEX WITH EACH OTHER?

Yes, it is a joy to see two beautiful women pleasure each other. I like the softness and romance of two women.

*Brandy, 24, retail salesperson*

It really makes me feel ill. I don't understand how a pretty, healthy woman can desire another woman. Ugly women might have few other choices, but give me a homely man over a homely woman any day.

*Inga, 54, cashier*

I like to watch women strap on dildos and role-play sexual positions. Unfortunately, most of the strap-on penises I've seen fall off, slip down, and become stuck inside the other woman. Someone should Super Glue a ten-inch dildo to herself and give it a real workout.

*Ellen, 37, computer programmer*

I like to watch the role-playing that goes on in most gay relationships. The women I know go through phases of being the dyke, the bitch, the submissive one, the delicate flower. It seems like such work to keep all the roles straight in gay relationships.

*Jan, 30, textile manufacturer*

I can't understand the sex these days. I know times are changing constantly and sex goes right along with changing salaries and everything else, but I just don't get it. I don't see anything sexually stimulating me, ever, other than a good man.

*Jane, 69, retired government administrator*

## Best Friends

I'm single, horny, wet, and a little bit wild at times. My roommate, Sherry, and I have been making a series of videotapes these past few months. We are just two college students in the Bible Belt who decided we'd rather make sexy tapes and take exciting photos of each other than work somewhere flipping burgers.

Though both of us are smart, creative, and educated, we are also two very single, very horny young ladies who simply love sex. So we sell tapes of ourselves playing around with each other. We aren't pros; we don't work for some big company. We even wore sunglasses in our first photos and tapes, because no one at school had any idea about our little hobby. If our parents knew what we were doing, they would absolutely kill us. We wear blond wigs and sunglasses to keep things safe.

I have loved photography since I was a little kid. I like to take pictures of animals, sunsets, and friends. I received a Nikon 35mm camera for my high school graduation, and it is probably my most prized possession.

Sherry loves her camcorder. She wants to be a movie director or an actress when she graduates. She is majoring in drama and has already been in two campus productions. She knows lights, directions, angles. Sherry and I are best friends, roommates, and have grown up together.

She is short (five feet two) and has small, pert breasts, a tight little butt, and a great tan. Her pussy is dark and looks like a rose petal. She's the shy one.

I'm taller (five feet six) and curvy, with large lickable breasts and a trimmed pussy. My clit jumps right out when I get hot. I'm not shy. I also do most of the talking. I love to talk dirty and play with myself. I also love to pinch my tits. We have made tapes of us bathing, stripping, playing, shaving our twats, and last week, after a couple of months of getting drunk and teasing, we finally actually performed oral sex on each other. Yes, we tasted forbidden fruit! It was a first for both of us, but the video is really amazing, if I do say so.

Sherry was embarrassed, but now I know why men like to lick women. Rest assured that we both still love men. But we are best friends and we do love sex. It wasn't planned. I hadn't been secretly lusting for my childhood girlfriend. We both have more men than we can handle. It's hard to describe the feelings of making love to another woman. The first time was scary but very exciting. Her body was like a miniature version of my own. She felt familiar. She felt warm and smelled sweet. We started kissing and rubbing each other all over. We had touched each other's breasts before while making our videos, but it was always fleeting. Just a tease. A come-on for the video camera in the corner of the dorm room. This time was different. I wasn't mad at my boyfriend and trying to get revenge. I wasn't coming out of the closet and discovering my gay inner self. I didn't really think about it much. I just did it. I was the aggressor. I'm not sure why, but I felt the need to taste her vagina. I have always loved oral sex with my boyfriends. I like to suck things—sodas, lollipops, pencils, probably my thumb if I think back far enough.

All I know is that once I flicked my tongue in her wet little love chamber, I went nuts. I wanted to devour her alive. I licked and sucked and swallowed all her juices. It was overwhelming. The smells. The heat. The moans. I thought she was going to pound my head all the way up inside her body before she stopped. When she came in my mouth, I felt a wave of pleasure engulf me. She tasted sweet and salty and earthy and so female. It was totally unlike any previous sex I'd had.

I seemed to know instinctively what she wanted me to do. When it was her turn to provide my pleasure, she took to it like a fish to water. We try to make new tapes and take new photos every week, and we continue to experiment. College is turning into quite an education.

*Kaye, 20, college student*

# chapter nineteen

# Kinky Sex: Fetishes and Bondage

143. *Do you have any fetishes?*
144. *Does your partner have any fetishes?*
145. *Does forceful sex appeal to you?*
146. *Do you like bondage?*
147. *Do you like to spank or be spanked?*
148. *Do you like to be bitten?*
149. *Do you like hickeys?*
150. *What do you consider kinky?*
151. *What's the kinkiest sex you have ever had?*
152. *Are you kinky?*

## 143. DO YOU HAVE ANY FETISHES?

I love rubber, specifically latex. I love the smell, the feel, the
squeaky noises it makes when I walk in my full-length bodysuit.
I was into latex way before it became mainstream in music
videos.

*Sheena, 28, model*

Tattoos turn me on. I love the whole forbidden nature of it. I like the
pain of the needle. I like the seediness of the parlors. A man with a tattoo will always be able to at least start a conversation with me. Especially if he has a tattoo on his ass.

*Elaine, 30, carpet salesperson*

I am a water sports enthusiast and I don't mean skiing or swimming. I like to drink as much wine as possible, hold it in till my bladder is about to explode, and then let the hot streams of piss gush out of my body onto the eagerly waiting body of my boyfriend. We usually enjoy this activity in the bathtub, but sometimes we do it outside at the beach or on a blanket. He likes to receive my gift as much as I love to give it. We always jump into a hot bubble bath afterward and have hot, passionate, wet sex.

*Jill, 25, retail salesperson*

I love to watch people shave their pubic hair. Maybe it started when I was a nurse, or maybe I became a nurse subconsciously to be closer to what I love. It makes me so horny when I watch men getting their hair shaved off before surgery. It really doesn't matter how old they are or even what they look like. Fat, thin—it really doesn't matter. Just seeing those clean, smooth pubic areas makes me moist. Perhaps more interesting is the fact that bare-pussied women turn me on as much as shaven men. It's not the idea of having sex with them that turns me on; it is the simple fact that they are bald down there. Bald on the bottom is beautiful.

*Joan, 40, nurse*

If being excessively clean is a fetish, then I have one. I can't stand to be sweaty, dirty, or smelly. I love to scrub all the dirt and bacteria from my skin before and after I have sex. I expect my lovers to be as clean or cleaner than I am. Many people disappoint me and fail to live up to my expectations. In a filthy world I like to keep myself clean and safe.

*Emily, 31, teacher*

## 144. DOES YOUR PARTNER HAVE ANY FETISHES?

My boyfriend has a huge foot fetish. He's always buying me spiked stiletto heels, and he always wants to rub and kiss my feet. He gets really turned on by silk stockings and loves it when I wear hose or wear sandals in the summer.

*Roni, 30, casino card dealer*

My husband is into golden showers. He loves to watch me pee. Sometimes, he asks me to pee on him, in his mouth, or I let him pee on me. I wasn't really into it, but it is kind of erotic. Once when he wanted to give me a golden shower, I spread my legs and opened up my pussy lips so he could aim the hot stream right on my clitoris. The way it pulsated on and tickled my clit sent me into one of the most intense orgasms I'd ever had. I begged him not to finish without drenching my breasts, my face, and my belly. He aimed at my face and pissed right into my open mouth. You would think it was disgusting, but it was sensuous. I'm really starting to get into it, too. Sometimes I "accidentally" walk in on him while he's in the bathroom. I jump right in front of him and sit down on the toilet so he can piss on me. Sometimes I order him to let me watch him pee, and I make him pee in bottles, on the floor, in the sink, standing in the shower, into a cup— you name it. It's fun, although a bit unusual.

*Cheryl, 37, photographer*

My boyfriend loves to have objects inserted into his ass right when he is ready to have an orgasm. Before he makes love, we always lubricate his anus and get something ready to jam up him at the right moment. We've used everything from soda bottles to walking sticks to dildos to a bamboo back scratcher from the Philippines. He doesn't seem to care what goes up his ass as long as it goes up him at just the right moment. At first I thought it was a strange but amusing side of his personality. But after two years I'm beginning to just think it is strange.

*Joni, 26, bank teller*

Me.

*Wanda, 35, receptionist*

## 145. DOES FORCEFUL SEX APPEAL TO YOU?

Sometimes I just want to be fucked hard and fast. I don't want to be romanced, wined, and dined. I want to be sitting on my lover's prick. I want my hands to be tied behind my back, and I want my legs to be thrown up in the air. I want him to take me hard, deep, and fast, and I want to come like someone stuck an electric wire up my ass.

*Lyn, 30, marketing supervisor*

No. I think lovemaking should be sweet, passionate, and gentle. I can't really see myself getting turned on by anything else.

*Kathleen, 35, restaurant owner*

Do I want to be raped? No. Do I want to be filled to the brim and fucked senseless? Yes, I do.

*Regina, 28, videographer*

I like to be the forceful one. I'm so submissive in my workplace and professional life that I like being in charge when we get home. I make my boyfriend give me oral sex in the kitchen. I grab his penis on elevators and forcefully remind him of who is in charge. I tell him what I want and when I want it. And he usually goes along with my desires, even though he is six feet tall and weighs about 260 pounds. The fact that I'm also his immediate supervisor at work probably has something to do with his eager compliance.

*Derry, 42, construction office manager*

Hell, yes. Threatening and forcing my husband to have sex is the only way I get it more than once a year. Something is wrong with that man.

*Georgia, 45, engineer*

## 146. DO YOU LIKE BONDAGE?

I like to act like an obedient slave girl and be verbally abused and humiliated until I reach the point of tears.

*June, 40, community service organizer*

I love to be tied and bound, then tickled and teased. I love being at the mercy of my lover. I trust and love him, and he knows just how far to go without scaring me, which is a very delicate balance. If he steps over the line just once, he knows our relationship will be over. I like to wear handcuffs and like to be bitten on my nipples.

*Gladys, 40, auditor*

Not the hard-core whips-and-chains, leather-and-latex scene, but a little hard, fast lovin' always does the trick.

*Daisy, 40, car salesperson*

Being tied up bores me. I think the games and the rituals of bondage are so strict and binding—excuse the pun. Plus if somebody really gets into it and tries to actually cause me pain, I will knock the total shit out of him when I get loose. Nobody hits this girl and gets away with it. Bondage, my ass!

*Sandra, 23, dancer*

I'd like to tie my husband to a tree and tie all of his girlfriends to his feet so that the neighbors could see and hear them screaming. Then I'd like to strike the match.

*Joan, 55, mother of six*

## 147. DO YOU LIKE TO SPANK OR BE SPANKED?

I love to be naughty and then get my bottom spanked by my husband. He does it with his bare hand, and it stings so wonderfully. A good six or seven whacks on my bottom will usually be enough to make me moist and attentive.

*Anna, 31, dating service operator*

My boyfriend loves to be whipped with my leather belt. His mother was a teacher who believed in strong discipline, and every weekend part of our sexual ritual involves my spanking his bare buttocks with my two-inch-wide leather belt with the oh-so-cruel brass buckle. Just the sound of my belt being unbuckled is enough to make my naughty student get an erection.

*Margie, 21, bartender*

My mother did not believe in spanking children. We were always sent to our room for time-out. So I have yet to experience a spanking in my life. From what I can tell, it doesn't seem very pleasant or arousing. It seems rather barbaric.

*Jennifer, 19, college student*

I keep at least one bruise on my ass at all times. It turns me on and my husband, too. It's our thing, and I really don't care if the whole world thinks it's fucked up.

*Terry, 38, courthouse circuit clerk*

## 148. DO YOU LIKE TO BE BITTEN?

I like to have my nipples roughly bitten during the middle of sex. I'm too sensitive when we first start, but after we've been going at it for a while, I practically beg my husband to chew my nipples.

*Naomi, 35, waitress*

I like to have my clitoris lightly bitten during oral sex. Light bites combined with deep, slow, full tongue licks send me over the edge.

*Hope, 25, student*

I like to have my tongue bitten when my boyfriend kisses me. Not enough to bleed, but enough to get my attention. It has turned me on since I was in high school.

*Tasha, 30, housecleaner*

I like to be bitten on my butt every once in a while. When my boyfriend and I play around, we usually tickle each other, rip our clothes off, grab each other's genitals, and I usually wind up with teeth marks on my bottom.

*Jeri, 22, art instructor*

A dog bit me when I was little, and I didn't like it very much. I still don't.

*Aubrey, 30, prefabricated housing manufacturer*

If I wanted to be bitten I'd sleep with a dog. On the other hand, my boyfriend isn't far from it when he's had too much to drink.

*Amy, 32, telecommunications*

## 149. DO YOU LIKE HICKEYS?

They bring back unpleasant childhood memories. Embarrassing moments in the cafeteria and even worse times in the locker room. I hate them.

*Lita, 32, janitorial assistant*

I love them when they are in plain sight. The bigger and blacker they look on my neck, the better. I like the shock value they bring to my stuck-up data processing unit.

*Henrietta, 37, data processor*

I like hidden ones placed on the underside of my left breast. Hidden, but always there for the right person's eyes.

*Charlotte, 29, medical assistant*

No. They're like wearing a big sign that says, "Hey, look at me. I'm white trash."

*Cherie, 32, product manager*

I like to put hickeys on my boyfriend's penis. Since there is usually so much blood trapped down in the area anyway when he has a boner, I find it quite simple to leave my mark on his privates.

*Sonya, 20, student*

## 150. WHAT DO YOU CONSIDER KINKY?

Anything I might do that I would blush about later, even thinking about it.

*Tonya, 34, factory worker*

Something a person does because someone talked them in to it. Something they wouldn't have had the nerve to do on their own.

*Tricia, 32, farmer*

If it involves old bald-headed men, animals, weird cheeses from Europe, or anything that wants to go in my out door, that is kinky.

*Tina, 40, product assembly*

Piss, diapers, snot, body fluids, ladies with blue hair and false teeth, or fish heads.

*Diane, 44, nurses' aide*

According to my husband, anything I want to do and he doesn't, that is kinky. Anything he wants to do and I don't, that is normal.

*Marilyn, 43, housewife*

Anything that turns me on.

*Queenie, 39, beautician*

## 151. WHAT'S THE KINKIEST SEX YOU HAVE EVER HAD?

Myself and two guys. That was pretty kinky in my book. They did everything to me. Two heads are better than one? Just a joke. I really had a great time. I was not bored.

*Vivien, 21, florist*

I let my German shepherd lick my bottom once for about ten minutes, until he tried to mount me. Then I sent him outside to cause terror with the neighborhood bitches.

*Sylvia, 45, engineer*

The kinkiest thing I ever did was perform oral sex on my girlfriend when she was on her period. I filled my mouth with her red juices and slowly drooled them back out on her creamy white breasts. It was messy but incredibly erotic.

*Crystal, 26, claims adjuster*

I used to have this little dog that loved to lick me. I'm not talking about my hands, I mean he liked to lick my vagina. He didn't bite, he didn't tell anybody, and he didn't try to fuck me. He was the perfect sex toy, and I always had a firecracker orgasm.

*Fay, 49, lawyer*

## 152. ARE YOU KINKY?

I don't know. I'd like to think I could be if I wanted to.

*Beth, 22, graduate student*

If you are asking me if I like to insert live goldfish in my vagina or do something strange with cold cuts, the answer is no. But if you want to know if I'm curious about different aspects of my sexuality, the answer is yes.

*Gloria, 28, insurance broker*

Kinky is as kinky does. I believe every woman has a little pervert screaming inside her with a whip and handcuffs.

*Catherine, 41, administrator*

With the right guy I can be one freaky bitch. I take my cue from the person I'm with. If he is willing to play a little, I'm right there with him. Just don't leave any permanent marks and don't make me puke.

*Angela, 30, computer programmer*

I don't think I would like to be tied to the ceiling or rammed by two or three burley muscle men or raped or beaten. I do, however, love to do it outside, in front of people and surrounded with candles, food, and wild music.

*Janet, 55, teacher*

## Love Marks

I know you probably think it is strange, but one of the sexiest things I've recently discovered is hickeys. Yes, I'm talking about those gross splotches on your neck from our teenage days of making out in the car. You may remember them as sorority badges of honor.

It started out innocently enough with my current boyfriend. We had both been enjoying some glasses of wine, watching TV, and playing around on the sofa. We were tickling each other, and then we started kissing. Soon we were soul-kissing and the passion was beginning to grow. For some reason I started to suck on his neck, and I guess I got a little bit carried away. By the time I stopped, my respectable boyfriend had seven dark red marks all over his neck. When I realized what I'd done, I felt horrible, but he didn't seem to mind at all. He went nuts and devoured me from head to toe.

The next morning we had to hide my love marks. We tried pulling his crisp white button-down oxford dress shirt higher on his neck. No good. The evidence of my passion was still visible. We tried putting makeup on to cover the marks. It just rubbed off on his collar and looked silly. We finally dug up an old white turtleneck from the closet and he went to his office with much fear and embarrassment, since this happened in the middle of July in the humid South.

It only took about six days for the hickeys to fade away, but the romantic scars are permanent. In fact, we never leave home without them. We've incorporated our love mark rituals into our regular lovemaking. He leaves his mark on my most private places, and I give him tangible signs of my affection. Our one concession to the business world is the fact that I always place my hickeys just below his collar.

*Connie, 31, nurse*

chapter
*twenty*

# Experimentation

153. *What do you do to keep the spice in your sex life?*
154. *What is the wildest sexual thing you've ever talked your partner into doing?*
155. *What is the wildest sexual thing your partner has ever talked you into doing?*
156. *Do you like anal sex?*
157. *Have you ever done anything sexual that you would never do again?*
158. *What experience did your mate initiate that you first hated, but later loved?*

## 153. WHAT DO YOU DO TO KEEP THE SPICE IN YOUR SEX LIFE?

The element of surprise has kept my twenty-year marriage alive and pulsing. It only takes a little bit of extra effort, but boy does it pay off with great returns! My husband never knows what little surprise I've worked up for him each week, but he has certainly come to expect it. Over the course of years I've welcomed him with wine and roses, edible panties, ribbons and bows, whips and chains, even ketchup and hot dogs. I try to surprise him with my treats on different days. Being unpredictable is a major part of the thrill. Some weeks I'll treat him two days in a row, sometimes it will be the last hour before midnight on Saturday. I think our little games are part of my sexual well-being.

*Marion, 46, travel agent*

I pour on the salsa. My husband licks it off my nipples, my belly, and my clit. The peppers make me tingle, and they turn my husband into a raging bull.

*Marcia, 38, tour guide*

My favorite element of spice is vanilla ice cream on my bottom. My lover gets out the satin sheets, slowly undresses me, and gently places me on my belly. He opens a pint of ultra-rich premium ice cream, puts a spoonful in his mouth, and lets it melt a little before he slurps down my backside. The white juice flows into my ass, down to my crack, and into my waiting pussy. We make love until we run out of liquids.

*Colleen, 26, music director*

I keep things spicy in my life by simply following the Golden Rule. I'm nice, receptive, loving, and supportive. I've been in a wonderful marriage for eighteen years, and it isn't because of any secret look or technique. And it isn't that I'm some super-religious idiot. I just treat my husband the way I want to be treated, and it gives me great satisfaction.

*Jenny, 39, librarian*

I got rid of my no-good scummy son-of-a-bitching husband. Then my sex life had a life.

*Belinda, 29, paralegal*

## 154. WHAT IS THE WILDEST SEXUAL THING YOU'VE EVER TALKED YOUR PARTNER INTO DOING?

Letting me give him a blow job while he was driving down the road.

*Roberta, 43, housewife*

I once talked my straitlaced boyfriend into tying me to his bed with some of his ties, spanking me, then fucking me. It was great!

*Jo, 25, public speaking coach*

I talked him into wearing a blanket around his butt like a diaper and then forced him to act like a three-year-old. It was humiliating, childish, and very erotic.

*Sarah, 43, investment adviser*

The wildest thing I ever did was talk my husband into letting me urinate on him. I convinced him it would make him hornier and harder than he had ever been. The fact was, I was simply mad at him for spending too much of our income tax refund on his stupid boat. I had him get down on the floor of his prized boat. I then took the most satisfying piss of my life on his naked chest. When I finished, I calmly got up, pulled my panties back on, and went upstairs. It took him about fifteen minutes to realize I wasn't coming back down.

*Lisa, 36, caterer*

Letting me ride in the trunk of his car tied up and naked. He drove me about two miles from our house and then took me out of the trunk, laid me down on the ground, on a blanket, and gave me the best sex of my life. First he made me beg him, and then he begged me for pleasures. It was completely wild and weird, but I loved it.

*Trish, 30, auto leasing agent*

We did it in front of the horses on our farm. They stood around sniffing and looking, and we ran the video camera, too. The dogs that were nearby were the problem. They kept getting closer and closer. They looked like they were thinking about having a little of me. My boyfriend thought it was hilarious.

*Jonnie, 26, bank teller*

## 155. WHAT IS THE WILDEST SEXUAL THING YOUR PARTNER HAS EVER TALKED YOU INTO DOING?

He talked me into letting one of his ex-girlfriends join us in an orgy.

*Samantha, 26, pharmacist*

She convinced me to lick her bottom and suck it really hard. It turned her on and she returned the favor. Now we do each other's asses all the time.

*Jeri, 32, hairdresser*

My former boyfriend talked me into swallowing his sperm. He said it would taste good and prove my love. It didn't prove anything but how little he cared about my feelings. I don't really remember how it tasted. I was too mad to notice.

*Dorothy, 19, cashier*

Going down on him. I couldn't imagine how I was possibly going to tolerate that. I had never done it before and it just seemed too crazy to me. My mother never talked about doing any kind of oral sex. I loved it. The way my husband talked me into doing it? He went down on me first. I loved it so much I had to return the favor.

*Misty, 19, student*

## 156. DO YOU LIKE ANAL SEX?

Once you get used to the weird feeling of having to go to the bathroom every time your lover thrusts in and out, butt sex is okay for something different.

*Amie, 21, temporary secretary*

Only if I'm highly drunk and terribly lubricated.

*Nikki, 29, ski instructor*

I believe that the only men who like anal sex are guys with very little peckers. I believe that the only women who like getting poked in the butt are girls with very, very loose vaginas. Very loose vaginas. Is there an echo in here?

*Rosalyn, 36, phlebotomist*

If I'm really comfortable with a guy, I'll let him have his way with my anus. He must take his time and go slowly. He must bring me to several orgasms before he gets anywhere near my butt. He must respect my desires and instructions. If he doesn't, I'll clinch down with my sphincter muscle and physically bruise his penis or break it in two pieces. And I can do it, too.

*Amber, 32, photo lab assistant*

My little hole is so little, I just cannot physically imagine putting a penis in there. I'm still trying to figure out how a penis fits in my tiny little tight vagina.

*Kelli, 20, fast-food server*

## 157. HAVE YOU EVER DONE ANYTHING SEXUAL THAT YOU WOULD NEVER DO AGAIN?

I slept with my husband's younger brother while he was going through a divorce and staying at our house. That was a mistake that continues to haunt and affect my life. To make things worse, the sex itself was lousy. It was like fucking my husband before he received my proper training.

*Kimberly, 34, newswriter*

Letting my boyfriend talk me into a threesome with one of his friends.

*Letitia, 31, government worker*

Faking an orgasm. My fake one was so much more convincing than my real one. Now I have to incorporate the theatrics of my fake one into my real one. It gets confusing.

*Melissa, 26, billboard designer*

Do not let a man fuck your mouth. If you do, he will always want to fuck your mouth, and nothing else will make him happy.

*Connie, 24, factory worker*

Yes. Take drugs or drink too much at a party. Been there, done that, and it still comes around to terrorize me. My boyfriend said he had to keep checking to see where I was and I was usually found in one of the five bedrooms fucking somebody. It was a nightmare. I don't remember a thing, but he continues to recap it for me. Actually, sometimes I get angry because I can't remember. Sounds like I had a damn good time.

*Dee, 42, savings and loan employee*

## 158. WHAT EXPERIENCE DID YOUR MATE INITIATE THAT YOU FIRST HATED, BUT LATER LOVED?

Anal sex. At first it hurt and I didn't think I would make it. I kept saying to him I didn't know about this—I didn't think this was working. He was real gentle and yet kept on going. Then when I began to relax and lubricate more, it was simply wonderful. The climax was great and very different.

*Patsy, 24, television producer*

Being in a threesome with my boyfriend and an old girlfriend of his. I thought she wanted my boyfriend back, but as it turned out, she was more interested in taking me away from him. She was a mean, spiteful bitch, but she knew how to make me come in her mouth. I decided to enjoy what she could do for me, and I never gave her anything in return.

*Gena, 21, finance clerk*

The first time I performed oral on a guy I thought I'd die. The mere idea of putting somebody's pee shooter in my mouth and tasting piss was enough to make me gag. I had smelled enough urine working in a nursery as a college student. The concept of actively licking and sucking a penis made me want to puke. Well, that was about ten years ago, and I admit that I've come to accept the idea with more enthusiasm. While I used to be a fanatic about cleaning off the penis beforehand, now I'll suck most anything put in my face.

*Linda, 32, talent agent*

Two couples having sex. My husband and I were out to the movies with another couple and there was a seductive scene in the movie about couples having sex together. We decided to try it, and all four of us went home together to do just that. Harry's wife took my husband and I took Harry. Trouble is, Harry is much better than my husband, and I was sorry when it was time to switch back. Oh, well, at least I got to try it.

*Angela, 48, bakery shop owner*

## In Search of Toads

My friends think I'm kinky, but I actually see myself as a great humanitarian. I'm a runway model. I make my living wearing fabulous fashions on the runways of New York, Paris, and Milan. My days are filled with beautiful people. I'm pampered, catered to, fawned over, and simply treated like a precious commodity, which I guess I am.

I'm tall, thin, and blond, and I know my looks are my fortune. I know the power of my appearance. People notice me wherever I go. I can walk into a room, and conversations stop. Men fumble and stammer. Women either hate me, compare me, or want me. Millions of young girls around the world would love to be living my life.

But despite the fact that I live the kind of life many people would kill for, I must admit that all is not perfect in my little world.

I'm often bored to tears by the fashion world. Being a product is not as glamorous as you may think. I have power, but it is very superficial. I can stop conversations, but what were they saying that was all that important in the first place? I am a pretty plaything for people with power. My friends are models who compete with me every day for jobs and assignments. They would stab me in the back in a second if it would help their careers. I know I'm expendable. I know I'm part of a big merchandising scheme to sell more products to people who can't afford them. And I gladly cash my paychecks for being part of the whole illusion.

Knowing all this, I often find myself in and out of relationships. Since I must be free to travel at a moment's notice, I'm always packed and ready to leave my apartment, plants, and obligations. Men seem to be both pleased and threatened by my lifestyle. I can, and often really do, spend my week on three continents. I tend to come and go with great ease.

Because my life is so transient, I guess I've become jaded toward relationships. I feel like a butterfly fluttering in and out of lives around the world. If things in New York are depressing, Paris is always waiting. I know if Ron is being too territorial in SoHo, Paulo is more than happy to give me my space in France. But without fail, within the week Paulo will be a raving lunatic, issuing demands and making radical declarations of passion.

People just seem to want to own me. They want to control me. They want to make me the center of their world. They want to put me in a golden cage.

It wears me out. It always has. That is probably why I've developed my kinky diversion. It keeps me sane. It makes me happy. And it is so totally unexpected.

The simple fact of the matter is that I love to go to bars and pick up physically unattractive men. I've been doing this for about two years, and it gives me incredible pleasure. Sometimes I take modeling friends with me. Sometimes I go adventuring on my own.

It starts with me getting really dressed up. I usually pour myself into a sexy red dress. I always look stunning. Unlike some models who like to dress down in public in baggy shirts and torn jeans, I love to flaunt my looks.

I don't go to biker bars, sailor hangouts, or honky-tonks. I'm not looking for danger. I'm looking for fun. So I go to popular singles bars. I like crowds, noise, and music.

I walk in, order a drink, and wait for reactions. It sometimes takes as long as two minutes before some Don Juan makes his move. Pretty men, confident males, self-appointed studs, obviously overinflated husbands—they all approach me and are rebuffed. I'm sweet, I'm kind, but I do dismiss their efforts. I politely say no to all who approach me. That is part of the game. If you approach me, you lose.

After the initial interest starts to diminish a bit, I begin my search. I check out the room and narrow down my choices. I look for guys who are in a group of friends. Part of the thrill is being able to totally surprise the guy's friends. I look for guys who aren't the center of attention. I want the man who is listening to the other friend's story. I want the guy who is the sidekick, the straight man, the good listener. The man who is going to have the pleasure of tasting my love is the guy who has never been the center of attention. In a world of doers, my winner is probably seen as a loser or an also-ran.

I watch my prey for a while. I look for basic grooming skills. I look for reasonable signs of intelligence. I like to see him laugh a bit. I want to see that he is happy and having a good time being on the sidelines. Then I look for the total lack of a wedding band.

They can be bald, short, too tall, geeky, disfigured, or just plain odd-looking. Some guys have big noses, big ears, big eyes. Some of them are plain. Some are plain ugly. Part of the game is finding a new physical variation I haven't yet explored.

When I finally choose my potential instant love, I make my move. Sometimes the crowds literally part when I make my way from the bar. Sometimes it isn't quite that dramatic. I walk over to the gang and say hi. The group stud usually assumes I'm there for him. The Don Juans try to make conversation, and they always fail miserably. I approach my conquest and, depending on the situation, either kiss him on the cheek or ask him what kind of drink he'd like. I focus all my attention on the guy and almost devour him with affection.

The reaction is amazing. Some guys become speechless. Some turn red. One guy in New York climaxed in his pants. They often think some joke is being played on them. Some think I'm a call girl. When I assure them that I'm not being paid to talk to them, conversations usually start.

I buy them drinks. I flirt, touch, whisper, laugh. I hear stories about their lives, their dreams, their adventures. I meet and sometimes come to know people I would never, ever come in touch with in my normal life.

Their friends get jealous, envious, mad, or awestruck. I change my conquests' lives. I make them special. I focus the attention back on them. I take the spotlight and let them jump into it with me. Maybe I'm giving them false hope. Maybe this is simply my charity work. Or maybe I'm really just a twisted, spoiled bitch. My friends think I'm a combination of all aspects.

I rarely go to bed with any of these guys. I kiss, hold, and fondle, but I don't have sex, protected or unprotected. Most of these guys are so appreciative of my simple attention that they never even imagine that they could have sex with me.

I have allowed a dozen or so to perform oral sex on me. You should have seen their performances. They always try so hard to please. I love to climax in their mouths. They drink my juices so emotionally. I love to watch their reactions and emotions.

My little adventures have become quite exciting. I look forward to my games. I'm not sure about the long-term effects these games have had on my life, but I am certain that I have changed the lives of over fifty men since I started my mission.

*Sara, 23, model*

# chapter twenty-one

# Sex, Drugs, and Alcohol

159. *Does alcohol make sex better or worse?*

160. *What is the best experience you have had with alcohol and sex?*

161. *What is the worst experience you have had with alcohol and sex?*

162. *Do you use drugs to enhance sex?*

163. *What is the best experience you have had with drugs and sex?*

164. *What is the worst experience you have had with drugs and sex?*

## 159. DOES ALCOHOL MAKE SEX BETTER OR WORSE?

Vodka makes every man look more handsome. Whiskey makes penises seem much bigger. Beer makes my puckered butt hole much more accessible. Hangovers the next day bring everything crashing painfully back into sober focus.

*Veronica, 34, telephone salesperson*

Beer makes me horny and sexy right up until the moment when I puke on my lover and pass out.

*Rochelle, 26, retail salesperson*

I love a good bottle of white wine, candles, and soft music. A mellow buzz will get me out of my panties quicker than anything.

*Bethany, 33, travel agent*

Beer gives me gas, and most guys aren't too thrilled about that side effect. Though there was this one guy who liked the sounds I made.

*Rhonda, 32, floral arranger*

If I'm the one who's drinking, then it's better; sex is definitely better. If he's the one who's drinking, I might as well be planning to play with myself. A lot.

*Shannon, 43, dentist*

## 160. WHAT IS THE BEST EXPERIENCE YOU HAVE HAD WITH ALCOHOL AND SEX?

When I got drunk with my husband on some cheap wine and then fucked his brains out and became pregnant with my daughter, Karen, now six years old. We had been trying to make a baby for eight years of marriage and were ready to go the adoption route. In fact, we had bought the wine to celebrate our approval by the agency for consideration as foster parents.

*Patti, 43, housewife*

My best experience with alcohol happened when I drank too much wine on a first date with the guy who became my husband. I was nervous, young, and inexperienced. I drank myself sick and discovered what a true gentleman really was. Steven took care of everything. He even held my head up when I was throwing up. He didn't take advantage of me. He didn't even try anything. He was just a perfect partner that night and has been for forty-five more years. If I hadn't made myself sick on that first date, things might have gone completely different for us. So I credit cheap wine with the success of my long and happy marriage.

*Lucille, 63, apartment manager*

My lover and I went to a club. After drinking a few too many beers he decided he was horny and began to seduce me. He was very frisky, like I'd never seen him before. He took me up on the stage, introduced me to his friends—he knew all of the band—and we sang a duet together.

It was very romantic, and the crowd loved us. Usually he is much too shy to ever do anything like that. Then he took me to his friend's minivan in the parking lot, and we had great sex. It really made me feel young again.

*Jonelle, 47, cigarette company employee*

## 161. WHAT IS THE WORST EXPERIENCE YOU HAVE HAD WITH ALCOHOL AND SEX?

When I passed out while giving head to my boyfriend. He must have gone to sleep also, because I awoke a few hours later with my mouth full of pee and a limp penis. It was highly memorable, but not highly recommended.

*Greta, 27, graphic artist*

I threw up all over my husband when he tried to kiss me after a night of Long Island iced teas, and what was worse, he was too drunk to even realize anything was wrong and kept trying to French-kiss me while I was throwing up in his mouth.

*Gina, 38, legal secretary*

I spent many nights in my youth drunk out of mind with guys I didn't even know. Looking back, it scares me to think of all the things that could have happened. I was lucky not to get hurt, pregnant, or diseased. And what is even more terrifying is the fact that my survival had nothing to do with my wits or skill. I was just plain lucky, plain and simple. I don't recommend following my example. Being wild isn't sexy, it is just stupid.

*Rosie, 34, barmaid*

It was our twelfth anniversary and I was still very much in love with my husband. All of our family was at the party and the food and decorations were gorgeous. Everything was perfect until I had too much to drink. While my husband and I were dancing, I got crazy and pulled his pants down on the dance floor of the private club we had rented—

the country club. Before he could stop me, I had his pants down and his dick out and headed for my mouth. He didn't know what to do but was trying to keep people from seeing us and get me under control. He finally got so frustrated he sat down in the middle of the dance floor, tried to get me off of him and his pants up. I don't remember anything. Thank God for small favors.

*Leslie, 34, homemaker*

## 162. DO YOU USE DRUGS TO ENHANCE SEX?

I had a boyfriend who loved to put cocaine on my clit and then lick it off me. He would go through two hundred dollars in about twenty minutes. He got off and I got off. I wonder if he is still alive. He was a very intense stockbroker.

*Marie, 35, executive secretary*

Being a child of the sixties, I still love a good pothead high. Pull out the bong, do a couple of bowls while listening to Led Zeppelin or Pink Floyd, and then fuck until we fall asleep. Even though I have two grown children and I'm pushing fifty, I still like to get high and make love to my rapidly balding husband on a weekly basis.

*Marti, 48, grocer*

When I'm on a caffeine high I have tons of energy and I want to have serious sex, but I'm too tense to climax. When I'm not drinking coffee, I'm too tired to think about it.

*Lorraine, 31, receptionist*

No way. Drugs can kill you, and what's sexy about that? I think people have to be pretty sexually limited in their mind in order to feel like they need drugs for enhancement. Use your imagination.

*Debbie, 22, employment agency counselor*

## 163. WHAT IS THE BEST EXPERIENCE YOU HAVE HAD WITH DRUGS AND SEX?

The best experience I had with sex and drugs was when I took so much speed over six months that I lost fifty-six pounds of fat and became a sexual creature once again in the eyes of my husband. I was lucky that I was able to stop my addiction once the weight was off. I'd never recommend it to anyone else. It was probably the riskiest thing I've ever done.

*Barbra, 30, math teacher*

Smoking pot with my husband is always a good aphrodisiac. He gets a hard-on like you wouldn't believe, and I get so horny I can't see straight.

*Robin, 28, consultant*

The best experience I've had with drugs was when I got on birth control pills. Despite the health risks, the Pill liberated my sex life. I didn't have to worry about unwanted pregnancies, dirty diapers, screaming children. I could enjoy sex for the sheer pleasure of it and not worry about the biological consequences.

*Pamela, 42, food service employee*

Not giving in to trying drugs. My sex life is good because I take care of myself and my body. At the risk of sounding like a "Say no to drugs" commercial, who the hell needs drugs? Stupid people.

*Tonya, 20, disc jockey*

## 164. WHAT IS THE WORST EXPERIENCE YOU HAVE HAD WITH DRUGS AND SEX?

I took a bunch of downers before going to a party and then passed out with a rum and Coke in my hand. I came to in the middle of the night with my clothes on the floor, my thighs sticky with sperm, and three total strangers snoring beside me.

*Candy, 24, receptionist*

I got so high at a concert one night, I decided to fuck my boyfriend right in the middle of the audience. We got arrested for indecent exposure. I was mortified.

*Andrea, 30, actress*

I got so stoned once I couldn't tell my husband was inside me. He thought it was one of his best fucks, until the next day when I told him I couldn't remember a thing about it.

*Victoria, 39, jewelry designer*

Quaaludes were in a candy dish at a party and I thought it was candy. Thank God I had only put one in my mouth when my boyfriend started yelling. I don't know what all I did that night, but I was really thankful that my boyfriend was the kind of guy he was and still is. (We've been married twenty years.) He did tell me that I was funny and the sex was stupendous.

*Jennah, 43, hot-tub dealer*

## Forget the Begging

Quaaludes. Worst experience I ever had. Period.

I was twenty-two and dating a guy who didn't do drugs. I never did them either. But a girl at work kept telling me how great sex was on Quaaludes. She said it was so great I would cry and beg for more. That sounded pretty enticing and interesting. The only thing I usually related to crying was pain and sadness. As for begging, I usually didn't want anything bad enough to beg for it. I told her I would take two and share them with my boyfriend, Luke.

He picked me up after work around six o'clock, as usual, and we went to a nearby club for a drink. I shared my newfound information with him, and he smiled as he began to imagine sex being so good I was begging him for it. He was pleased at the idea more than just a little bit. Maybe too much.

We shared the Quaaludes, sipped our drinks, danced a few, and headed for home. The car was just outside the club door—good thing because I was feeling pretty woozy. I asked Luke if he could drive and he kept saying he was fine and dandy. That should have been my first clue that he wasn't. He never said things like "fine and dandy."

We made it back to the car, got in, and shut the doors. Luke put the car in reverse, backed into another car, tried to get unlocked from that one and ended up going forward into another car.

Now people are coming out of the club hollering for us to stop and get out of the car. Luke finally put the car in park just seconds before he passed out. The shocked observers called the police to intervene, and from that point on, all I remember is waking up with Luke in a local police department cell with a major headache. I heard my father's voice, felt sick, and threw up—not what I call a quality evening!

Luke and I decided to try a different approach the next time we were in need of some romantic enhancement. If we couldn't get the lusty excitement that makes me want to beg for more without getting arrested, we would gladly do without. Luke said he really saw no need for me to beg anyway.

*Sharon, 25, waitress*

## The Element of Surprise

I recently learned about putting a little bit of the unexpected into my sexual relationship, and I can honestly testify that it was a memorable experience.

My lover of two years recently surprised me with two tickets for the upcoming Michael Bolton concert. Actually, he surprised me and himself with four tickets to this sold-out concert. He took off from work to wait in line with Michael's screaming female fans the day the tickets went on sale. After waiting in line and hearing more gossip about Michael's this and Michael's that, when he finally made it to the ticket counter, all the reserved seats were sold out! The only tickets left were grass passes, which he promptly bought with a fair amount of disgust.

I didn't care. I was thrilled to just be in the same city with Michael Bolton, and I told my lover how happy I was to even have any kind of ticket.

Well, with the concert three weeks away, we both went about our daily rituals, going to work, eating, sleeping, just plain living. But I was counting the hours until the concert came. It was like waiting for Christmas. I hadn't been to a concert in years, and this was going to be *the* concert. Michael Bolton live onstage in person!

Three days before the show, my lover told me he had a surprise for me. Since we already had the tickets, I wasn't sure what he was really up to. I already had every CD, single, and video Michael had ever made, so I couldn't imagine anything better.

My lover came in and put an envelope in my hand. Inside were two reserved seats right in front of the stage about four rows back. I was beside myself. A co-worker of his had won these prime seats in a radio contest. He had paid her one hundred dollars apiece just so I'd have a night to remember. I decided then and there to give my lover a night he would remember too.

The day of the concert finally arrived. All day at work I was tingling and excited. All my friends were envious. Most didn't have tickets, and those who did had grass passes way out in Outer Mongolia, beyond the nosebleed section. I couldn't wait for the workday to end.

At four-thirty I flew out of the office and raced home to get ready for the big event. I called my lover, told him not to be late, and told him to get himself home as soon as possible.

While he navigated the freeway traffic of rush hour, I took a hot bubble bath, put on my favorite perfume, and poured myself into a sexy little black miniskirt I'd bought just for the occasion. I'd bought everything new for this concert. I had new shoes, skirt, blouse, necklace, even a new pair of red silk panties. I frizzed and teased my shoulder-length red hair to just the right attitude and altitude of sexual rebellion.

Then I went downstairs, poured myself a glass of Chardonnay, and waited by the door. When my lover came in, I attacked him. I gave him the biggest hug, the hottest kiss, and then whispered in his ear, "I'm going to fuck your brains out." So much for foreplay.

The poor man didn't even have time to put his briefcase down. I grabbed his hand and put it under my dress. I had left my silk panties upstairs, and when he touched my wetness, he went wild. He hiked my dress up to my belly button, threw me on our oh-so-fashionable sectional sofa, and impaled me on his erection. He didn't take off his shoes. He didn't take off his tie. He didn't care about his belt, keys, wallet, or anything. He just pumped and kissed and groaned and filled me to the brim.

The only thing that brought us back to reality was a loud banging on the door. It was my thirty-five-year-old sister and her friend coming over to pick up the grass seat tickets my lover had first bought for me.

I'd forgotten that they were going to the concert with us! My sister knocked again and then came on in. We hadn't even had the time or the wits about us to lock the door. There we were scrambling around to pull my dress down and to put his pecker back in his pants. It was a wonder he didn't catch his special part in his zipper as we tried to gain some composure.

The room smelled like pure sex. My wineglass had fallen over and made a puddle on the beige carpet. I didn't care. We were caught quite literally with our pants down and legs in the air. I loved it. My sister and her friend didn't know what to say. I started laughing until tears fell down my face.

For the record, the concert was great. It was almost secondary. I never did quite get around to putting my panties back on.

*Anne, 27, legal secretary*

# chapter twenty-two

# *Inhibitions*

165. *If no one was looking, what would you be apt to do that you have never done before?*
166. *What "forbidden" sexual subject would you love to talk about?*
167. *What do women have a hard time requesting from a man?*
168. *What do men have a hard time requesting from a woman?*
169. *Have you ever had a sexual experience that was too embarrassing to enjoy?*
170. *If a sexual experience is embarrassing but feels great, do you keep it on your sexual menu?*

## 165. IF NO ONE WAS LOOKING, WHAT WOULD YOU BE APT TO DO THAT YOU HAVE NEVER DONE BEFORE?

Have sex with a very young man. One young enough to induce rumors.

*Erica, 36, freelance photographer*

Masturbate. I've never tried it.

*Betty, 53, housekeeper*

Rent porno movies and buy dirty magazines.

*Joni, 35, stockbroker*

If it was physically possible, I'd like to lick my own vagina. I know what my juices taste like, but I'd like to know what it actually feels like to taste and probe my own sex organs.

*Marla, 23, auto detailer*

If no one was watching, I'd strap on a dildo and fuck my next-door neighbor. He is such a self-righteous prick. Since he has an opinion about how I raise my children, mow my yard, and plant my garden, I'd like his reaction to my shoving a cold fake dick up his ass.

*Gloria, 33, factory worker*

I'm curious about adult bookstores, what the men do in them and what is for sale in them. I just can't take the chance on being seen in one.

*Patricia, 23, advertising executive*

## 166. WHAT "FORBIDDEN" SEXUAL SUBJECT WOULD YOU LOVE TO TALK ABOUT?

Being with another woman. I would like to hear, and maybe know, what it is like, but I just can't bring myself to ask someone who really knows.

*Mikasha, 30, x-ray technician*

Being orgasmic.

*Lillian, 43, traffic cop*

I'd love to find somebody who shares my fetishes. They're too weird for me to bring up with my current boyfriend.

*Dawn, 30, shoe designer*

My secret desire is to be filled with a large, hard penis. My husband is loving, but not very well endowed. I know it wouldn't threaten our marriage if I was probed by a well-hung stud, but I'm not sure my husband would agree.

*Teresa, 39, customer relations employee*

I would like to know why some men, even after a shower, have an odor around the head of their penis and some don't. The way some penises smell makes me gag, and others are great and smell wonderful and even what I would call erotic. I don't understand the difference.

*Mary, 49, travel agent*

## 167. WHAT DO WOMEN HAVE A HARD TIME REQUESTING FROM A MAN?

Help. Women are tired of being damsels in distress to haughty men. Too often it is held over their heads long after the help is given.

*Sue, 29, auto salesperson*

I like my man to kiss my bottom and then flick his tongue up my crack. I love it, but I feel funny asking the man I share my life with to suck my ass.

*Amber, 25, teacher*

I like to be sucked to orgasm and then go to sleep. I feel selfish sometimes, but that is really all I want to do on some nights. I have a hard time asking my husband to make me come without feeling like I should return the favor, so I usually give in and make him happy. But I'd like to be able to just tell him to make me happy and be free enough to go right to sleep.

*Kim, 22, housewife*

Most women are afraid to ask their men to please them. Somehow it just doesn't seem ladylike to expect your man to bring you to orgasm. I think such an attitude leads to massive frustration and built-up resentment.

*Natalie, 34, social worker*

Money. When a man you love and respect has lots of money and you don't, it's hard to keep up. Clothes, makeup, baby-sitters, and other things you need to be with him and dress for him. I find it hard to do sometimes. I just can't see myself saying anything about money to him.

*Ginger, 36, dental assistant*

## 168. WHAT DO MEN HAVE A HARD TIME REQUESTING FROM A WOMAN?

They have an extremely hard time asking for sex—no emotional involvement, just sex. They are afraid of rejection and can't seem to just ask for exactly what they want. So they pretend to be interested in more. It turns out much worse in the long run for both.

*Victoria, 23, aerobics instructor*

My lover can't ask me to give him oral sex. So I just always assume that he wants it and give it to him without his asking.

*Debi, 45, illustrator*

Men have a hard time asking for something different. They don't want you to think they are perverted, so they just do the same old thing all the time. I might be into their fantasies if they'd just share them with me.

*Helen, 31, record promoter*

Nothing. Most men I know will ask you—no, make that *tell* you—what they want any time of the day. They want money. They want dinner. They want sex. Then they want respect. I say you have to earn respect. The lazy bums only have a hard time asking for a job or an honest day's work. I don't need anyone to help me spend my money.

*Brenda, 40, metalworker*

Sympathy. Men are too macho. Emotionally, I wish they could let their hair down and talk more about normal feelings: someone hurt their feelings, made them sad, they miss someone in their family—stuff like that.

*Belinda, 40, hotel manager*

## 169. HAVE YOU EVER HAD A SEXUAL EXPERIENCE THAT WAS TOO EMBARRASSING TO ENJOY?

Yes! Oral sex. It's just too intimate. And the smell. How embarrassing.
*Jillian, 30, bakery owner*

No. All sex is embarrassing. But if you enjoy it, who cares?
*Emmy, 28, acting coach*

I think it's embarrassing to do it doggie-style. I just can't feel comfortable sticking my butt in my husband's face. I don't like it that much anyway.
*Eve, 29, ad salesperson*

I can't stand to see my husband having intercourse with me. He likes to see himself in the bedroom mirror, but I think two people having sex just looks like animals grunting. I'd rather turn off the lights or shut my eyes and try to concentrate on how it feels. I don't want to see hairy butts, fat guts, and flabby, pale thighs bouncing back and forth.
*Jackie, 33, diet counselor*

I think I could get into anal sex if I could relax about it. It makes me so self-conscious. My husband wants to try it and I'm trying to get up my nerve.
*Reba, 39, cosmetics consultant*

## 170. IF A SEXUAL EXPERIENCE IS EMBARRASSING BUT FEELS GREAT, DO YOU KEEP IT ON YOUR SEXUAL MENU?

Of course. If it feels good, who cares what it looks like, and besides, who's looking anyway?
*Toni, 40, physical trainer*

All sex is embarrassing. Have you ever watched two people fuck? It's disgusting. Turn the lights off and hide your skinny butt.
*Virginia, 33, optometrist*

If it feels so good I want to pass out, I don't care how dumb I look or who sees me. As long as I get mine, I don't care what the neighbors think.

*Janine, 28, service counter clerk*

If I'm embarrassed, then it can't possibly feel good. My reaction to embarrassment is acute and extreme. I turn ten shades of red. I hide my head and I start to cry. I feel the blood rush to my head and experience a tingling in my ears. It was that way when I was a little girl, and I can still blush faster than anybody in my office. So if I'm embarrassed, you had better believe that all action will come to a complete stop.

*Donna, 21, data processor*

You bet. If it feels good, we go for it. There's enough trouble in the world, and I don't want any trouble in my bedroom.

*Nicole, 39, bridal shop owner*

# chapter twenty-three

# *Love versus Sex*

171. *What is the biggest difference between making passionate love and having great sex?*

172. *Do you think it is necessary to be in love with somebody before you sleep with him?*

173. *Which part of sex is most important to you—cuddling, foreplay, talking afterward, how you are treated after sex, or the physical details?*

174. *If you love your mate but he is not a good sexual partner, what do you do?*

175. *Do you stick with someone you love and care about even if the sex is terrible?*

176. *Is great sex or a good relationship more important? Can you have a great relationship if the sex is bad?*

## 171. WHAT IS THE BIGGEST DIFFERENCE BETWEEN MAKING PASSIONATE LOVE AND HAVING GREAT SEX?

Emotions, the right man, the right time. If my heart isn't involved with the man, it is easier to concentrate solely on great sex.

*Sally, 23, art instructor*

There is no difference. Passionate love and great sex are one and the same. I love my husband, and sex with him only makes our love stronger. That is why we were put on this earth: to fall in love and make babies. God's plan is so pure and beautiful.

*Rosie, 20, medical technician*

Passionate love is when you care about the person after the sex is over. Great sex is when you don't even care about the person's name until after the sex is over, and even then his name doesn't really matter.

*Tammy, 33, production manager*

The biggest difference between passionate love and great sex is the same as the difference between a romantic poem and an action thriller. They both have their place.

*Courtney, 21, art history major*

The two go together for me. The love of my life, the man I fell so very deeply in love with, was also the best sex for me. We had intense, hard-riding, and soft, delicate, stroking sex. We did it all, and the inhibitions were never there. We loved each other completely, every inch of our bodies. We kissed deep and hard and we kissed teasingly and hot. He spanked me, he loved me, and we played together in bed. Our bedroom was always our private playground.

*Tammy, 40, sewing machine salesperson*

## 172. DO YOU THINK IT IS NECESSARY TO BE IN LOVE WITH SOMEBODY BEFORE YOU SLEEP WITH HIM?

Love is love. Sex is sex. Don't confuse the two.

*Ella, 37, veterinarian*

It's not necessary. But it sure helps.

*Yvonne, 30, gymnastics coach*

No way is it necessary. It makes a big difference, though.

*Sherry, 24, graduate student*

Not only should you be in love, but you should have a blood test and hire a private investigator before you have sex. Then make him wear two condoms for safety.

*Alice, 26, health worker*

If you are sleeping, you're sleeping. Period. If you are having sex, that's sex. If you want to make love, you must be in love. Easy question.

*Joni, 48, horse trainer*

## 173. WHICH PART OF SEX IS MOST IMPORTANT TO YOU— CUDDLING, FOREPLAY, TALKING AFTERWARD, HOW YOU ARE TREATED AFTER SEX, OR THE PHYSICAL DETAILS?

Definitely the details. He has to be prepared, if you know what I mean.

*Lucille, 21, day-care worker*

I like the cuddling. If I'm not emotionally satisfied, then sex alone just doesn't do it for me.

*Jolene, 33, waitress*

I like being filled to the max. I like the hardness, the texture, the feeling of being on a skin pole. I love the friction.

*Kitty, 47, realtor*

I like the whole production. I like the teasing, the physical aspects, the emotional roller coaster. I like the afterglow and the intimacy. I even like brushing our teeth together and putting fresh sheets on the bed. I love it all.

*Alexandria, 24, newlywed*

Intercourse, of course, is very important. No one will deny that it is vital to every good marriage. But making love is an around-the-clock activity. Without touching me, my husband makes love to me and I to him. We also place a high value on cuddling and kissing. All of the different methods people use to show their affection are important. I don't think you can dissect it. Do you?

*Betty, 67, seamstress*

## 174. IF YOU LOVE YOUR MATE BUT HE IS NOT A GOOD SEXUAL PARTNER, WHAT DO YOU DO?

I give him three strikes and he's out of here.

*Nan, 34, housewife*

I'd try to teach him to be a stud puppy and keep practicing till he got it right.

*Leslie, 29, printing salesperson*

If he was rich and handsome, I'd put up with it. If he was poor and ugly, I'd neuter him.

*Doreen, 27, shoe salesperson*

With training and devotion, any man can learn to make great sex. If he is willing to take instruction and follow the advice of others, he can improve his endurance, sensitivity, and pleasure. Sexual ability can be taught if you have an enthusiastic student. Why should sexual knowledge be seen as a threat to a man's masculinity? If he didn't know how to fix a car, he would certainly seek out help. The same thing applies if he is a lousy lover.

*Annette, 40, sex therapist*

It depends. If he filled enough other shoes, I might keep him. Humor is one asset hard to find in a mate. Real good humor. On the other hand, sex is pretty important and I like the white-hot kind. Maybe I would get him an instructor.

*Laurie, 54, realtor*

## 175. DO YOU STICK WITH SOMEONE YOU LOVE AND CARE ABOUT EVEN IF THE SEX IS TERRIBLE?

It depends on your age. I'm fifty, and frankly, sex is fine, but I'd much rather have love and devotion. I can always take care of my own urges.

*Mary, 50, housekeeper*

No way. Life is too short to go without good sex.

*Sam, 22, hairstylist*

There is no blanket answer to this question. If the causes are physical, then that is like asking if you should stay with someone who has cancer or a terminal illness. Each answer is a personal choice. Each relationship is unique. Now, if the man is just lazy and totally unwilling to improve himself or his skills, then maybe there are more problems than just the sex.

*Diane, 55, psychiatrist*

Passionate, hair-raising sex is absolutely the best thing ever discovered in America or elsewhere. However, it is very hard to find. Chemistry, I think they call it. But you can't just throw away love and a good man because he doesn't happen to have it. Get over it. There are other great things in life. You can't have everything.

*Gracie, 59, dental secretary*

## 176. IS GREAT SEX OR A GOOD RELATIONSHIP MORE IMPORTANT? CAN YOU HAVE A GREAT RELATIONSHIP IF THE SEX IS BAD?

Maybe, but who wants to find out?

*Katherine, 32, musician*

Great sex can make any relationship good.

*Myra, 34, financial adviser*

The human spirit can endure almost anything, but I can think of nothing sadder than a relationship built only on sex. The mind needs so much more than just sexual stimulation. The need for companionship, shared interests, and seeing mutual challenges met is so much more important than just the physical sensations.

*Eugenia, 60, physician*

Great sex is very, very, very important to me. I can't imagine living without it. The first time my lover and I made love it was as if we had known each other forever. And it seemed he knew my body better than I did myself. A good relationship will keep you together. Great sex will keep you alive.

*Lynn, 27, realtor*

## Heart, Be Still

Some people think there is a huge line between love and sex. I'm one of those people. I've had sex with boys, guys, and men throughout my lifetime, but loved only one man—my husband.

Men have chased me since I was in grade school, and I've loved the attention. But only one man captured my heart, body, and soul.

I've had sex with many men, but made love with only my husband. Nothing compares to our lovemaking. Sex without love is empty. Sex without love is cold.

Intercourse alone, the physical putting-it-in and taking-it-out, in my opinion, is nothing. You can have an orgasm, but the quality of it is boring and void. Give me the man I love and I have the greatest variety of sexual pleasure you could ever imagine. We have fast sex, slow sex, playful sex, intense sex, any kind of sex we want and need. The variety is there for the taking. The love between the two of us is the key that opens the door to the sexual pleasure that takes me to a level of consciousness unlike anything on earth.

I feel weak in the knees at the mention of his name. The mere thought of his hands touching my body can and does make me wet. His warm, loving smile, his intense brown eyes sliding up and down my body, his attention to my every whimper, my every move, my every need, is unbelievable. He can read my body, knowing what I need and what I want, even before I know myself.

His moves are slow and precise. He knows what he is doing and why. He is consistently aware of who I am and why I am there with him. He knows himself; he knows me.

With deep resonance, passionate words roll off his tongue without pause. He knows just what he wants to say. He tells me how he feels about me while he makes love to me. He openly expresses his love of my body, taking what is his and giving me what is mine. There are no rules when we are making love.

"I love the way you move your body, the way you arch your back a certain way when I eat your pussy. The way you whimper and squirm, the way you stand in front of me while you bring your pussy next to my lips. The way you finger yourself when I suck your nipples. The way you hold your breasts when my finger is inside you. You're so warm and wet, baby. I want you. I love you. You're so good."

Give me my man, the man who loves my heart, my body, and my soul, and forever we will grow together, learn together, love together, and I'm the luckiest woman alive.

*Lisa, 36, musician*

# chapter twenty-four

# Dressing Up

177. *Do you like to dress in sexy clothes?*

178. *Describe some of your favorite sexy outfits.*

179. *What type of lingerie does your partner prefer?*

180. *Does your partner ever cross-dress?*

181. *Do you ever cross-dress?*

182. *What do you like to wear that belongs to your partner?*

183. *What does your partner like to wear that belongs to you?*

## 177. DO YOU LIKE TO DRESS IN SEXY CLOTHES?

I love to wear sexy, revealing dresses and lingerie. It makes me feel feminine and beautiful.

*Peggy, 45, fund-raiser*

Dressing in sexy clothes is an easy way to get my man into bed. He loves it when I wear low-cut blouses, no bra, tight jeans, short skirts, high heels. It's fun to dress seductively.

*Teresa, 42, high school principal*

I like to wear my revealing clothes to show off my seventy-pound weight loss. I worked hard for eighteen months to lose the weight, and I am proud of the results. At first I felt like a complete alien in my new body. I was actually a babe in the woods. I bought slutty, slinky clothes totally inappropriate to my age and profession. I became a vain fashion victim. I'd buy anything that showed off my slim thighs and firm stomach. I'd buy any dress that had a slit running up the side. And you know what? I'd do it again. After decades of wearing tents, baggy sacks, and converted parachutes for beached whales, I'm proud of my figure and I want people to see it.

*Lori, 43, merchant*

He loves to buy them and I love to let him. I wear anything and everything he brings me. It keeps things interesting and exciting. Doesn't make me look too shabby, either.

*Carolynn, 37, contractor*

## 178. DESCRIBE SOME OF YOUR FAVORITE SEXY OUTFITS.

I like to wear a short, tight skirt with tall boots. It makes my legs look long and lean. I've got really long blond hair, and guys love it. Black skirts and blouses look good on me. I wear red a lot, too.

*Charlotte, 25, teacher*

I like sexy lingerie. Sexy, silky, soft lingerie makes me feel very womanly. Even if no one sees it but me, I feel very feminine when I have sexy panties and lacy things on underneath my clothes. And who knows when a girl might need them?

*Joyce, 22, food service worker*

Red! I love red clothes. Even if I'm wearing blue jeans, I will have a red scarf or blouse on. It brings out the devil in me.

*Lynette, 19, tour guide*

My favorite sexy outfit consists of wearing my wedding ring on my finger and my tennis bracelet on my ankle. And that's all. My husband loves it.

*Renata, 31, tennis instructor*

Crotchless panties and bras with no cloth around the nipples make my husband have an instant erection. What is there to complain about when your man does that? I am presently trying to find some of those edible panties I've heard about.

*Gladys, 55, banker*

## 179. WHAT TYPE OF LINGERIE DOES YOUR PARTNER PREFER?

My husband loves thong underwear and anything black or red.

*Ginger, 36, jeweler*

My boyfriend loves crotchless panties and lacy bras that show off my perfect breasts and nipples. He also likes garter belts and stockings.

*Heather, 23, model*

I always thought that men liked fancy, expensive lingerie. But every man I've ever dated has preferred plain cotton panties and bras. So much for spending money on fancy lingerie!

*Jennifer, 26, sportswriter*

My boyfriend likes it when I wear his briefs. He likes to stick his finger in the penis opening and insert it in my wet pussy. It really gets him excited. Maybe too excited.

*Ruth, 19, fashion apprentice*

I couldn't believe it when I first heard from my boyfriend's lips the lingerie that turned him on the most—panty hose. He likes to rip the crotch out of my panty hose while I have them on. Then he gets torn up and eats me and rides me with his shaft like a wild horse.

*Paulina, 38, teacher*

## 180. DOES YOUR PARTNER EVER CROSS-DRESS?

My lover wears my crotchless lace panties to work every Wednesday. He calls me from work, talks dirty on the phone, jerks off, and then brings home the crusty underwear for my approval. We know it is sick, but we love it.

*Cindy, 37, purchasing agent*

We like to play dress-up and put makeup on each other. I make my handsome stud puppy into my little party girl and we giggle and play ourselves into a frenzy. Then we smear our makeup all over each other's private parts and fuck.

*Helen, 26, travel agent*

My girlfriend occasionally dresses like a man and actually believes she is convincing. It is hard to keep a straight face when she gets in these delusional moods.

*Lena, 30, illustrator*

Red lipstick and jewelry is my hunk's favorite. He loves to leave lipstick marks all over my body. Sometimes the jewelry concerns me. He likes to bury my long strand of pearls in my pussy. Then while he is stroking himself to an all-time climax, he is slowly pulling the strand of pearls from deep inside me. Needless to say, I have an all-time climax, too.

*Dora Jean, 40, proofreader*

## 181. DO YOU EVER CROSS-DRESS?

My gay lover and I love to dress up like businessmen and go out to biker bars. I know we look silly, and I'm sure that no one really believes that we are males, but it makes us hot to enter a dark, sweaty butch bar full of rough gay men, act like homo lovers, and seduce each other on the dance floor. Some men really have a violent reaction toward us, but others seem to admire our boldness. All I know is that it makes me come buckets.

*Amanda, 23, merchandiser*

No. I don't think that cross-dressing is that common among women, anyway. It is much more a man's thing.

*Vanessa, 28, court reporter*

My husband makes me wear his most conservative business suit in one of our favorite fantasy trips. He is dressed as my male secretary, and I am the stern superbitch, the female boss from hell. I demand that he service my sexual needs, which basically means he crawls across the floor on his hands and knees, unzips my trousers, and licks my pussy. I tell him to do it better, harder, blah, blah, blah. Anyway, he really likes the whole ordeal, and I usually climax in his mouth. So I'm not complaining too much.

*Michelle, 36, antiques dealer*

I'd love to have the nerve to try it, just for fun. My guy likes to try new things and so do I. Trouble is, I don't know if he'll try this one, because he doesn't like clothes very much to begin with. He has to wear three-piece suits every day to work, with every hair in place, so when he comes home he really appreciates not having to dress for anything. He runs around the house and yard with no shirt, no shoes, and just his boxers. The neighbors love it.

*Gina Marie, 35, delivery service employee*

## 182. WHAT DO YOU LIKE TO WEAR THAT BELONGS TO YOUR PARTNER?

I love to wear his shirts. They always smell like him.

*Elizabeth, 40, housewife*

Boxer shorts are my favorite. They're so cute and so comfortable.

*Emily, 24, graduate student*

It probably doesn't count, but give me my lover's credit cards, and I'll wear them out.

*Donna, 30, designer*

My husband used to be a long-haired hippie before he discovered mutual funds and futures options. So even though we have a grand home and the required twin Mercedes in the driveway, I keep a lock of golden hair from his surfer days in a gold locket around my neck. I wear it proudly to my stockholder meetings and remember the days of incense and jug wine.

*Anita, 42, investor*

## 183. WHAT DOES YOUR PARTNER LIKE TO WEAR THAT BELONGS TO YOU?

My boyfriend likes to wear my athletic bra under his three-piece suit. It turns me on to know that under his tweed vest with the gold-chained watch, my hot pink titty protectors are making his nipples hard.

*Shannon, 27, gym instructor*

Absolutely nothing. You can bet if he got off on dressing up in my clothes, he would be gone in the blink of an eye. That's just not right.

*Jill, 36, historian*

My husband likes to wear my diamond tennis bracelet around his ankle. I've never heard of anyone else having this desire. But as long as it makes him happy, who cares? I don't even think it is a sexual thing. Maybe it's just his insurance if he gets robbed and loses all his cash.

*Alicia, 43, florist*

My boyfriend likes to wear my lipstick impression on the end of his penis. I leave each day for work by placing a big, juicy kiss on his dick. I use ruby-red lipstick that almost glows, and he loves it.

Every night I carefully suck the lipstick off my baby before he goes to sleep.

*Monica, 22, food server*

My husband cheated on me about three years ago. I haven't made him leave, but things were really strained for about two years after that. The past year has been much better. I love him and want our marriage to last, but since the day I found out about his infidelity, I refused to ever wear my wedding rings again. He wears mine and his. His on his finger and mine on a gold chain.

*Polly, 49, computer programmer*

# chapter twenty-five

# *Forbidden Sex*

184. *What do you consider the most forbidden form of sex?*
185. *What forbidden sex act have you heard about a friend performing?*
186. *Have you ever performed a sexual act that you consider forbidden?*
187. *Have you ever cheated on a lover?*

## 184. WHAT DO YOU CONSIDER THE MOST FORBIDDEN FORM OF SEX?

Sex with animals and rotten fruit at the same time.

*Annie, 34, data processor*

I think of forbidden sex as something that is hot, enticing, exciting. I like to break society's rules, and just the idea of illicit, taboo sex is very appealing to me.

*Sharon, 43, sales representative*

I think performing oral sex on a dog would probably be the most forbidden and disgusting type of sex a person could have.

*Shirley, 45, transportation specialist*

A very young person having sex with a very old person is extremely forbidden and gross in my mind. I mean an eighteen-year-old having sex with an eighty-year-old. That is repulsive.

*Andrea, 19, student*

To me the most forbidden kind of sex is selfish sex where only my boyfriend enjoys himself. I'm not his toy, and I think he should be concerned about my feelings and needs. So I forbid him to take his pleasure at my expense.

*Jamie, 22, teacher's aide*

Extramarital affairs are taboo. Men who cheat should be castrated, and women who cheat should have their vaginas sewn up.

*Jennie, 30, high school guidance counselor*

## 185. WHAT FORBIDDEN SEX ACT HAVE YOU HEARD ABOUT A FRIEND PERFORMING?

One of my friends had sex on a regular basis with her junior college music teacher, Mrs. Anderson, our entire freshmen year. Everyone knew about it and the whispers were scandalous. She definitely pursued my friend with recklessness. My friend claimed to hate the teacher and the idea of gay sex, but for some reason, Mrs. Anderson had an almost perverse power over my friend. And what's more, my friend was sincerely attractive and Mrs. Anderson was just plain ugly. I still don't know what the attraction was.

*Julie, 22, teaching aide*

My best friend used to perform oral sex on the anus of her boyfriend whenever she was very horny. I always thought it was extremely disgusting.

*Shelly, 27, driver*

I think all sex is forbidden. Ever since Adam and Eve were thrown out of the garden, sex has been shameful, dirty, and a sin. Celibacy is the only option for a pure life.

*Tonya, 33, researcher*

My sister had sex with my husband while I was in the hospital giving birth to my daughter. That bitch got pregnant, and nine months later to the day she gave birth to a son who looks more like me than he does his own mother. She got a divorce from her husband and stole my husband from me. They married each other as soon as the state would allow it. That marriage lasted all of five months before my ex-husband came home early one day and found my sister screwing one of his fishing buddies. Now I'm a single mother raising my own three children.

*Amanda, 30, collections agent*

A girl in our church choir used to perform oral sex on her next-door neighbor until he came in her mouth and went to sleep. They would sneak out their windows every night, and she'd blow him. She started doing it when they were both sixteen and kept it up until he joined the army. She used to brag about the power it gave her. I don't think she ever had intercourse with him because if she had, she would have been bragging about it to anyone and everyone.

*Tabitha, 22, student*

My friend had sex with a complete stranger at a party back in the late seventies. In fact, most of my friends had sex with people they didn't know. Then it was no big deal as long as you didn't get pregnant or catch a venereal disease. But if her daughter or mine tried to do the same thing today, it could lead to AIDS and slow death. So recreational sex is now forbidden for an entire population. I don't know if that is a bad thing or not.

*Emily, 42, software designer*

Wife- and husband-swapping is strange and, in my mind, very forbidden. Sick men usually get that started and use all sorts of reasons, even religion, to justify it. They need to be locked away or sent out west to die in the dust and heat and tornadoes.

*Dena, 42, funeral director*

## 186. HAVE YOU EVER PERFORMED A SEXUAL ACT THAT YOU CONSIDER FORBIDDEN?

No. I've been pretty strait-laced.

*Mia, 30, claims adjuster*

Yes. I once screwed two guys at the same time. I still feel really guilty about it. I was really drunk, and it seemed like a good idea at the time. It happened over ten years ago, and it still embarrasses me.

*Collette, 45, loan officer*

I had sex with one of my high school teachers. He was married, and it was an awful thing to do. I couldn't even enjoy it.

*Laura, 28, secretary*

I had sex with a person who turned out to be my cousin. I was very disappointed when I found out he was family. I knew we had a lot in common, but not that much. I kept hoping one of us would turn out to be adopted. It was a summer fling that should have been much more.

*Patty, 24, garden specialist*

I got mad at my boyfriend and went to this dumpy dive-bar and picked up a guy. Took him to a motel and fucked all night. It was great sex. Anger is a good and a weird motivator, but I worry to this day about AIDS. It's been six years, and I still worry and get checked every three months. Don't want to do that again—without protection, that is.

*Irlene, 37, flight attendant*

## 187. HAVE YOU EVER CHEATED ON A LOVER?

Yes. I got caught in the act with Troy, one of my boyfriend's friends. I have no regrets. My boyfriend broke up with me, and Troy and I are still together. Troy treats me better anyway, so I feel no remorse.

*Donna, 25, prop designer*

No. I have a terrible conscience. I could never cheat. I'd be so guilty. I know it would be written all over my face.

*Kristine, 34, pet groomer*

I try not to cheat, but sometimes I slip up. If I'm not getting enough attention from my boyfriend, I have to go out and find it somewhere. I know it's dishonest, but I can't help it.

*Louise, 22, student*

I don't consider having sex with other women cheating on my boyfriend. He doesn't know I'm bisexual, and I don't feel any real need to tell him. I do know that my gay relationships aren't any threat to my relationship with him. I love him and enjoy being with him. I can see spending the rest of my life devoted to him. That doesn't mean I won't have sexual relationships with many more women in my life. If we do marry, the line about "forsaking all others" may need a little modification.

*Allison, 20, beauty school student*

Men are so selfish. My fiancé told me he wanted to be apart for a little while, about a month, to see how much we missed each other. No talking, no sex, no seeing each other at all. I thought it was strange and was going to be hard, but agreed to it because I love him. He cheated with an old girlfriend, and I didn't cheat with anyone. What a fool. I sent him packing.

*Amanda, 26, radio copywriter*

## Higher Learning

For the past two years I have been involved in an intense affair with my professor and mentor. I am a few months away from receiving my Ph.D. in chemistry, and already I have a job in research lined up at a leading Ivy League university.

I'm smart, well read, well mannered, cultured, and pretty. I win awards for excellence, scholarships for my research, and I am even good at applying for esoteric grants in obscure fields of study.

I know how to play the game in academia. Why I'm such a loser at relationships is totally beyond me.

I took my undergrad studies in Oklahoma and married my dream guy during my junior year. I took my studies and my vows seriously. Unfortunately, he didn't. We divorced after fourteen months of my denial and his disregard.

I earned my master's degree after two more years of intense effort. Being in a new town, new college, and new environment, I studied around the clock and kept my nose directly on the grindstone. I had two dates the entire time. Both of them were complete flops.

When I decided to go for my doctorate, I pulled up stakes again and moved down south. The whole experience was the closest I've come to culture shock yet. Having never fit in with most people, it didn't amaze me to find people hostile and petty in the home of "southern hospitality."

I was alone in a strange town. If Leland hadn't been so sweet, I probably would have spent my entire time in seclusion, with my head buried in books and research papers.

But Leland was not only my professor, mentor, and best friend, he was also my lover. He was older, wiser, and totally nonjudgmental. He took me in his office and made sweet love with me at least twice a week. While grading papers, he would call me and spend hours seducing me with his voice. He arranged lab sessions where we could conduct intimate sexual marathons. He brought out the female in my soul. He made me tingle and swoon. He was forceful and instructive and demanding. He was supportive and educational and revitalizing. I loved his touch. I loved the smell of our sex in the classroom. I loved hiding my panties in his lab coat.

What I didn't love about Leland was his total devotion to his wife. He had told me up front that he was happily married and the proud father of three. He was honest about his relationship with his wife. He told me that I could be his friend, his student, his co-worker, and his sexual partner, but I could never replace his wife. I would always be on the outside looking in.

At first it didn't matter. I just needed the companionship, the warmth. I needed to be close to someone. I needed to be sexual and aroused. I craved the physical aspects and figured the emotional attachment would come later. I was wrong. His wife had his respect, his house, his children, his warm body at night. I had stolen moments. I had hot intense passion. I had quickies.

He spent holidays with his family. He spent spare time with me.

The final blow came when I went to a four-week seminar in Europe a few weeks ago. I sent him seventeen postcards. I called his office twice and talked dirty for about an hour. We had transatlantic phone sex. I had sexy photos taken in France and sent them to his office. As a homecoming gift I sent him a dozen roses.

He didn't meet me at the airport. When I made it home, there was only one message on my answering machine after I'd been away from home for four weeks. Leland had just phoned to say how much his wife loved the roses. She thought they were for their wedding anniversary, and he assured her that they were.

Maybe life in New England will be better.

*Jenny, 25, researcher*

# chapter twenty-six

# *What If . . .*

188. *If money were no object, what sexual fantasy would you like to experience?*
189. *If you were a man, what kind of woman would turn you on?*
190. *If you were a man for a week, what would you do differently than your mate?*
191. *What would you like to do sexually if you were a man for one week?*
192. *If you could go anywhere in the world with your lover for a love fest, where would you go and how would you travel?*
193. *If your mate could pretend you were his mystery lover, what do you think he would do differently?*

## 188. IF MONEY WERE NO OBJECT, WHAT SEXUAL FANTASY WOULD YOU LIKE TO EXPERIENCE?

I'd have twenty bodybuilders get naked and oiled up and form a human carpet for me to roll on. I'd make each one please me with his mouth, and then I'd force the entire bunch to form a circle and perform oral sex on each other.

*Miriam, 33, bookkeeper*

I'd take ten million dollars in cash and roll around on it.

*Suzette, 29, bank teller*

Oils and perfumes and diamonds and mink would become my
sex toys.

*Monica, 35, housewife*

I'd simply walk through a construction area and snap my fingers at all
the sweaty hunks. I'd dangle thousand-dollar bills in front of their
noses and tell them to bark like dogs and make my pussy happy. After
I was through with them, I'd tell them how lousy they were and hu-
miliate them to their very core. Then I'd dangle another thousand-
dollar bill in front of their noses and tell them to cry like babies and
suck their thumbs.

*Helena, 25, design student*

If money were no problem and AIDS didn't exist, I would form a
United Nations of Sexual Males. I'd have a lover from every race.
I'd taste the sperm of the world and experience the sexual abilities
of the entire male sex. I'd enjoy it so much more than an exotic cook-
book.

*Charlene, 32, translator*

I'd start the week with a maid to clean my home. That always makes
me feel good. After my home was in order I'd concentrate on myself.
Then to the hairdresser, nails, pedicure, full-body massage, the works.
I'd have someone at home packing for me, selectively choosing just the
right clothes for a sexy, luxurious trip. Then to a romantic spot like
Paris, the Bahamas, Bermuda, or Jamaica. Did I forget to mention my
husband? I'd take him, too. I've got another list for him. Particularly
things I would let him do to me.

*Wendy, 31, political analyst*

## 189. IF YOU WERE A MAN, WHAT KIND OF WOMAN WOULD TURN YOU ON?

Coy. A wolf in sheep's clothing.

*Elaine, 24, nutritionist*

I'd want a woman like the woman my husband left me for—young, blond, and dumb. Then I'd fuck the life out of her and dump her and her fake tits.

*Dorothy, 37, telemarketer*

I'd like to fuck a clone of myself. I'd take care of my needs and really think all my jokes were witty and insightful. I'd compliment myself on how sexy my body was and how trim I looked in my new outfit. I'd know where to scratch before I even itched. And I would positively know how to use a penis to make myself come.

*Erin, 29, art instructor*

I'd be turned on by all the same tall, thin, blond models that men now desire. I'd want youthful, flawless bodies. Wet, eager lips. Round, firm breasts. Why should I desire anything less than the other male pigs grunting around out there?

*Marian, 25, researcher*

Brains turn me on. Loyalty, motivation, commitment. Now turn this around and look for a man with these qualities and we've instantly got a problem.

*Jeniffer Lee, 47, insurance agent*

## 190. IF YOU WERE A MAN FOR A WEEK, WHAT WOULD YOU DO DIFFERENTLY THAN YOUR MATE?

I'd be more sensitive to a female's needs. I'd go slower and focus more on pleasing her.

*Francine, 40, consultant*

I'd explore my feminine side and my masculine side and have an internal battle of sensitivity.

*Paulette, 49, teacher*

If I were a man for a week I'd write my name in the snow with piss. I'd drink gallons of beer and stand as far back from the toilet as possible, trying to hit the pot. I'd scare women with my massive penis. I'd climax as many times as possible to feel the sensation of sperm shooting out of my body. And just to know what it felt like, I'd fuck some guy in the butt. I don't think my husband has ever done any of these disgusting things, but I could be wrong.

*Margaret, 38, stockbroker*

I'd be able to live with myself for starters. I would not be this mindless macho fuck who manipulates women while selfishly indulging my every whim. I'd have a clue as to where my emotions are and what the hell my feelings are. Then I'd do something really original to the male sex: I'd tell the truth.

*Brenda, 30, legal secretary*

## 191. WHAT WOULD YOU LIKE TO DO SEXUALLY IF YOU WERE A MAN FOR ONE WEEK?

If AIDS disappeared in this hypothetical situation, I'd sleep with every slut I could find. I'd come so much I'd run out of sperm. I'd be a complete dog, licking, sniffing, and putting my nose and penis in everything and everyone. I'd be a pig and I'd scratch my balls a lot in public places.

*Juanita, 40, store manager*

I'd be much more concerned about my woman's desires than my own. I'd try to use my body parts to give her extreme pleasure. I'd worry less about pleasing myself.

*Tracy, 26, dental assistant*

I'd wear my penis out. It would be useless by the time I got through with it. I'd fuck a fence hole if I could reach it. I'd be little Johnny Apple Sperm if I had a dick for a week. The neighborhood cats would run in horror.

*Helen, 19, day-care assistant*

If I were a man for a week, I would be something rare. I'd be totally and completely faithful and devoted to my girlfriend. I'd be considerate, loving, and giving. I would be a woman in a man's body. I'd be nice.

*Marie, 33, events coordinator*

I would love to show men, by being one myself, what it would be like to be honest, compassionate, tender, and still sexy and manly. They could be human and kind and still be those other things we women adore. Why they can't see that is beyond my comprehension.

*Tracey, 28, computer sales associate*

## 192. IF YOU COULD GO ANYWHERE IN THE WORLD WITH YOUR LOVER FOR A LOVE FEST, WHERE WOULD YOU GO AND HOW WOULD YOU TRAVEL?

I'd go to the Garden of Eden and tell that snake to go to hell. We'd arrive on the wings of angels and never leave the eternal bliss of innocence.

*Darlene, 37, office manager*

I'd take a champagne flight in a hot-air balloon to a tropical isle and leave my beeper, cellular phone, and fax in the office. I'd make love all night, sleep all day, eat fabulous raw oysters, and stay mildly buzzed on good red wine.

*Jana, 29, executive secretary*

I'd go back in time to my childhood home. I'd still be the age I am today, and I'd take my husband and children with me. I'd take them back to meet the grandparents my children never knew. I'd show my husband off to my sure-to-be envious girlfriend who died in a car wreck our senior year. I'd give my long-dead older brother a gigantic hug and tickle him. I'd tell Aunt Dale not to believe the doctor when he said the spot on her left breast was nothing to worry about. Then I'd probably spend the entire fantasy crying and remembering everyone. My sex life is fine. It is the death of so many people I loved that hurts so much.

*Kitty, 41, teacher*

We'd go to Paris and travel on a little of everything—airplane, cruise ship, train, car, limo, and a bicycle built for two.

*Maimmy, 59, high school principal*

## 193. IF YOUR MATE COULD PRETEND YOU WERE HIS MYSTERY LOVER, WHAT DO YOU THINK HE WOULD DO DIFFERENTLY?

He would take me from behind and up my bottom.

*Caroline, 40, switchboard operator*

He would be forceful and demand more pleasure instead of worrying about my reactions or feelings.

*Sasha, 25, time management consultant*

She would be a true dyke and torture me with dirty words, rough actions, and a black dildo.

*Linda, 30, teacher*

He would probably do things exactly the way he has been doing them for fifty-three years. And that is perfectly all right with me.

*Betina, 76, retired grocer*

Cheat, but it wouldn't be anything different. He'd feel right at home because he would feel like he was cheating. He'd love that.

*Diane, 53, chemist*

## Surprise!

As I was growing up, I watched my parents and how wonderfully good they were to each other. They always gave each other respect, courtesy, and love. Loving each other was something they did very well.

The only element missing was surprise. They knew each other so well they could speak without words, send private messages back and forth across the dinner table or in a crowded room, and no one was ever the wiser. Then, on their twentieth anniversary, my father surprised everyone. I remember it as if it were yesterday, carry it with me, and think of it when the subject of romance is at hand. My father tells the story like this:

My wife is the most important person in the world to me. I love her unconditionally. There was a day when I began to see we needed just a little spice, and I began thinking about creating a little, just for the two of us. I started thinking, What if I could orchestrate an evening, a day, an adventure, something brand-new for us both, something so far out of the ordinary that she would never expect it? Could I pull it off? Could I think of something brand-new? I'd have to let my imagination run wild, which I did. I'm glad I did.

I sent her roses at work. I sent her candy the same week. One week prior to our anniversary, I started romancing her like it was a brand-new love affair. She was surprised, but she loved it! One day I sent her reservations for her favorite beauty salon—hairdo, manicure, pedicure, massage, the whole works.

Next, I hired a chauffeur to pick us up, and we went out for dinner and dancing. Looking into her eyes, I can still see it now after all these years. She was beautiful then and even more so now.

Making love was something we never had to think about. When we were making love, the world stood still. The last night of our romantic week of surprises I presented her with a pair of plane tickets for Las Vegas. We flew to Vegas and did our wedding ceremony all over, just like the first time. I was excited and nervous and almost forgot the ring. There is something very sacred about wedding vows the first time around and something very romantic about the second time.

I would marry my wife every week if she wanted me to. I love her very much. As we were leaving Las Vegas, sitting in the plane, holding hands, and talking about our week, I slipped a penny in her hand and said, "Pretend this penny is magical. You may make one wish and ask for anything in the world. What is your wish, my dear?" She held the penny in her left hand and with her right hand holding mine tightly, she looked at me and smiled, "I want nothing. I would wish for nothing." When two people have been married as long as we have, it is a feeling beyond words to genuinely know your wife, your lover, your friend, is truly happy. If you can accomplish that for your mate and yourself, you have lived a wonderful life."

*Deborah Ann, 40, teacher*

## The List

I am a social worker who specializes in domestic abuse. All day long I hear the most terrible stories of pain, hardship, and struggle. My caseload is filled with sad stories of hard times and unbelievable violence. In my twenty-three years on the job, I've seen about everything.

My friends told me about the book you are working on. We all read your questions and had a big time talking about men and sex. We tried to share our most secret thoughts. I will admit that it was a lot of fun.

I especially liked the fantasy questions. They made me think about my own fantasies. I haven't thought much about fantasies or dreams in a long, long time. I guess the facts of life are so overwhelming I don't have time to indulge in much dreaming.

I've been thinking about what my fantasies are for the past couple of days. The whole process has actually been a bunch of fun. Do I dream about tropical isles, bronze lifeguards, exotic foods? Do I fantasize about movie stars and money? Not really.

After much thought and mind-searching, here is my fantasy. I call it "The List."

I'd love to have a vacation and invite all my former lovers and sexual partners to be with me. I'd like to have them all freeze their individual lives and just take a lost week with me.

In my fantasy we are all our present ages. Part of the fun is to see how they have all turned out. I don't want to see my nineteen-year old Jimmy, the love of my high school life. I want to spend some time with Jim, the forty-seven-year old man I hope he has become.

I'd invite them all to play with me at a lush resort hotel. I'd pay all their expenses and even give them each a thousand dollars for spending money. They would all know what was expected beforehand, and there would be no secrets. I wouldn't pretend that Ralph was the only one from my past I wanted to see. I'd proudly display him to all the others in my room of former lovers. I'd introduce each of them by name and shine a bright light for everyone to see. They would all be aware that the thing they had in common was having had intimate sex with me at least once.

I wouldn't try to wreck their lives, ruin their marriages, or upset their cozy little worlds. I would just invite them all to have the most wonderful, stress-free vacation of their lives.

And I would make love to each and every one of them. I'd probably make them all choose a number out of a hat. Then I'd give each of them their designated two hours to please me and make me exceptionally happy. In order to ensure my pleasure, I'd probably hold their passports and return tickets in my safe until I was satisfied with their performances.

I would be the center of their attention for the entire week. I'd also be the only woman, so there would be no temptations. They couldn't call home. Their only contact with the rest of the world would be through me. And since this is my fantasy, they wouldn't have any interest at all in anything but me. Just me. Selfish, horny me.

After our initial reacquaintance sessions, I'd start comparing notes. I'd judge them on their enthusiasm, technique, attention to detail. If Frank has learned a new way to give women pleasure in the last thirty years, I'd make sure he taught Jeremy how to do it too. It would be an education for all of us. If Larry knew how to hit my special spot, I'd make sure Melvin did his best to find it too. This would be their last time to get it right. No more excuses, Arnie.

There would be joy. There would be tears.

I'd see guys I only fucked once and didn't even remember their names. I'd see men I have spent years with in misery and silence. I'd be with my three ex-husbands and relive all that excess baggage and pain. I'd see the father of my precious baby—the father who ran off three weeks after our daughter was born and never looked back.

I'd meet all those guys from all those bars who promised to love me, who promised to need me, who always forgot to call the day after.

I'd see my loves who died from cancer, bullets, and alcohol. I'd spend time with James, who died in a car crash on a rainy night. I'd hold Tony, who went away to war and came back in a hero's body bag. I'd fuck Jerry, the married guy who never quite could break up with his wife.

And last but certainly not least, I'd see Paul, my dear, dear stepbrother. He was my first sexual partner, to whom I gave my virginity when I was fourteen and he was sixteen. I'd tell him that he didn't have to run away from the family when Mom found out what we did. That he could have kept in touch with his new brothers and sisters these past thirty years, and watched us all grow up.

I'd tell him that his father died fifteen years ago, calling his name. That Mom happily remarried and is now a proud grandmother. I'd tell him that I never go a day without loving him and thinking about him and wishing he was back in my life. That I was glad he was alive and that I have spent my life missing him. Then I'd probably cry my eyes out for all the lost moments.

Maybe this isn't such a good fantasy for me after all.

*Marilyn, 47, social worker*

# chapter twenty-seven

# *Safe Sex*

194. *How has the AIDS epidemic changed your sexual habits?*
195. *How important do you think it is to practice safe sex?*
196. *How much of your partner's sexual history do you like to know before you engage in intercourse?*
197. *Do you practice safe sex all the time?*
198. *What do you consider the safest form of sex?*
199. *Have you ever had phone sex?*
200. *Have you ever had cybersex?*

## 194. HOW HAS THE AIDS EPIDEMIC CHANGED YOUR SEXUAL HABITS?

I'm a lot more careful than I used to be. One-night stands used to be okay; now they're just too risky.

*Gretchen, 35, chef*

I don't fuck around as much as I did at one time. I'm a lot more selective about who I will and won't go to bed with.

*Sandra, 30, mechanic*

AIDS hasn't changed my lifestyle at all. I never was promiscuous and I sure don't intend to start now.

*Cheryl, 36, hospital administrator*

All I've ever heard about is safe sex and AIDS. I've never known a time when the threat wasn't constant. I am twenty years old and I have never felt the skin of a penis rub against my vagina walls, flesh to flesh. I've had three relationships, and condoms were used each and every time. I know I'm missing out on something. I'm missing the elemental need to join my flesh, juices, and soul with another human being without a latex barrier. I feel angry. I feel cheated.

*Melissa, 20, college student*

I used the threat of AIDS originally to justify my gay tendencies. I told my parents that they should be happy I loved other women because AIDS didn't affect lesbians. And in 1985 I believe most people thought the same way. AIDS was a guy disease. Now we know better, and I'm ashamed that I used the death of others to give validity to my sexual urges.

*Barbara, 29, nursing home assistant*

AIDS is awesome. It has completely freaked out my generation— totally. We can't do the things my mother and dad could. We can't make mistakes. We will die if we do. We have to be responsible and safe. I'd say the world's sexual habits have changed, not just mine. Everything is completely different.

*Rebecca, 19, art student*

I think sex has changed from a participant sport to a spectator sport. Swinging clubs are houses of sexual Russian roulette. People are hesitant to join in orgies and group circles. Now they would rather watch other couples and videotape the action for repeated safe viewing. I miss the old days when you could just grab any swinging dick and play with it until a bigger one came along. Swinging weekends are more about learning new dance steps and testing new camera equipment than good old-fashioned physical sex. I miss the thrill of an attractive stranger with a drink in one hand and a firm erection in the other.

*Gertrude, 59, social director*

## 195. HOW IMPORTANT DO YOU THINK IT IS TO PRACTICE SAFE SEX?

I don't think "important" is the right word. It's not important. It is a matter of life or death.

*Tricia, 27, veterinary assistant*

It's either safe sex or no sex. There is absolutely no reason to gamble.

*Mary, 42, nurse*

I feel lucky to have been in a faithful marriage for the past fifteen years. Who would have believed that monogamy would ever be popular after the sexual revolution of the sixties?

*Leslie, 44, administrator*

"Practice" is a funny word choice. Kind of makes me think of medical practice. If doctors are experts, why do they call it "practice"? If I "practice" safe sex, it implies I might make a mistake. I can't afford mistakes. I have safe sex every time I have sex. I don't "practice" anything that involves my life. I just do it. And I do it right.

*Martharaye, 30, kindergarten teacher*

## 196. HOW MUCH OF YOUR PARTNER'S SEXUAL HISTORY DO YOU LIKE TO KNOW BEFORE YOU ENGAGE IN INTERCOURSE?

I don't know. That's a hard question. It's not an easy subject to bring up when you're in the throes of passion with someone.

*Helen, 43, marketing consultant*

A lot. Enough to know I'm not putting myself at risk.

*Eleanor, 36, loan officer*

I won't sleep with someone on the first date. Or probably the second, third, fourth, or fifth date, for that matter. You have to get on a level where you know whether or not you can trust them before you ask them a question like that. They can always lie, of course. Even if I do believe they're telling me the truth, it's still important for me to practice safe sex.

*Sylvia, 30, veterinarian*

I'd love to start with a clean slate. If I could, I'd find me an eighteen-year-old virgin and train him in the art of love. I'd keep a twenty-four-hour watch on him and make him so sexually happy that he could never even imagine having another lover.

*Candice, 39, projects developer*

Women my age are starting to see the wisdom in dating widowers who have had at least twenty years of a happy, faithful marriage. If they aren't lying about being faithful, they should be at low risk for AIDS. And the fact that they usually have plenty of money and nice houses doesn't hurt. You could do worse.

*Maxine, 50, business owner*

I find myself in a unique position. I don't believe in sex before marriage. And since my husband's death I have finally started dating. In my day and even now the people of my generation just never have sex before they commit to marriage. The problem is that it used to be people dated, fell in love, and married. Now, because of the sexual diseases out there, I fully intend to know everything about the man I consider marrying before marriage. Blood tests, urine tests, and the works. I also feel I would have to be engaged for a longer period of time to be more certain he was healthy. It's sad, but a fact.

*Ethel, 62, retired elementary teacher*

## 197. DO YOU PRACTICE SAFE SEX ALL THE TIME?

Absolutely. But not necessarily because of AIDS. I'm more worried about getting pregnant.

*Brandi, 19, student*

If you call being in a monogamous relationship with one person all your life and intending to be for the rest of your life, I do.

*Louise, 56, housewife*

I know condoms are a bother, and despite all the ads trying to make them look glamorous, the fact is, no one would use them if they didn't save lives and prevent pregnancies. I make my boyfriends wear them. They don't like it, but if they want some of the good stuff, they will wear their rubbers. I even make them wear condoms when I perform oral sex. It is my mouth, so I can be choosy.

*Erica, 24, graphic artist*

Every time an erect penis is in my bedroom, a rubber waits ready and able to prevent the exchange of body fluids.

*MaryLynn, 36, editorial director*

No. It makes me nervous when I think about it, but it's amazing how I and other people I know seem to draw a line between love and casual sex. It seems not to worry me if I love the man. I tend to automatically throw caution to the wind. If I don't love the man I'm dating, I'm careful. I practice safe sex and insist on condoms and so forth. Now that I think about it in these terms, I think I'll start being careful all the time.

*Clara, 39, apartment manager*

## 198. WHAT DO YOU CONSIDER THE SAFEST FORM OF SEX?

I guess monogamy is pretty safe.

*Katy, 28, receptionist*

Masturbation is just about the only safe form of sex. It's too risky to sleep around. Condoms can break. You never know who your partner has slept with before you. That leaves masturbation, which is my favorite form of sex anyway.

*Alisha, 30, bank teller*

Celibacy seems to be a pretty good route to take, though not necessarily the most enjoyable route.

*Penelope, 46, pet groomer*

My husband and I practice safe sex. There's no risk if you haven't had sex in twenty years and probably never will again.

*Jean, 52, teacher*

I watch television and dream of better days.

*Diane, 18, unemployed*

Condoms are safe if you use the right kind. I always use creams and lotions that are treated, as a backup. You can't be too careful. AIDS kills.

*Joanne, 22, student*

## 199. HAVE YOU EVER HAD PHONE SEX?

No, not the kind you have to pay for. But when my boyfriend and I had a long-distance relationship we used to have some really hot, sexy conversations. We would get on the phone, talk about how much we wanted to fuck each other, and masturbate. It sounds silly, but it was really satisfying.

*Barbara, 26, actress*

Yes! Phone sex is terrific. You can talk as long or as dirty as you want to and you don't have to worry about relationships, diseases, getting pregnant, or dealing with the person on the other line. It's a great sexual release.

*Lee, 28, computer programmer*

I think I'd be too embarrassed to call. I've been tempted to call one of those really kinky fetish lines once or twice. I have some pretty strange fetishes, and I'm too ashamed to tell my boyfriend about them. I always thought it would be nice to talk to somebody who has the same fetishes or at least pretends to. I probably never will. They're too expensive anyway.

*Val, 30, furniture salesperson*

I get a lot of "wrong number" phone calls, since I'm listed in the phone book under my real name, so I guess I could have all the phone sex I could ever want. I just think the whole concept seems so silly.

*Holly, 21, art gallery assistant*

Yes, and it's great. I am a professional and don't have much time to date. Being a young widow has been challenging at my age. I have long workdays, am still raising four children—teenagers and college age—and just don't have enough time to go out and date. I see several gentlemen and have phone sex regularly. You can have bad hair and be tired and still have great sex on the phone. I think it's one of the things that best helps me relieve tension and feel good. Then I go right off to sleep and have great dreams, too.

*Andy, 45, lawyer*

## 200. HAVE YOU EVER HAD CYBERSEX?

Cybersex? I don't even know what that is. I guess that means no.

*Rochelle, 36, teacher*

Yes! Yes! Yes! And it's great. I get so hot sometimes it gets hard to type. Wish I could type with one hand.

*Heather, 28, writer*

I'd like to, but I think I'd have to be pretty drunk. It's hard to be uninhibited.

*Carolyn, 30, ad salesperson*

I have cybersex a lot. I like to get guys or girls on line and tease them until they can't stand it anymore. I talk as dirty as I can and get really, really wet. Usually I start masturbating and tell them every little detail. It gets them going, too. I've actually met a couple of dates that way. Unfortunately, they didn't get me as hot in person as they did during cybersex. Most of them were complete losers. I think I'll stick to the computer from now on.

*Wendy, 22, student*

I think the Internet is the 1990s version of the citizen-band radio craze. It seems to be filled with nerdy guys who lie about their age, looks, background, profession, and financial status. So the idea of having make-believe sex with these phonies is about as appealing as making love to my blender. I think the whole system will go back to being like it was in the beginning, mainly academic and technically oriented, once the jerks have run out of fantasies and lies.

*Kristina, 35, technical writer*

I think it's sick. Wasted time. For the life of me I cannot understand what makes people tick who enjoy stuff like that. I wonder who does that and do they live right next door to me? You never know who the weirdos are, do you?

*Tonya, 28, advertising executive*

## Reach Out and Touch Someone

"Hello, baby. I miss you. Yes, I have the camera turned on. You know I am rock-hard and I'm thinking of you while I jerk off for the video. Of course I'm naked. Tell me what you want me to do."

My husband and I have found a high-tech means of sharing our love long-distance and creating some memorable family tapes that put Aunt Ruth's vacation memories to shame.

Jerry has been on temporary assignment in Seattle working on a new software package that could revolutionize home banking. Meanwhile, I'm here in Saint Louis, working at the hospital and taking care of the cats. So for the last three weekends we have reached out and touched each other in a very intimate but safe sexual way.

It started the first Friday night Jerry was away. Fridays have always been our sexual delight days, and this was the first time in three years of marriage that we were going to miss being in each other's mouths and other love openings.

I was resigned to a night of bad movies and cheap wine when the phone rang. From the Caller ID I could tell it was a long-distance caller. I anxiously grabbed the phone and said, "I love you, honey."

The voice on the other end was deep and lusty. "I want to fuck you until you scream for mercy."

"Excuse me?"

"You heard me, you hot, sexy thing. I want to run my rough, wet tongue up and down your creamy little body from head to toe. I want to lick your clit and gulp your juices until you fill me up. I am starving for your love. Feed me."

I knew it was Jerry. He knew I knew it was him. But that was part of the kick. He spent the next ten minutes talking trash. He growled and smacked his lips. He was rude, crude, and outrageous. He told me he was completely naked and that he was masturbating and was going to come all over the phone. He described his hot room, his hot body, and the tingling sensation in his testicles.

As stupid as it may sound, I was aroused. I was already a little tipsy, and I had been horny ever since I put Jerry on the plane. With his encouragement, I played the role, and I played with my body. The more I explored, the more he talked. My wonderful lover led me up a climactic mountain and let me come all over my fingers, panties, and sofa. It was the best twenty minutes I've spent on the phone in years. After we had regained our senses, he asked me how the cats were doing and said good night.

The following Monday I came home to find a package waiting on my doorstep. The note inside read, "Thanks for being there when I needed you. I miss you. You can expect an encore performance this weekend. Until then, watch this tape and remember that you are truly loved by a man temporarily in Seattle. Always, Jerry."

I ran to the VCR, hit Play, and watched with amazement as my stuffy, computer-programming husband appeared stark naked with his erect penis firmly in hand. I saw him pick up the phone, dial my number, and talk dirty to me. I watched my lover stroke, squeeze, and bring himself to a thundering climax.

I must have watched that tape a dozen times before he called the following Friday and produced the soon-to-be-legendary sequel. By the time Jerry comes home in six weeks, I'll have to buy more batteries for the remote. I'm already assembling a new bookcase to hold our growing collection of special moments.

*Jean, 32, medical administrator*

# And Finally . . .

Congratulations! You survived. Did you answer all the questions? Did you learn anything about your sex life that surprised you? Did you blush, laugh, get embarrassed, and think one answer was the most outrageous thing you'd ever heard?

Well, good for you!

The purpose of this book, survey, and entire project was to explore and have fun. We certainly had our share of good times putting this project together. Thanks for coming along for the ride. We hope it gave you some much-deserved pleasure.

We'd love to hear from you. A sequel to this book is in the making. Send us your comments, questions, and stories. We are alive and kicking and always looking for more friends, projects, and adventures.

Good Girls' Guide
P.O. Box 50214
Belle Meade Station
Nashville, TN 37205

This book makes a great gift for friends, family, and co-workers. We look forward to hearing from you and including you in our next book!

*Best to you,*
*Debbie and Thom*